TURKISH COAST

Bodrum to Marmaris

Third edition

Michael Bussmann and Gabriele Tröger
with walks by
Brian and Eileen Anderson
and Dean Livesley

SUNFLOWER BOOKS

Third edition © 2012
Sunflower Books™
PO Box 36160
London SW7 3WS, UK
www.sunflowerbooks.co.uk

ISBN 978-1-85691-403-1

Important note to the reader

Apart from the walks, this book is a translation from a series of *general* guides originally published in Germany (see Publisher's note on page 6). We have tried to ensure that the descriptions and maps are error-free at press date. The book will be updated, where necessary, whenever future printings permit. It will be very helpful for us to receive your comments (sent in care of Sunflower Books, please) for the updating of future printings.

We also rely on those who use this book — especially walkers — to take along a good supply of common sense when they explore. Conditions change very rapidly in this part of Turkey, and ***storm damage or building works may make a route unsafe at any time***. If the route is not as we outline it here, and your way ahead is not secure, return to the point of departure. ***Never attempt to complete a trip by car or on foot under hazardous conditions!***

Cover photograph: Bodrum harbour

Text (except the walks) translated and adapted from *Türkei — Lykische Küste, Türkei — Westküste* and *Türkei — Südägäis;* text, town and site plans © 2005, 2006, 2008, 2011 Michael Müller Verlag, Erlangen, Germany; translation: Thomas Wilkes and Pat Underwood
Photograph credits
© Michael Bussmann: pages 9, 10, 12, 18, 26, 29, 31, 32, 43 (bottom), 59, 63, 86, 106, 122, 124, 138, 142, 155, 156, 162, 168 (top), 176
© Brian Anderson: pages 20, 48, 71, 84, 87, 92, 93, 95, 101, 114, 117, 131, 132, 148 (both), 160
© Shutterstock: cover; i-stockphoto: pages 16, 23, 24, 30 (both), 36, 39, 43 (top), 44 (both), 46, 55, 60, 90, 137, 156, 164-5, 168 (bottom)
Walking maps: © Sunflower Books
Sunflower Books is a Registered Trademark.
A CIP catalogue record for this book is available from the British Library.
Printed and bound in China: WKT Company Ltd

Contents

Preface

The Turkish poet and writer Cevat Şakir Kabaağaçli once described the area between Bodrum and Marmaris as 'terrifyingly' beautiful. Silver-leaved olive groves and wild inland mountains yield up the stone remains of ancient civilisations. The dazzling multi-coloured bays, framed by fissured cliffs and collared with golden sand, are the stuff of dreams. Snuggled into the coves are romantic fishing villages, where you will be greeted with genuine Turkish hospitality. And in Bodrum and Marmaris you can mix with the Turkish jet set.

The region has so much to offer that of couse there is a 'down' side: some dreadful over-development. Many of the once-idyllic fishing villages have changed substantially in recent years, some have even become centres of international mass tourism. But there is a new surge of ecological tourism afoot. In some old mountain villages and along isolated sections of the coast there are more and more small quiet places to stay — with the flair of 'Tuscany meets the East'.

This book covers the ground from the Bodrum Peninsula to Marmaris, 100km east of Dalaman Airport, and includes several excursions and walks in outlying areas. A companion guide, *Turkish Coast: Kaş to Dalyan*, explores the area between Marmaris and Kekova. When you've taken in all that, you might like to move further east to visit eastern Lycia and Antalya, covered in a third guide.

Bodrum and Marmaris highlights ...

... for lovers of beautiful beaches

There are hundred of kilometres of coast, and away from the large resorts plenty of still-peaceful coves and bays. Even more opportunties for sun, sand and sea are offered by the many boat trips to nearby islands. Here are a few of the top choices:

Gulf of Gökova — with the two bays of Mazıköy, this is one of the most beautiful stretches of coastline in Turkey.

Hayıtbükü Bay — a favourite with the yachting fraternity. There's Greek flair and not a trace of mass tourism in this small protected bay on the Reşadiye Peninsula west of Marmaris.

... *for archaeology and culture freaks*

Numerous ruined cities, among them some of the most imposing in Asia Minor, are evidence of the importance of this region in ancient times. Among the major sites covered in this book, the following stand out.

Knidos — a spellbinding combination of stone remains and the grandiose landscape of a dramatic coastline. This site lay undiscovered on westernmost tip of the Reşadiye Peninsula for two thousand years.

Ephesus and Aphrodisias — the former a major city before Rome was even founded, the latter with the best-preserved ancient stadium in the Mediterranean area. Both sites are among the most important in all Turkey and easily reached by bus or car.

... *for nature and landscape enthusiasts*

The tiny Bodrum Peninsula is full of contrasts, with a limestone west and volcanic east. The countryside around Marmaris is totally different, with swathes of green pine cloaking the hills like giant waves frozen in motion.

Reşadiye Peninsula — steep mountains, gorgeous bays. The sparsly populated peninsula, which separates the Aegean from the open Mediterranean, offers magnificent views to the Gulf of Gökova.

Pamukkale — Even if these white sinter terraces don't lie right in the Bodrum/Marmaris area, they are easily reached on a day trip. The sight is something special, even though you can no longer bathe in the travertines.

Publisher's note

A couple of decades ago, we published Brian and Eileen Anderson's 'Landscapes' walking and touring guides to the Antalya and Bodrum/Marmaris areas. Brian and Eileen are still Sunflower authors, but these guides eventually went out of print. There was so much building work going on from the 1990s that the books really needed revision annually, but because of the long distances involved, coupled with rising car hire, petrol and accommodation costs in Turkey, this was no longer practical for UK-based authors.

We've been able to remedy the situation by finding two German authors who have been visiting and writing about Turkey for many years, and an Englishman who has his own guiding business in the area. So this book has five authors, all with different interests. The walks were originally devised and written by Brian and Eileen; all were checked and rewritten where necessary by Dean just prior to publication, and everything else is down to Michael and Gabi, the main authors. Naturally this can lead to slightly different writing styles, but we hope it won't be a case of 'too many cooks'. A few notes follow.

Keep in mind that if a hotel or restaurant entry says 'recommended by readers', this refers to recommendations by *German* users of the original guides (in print for decades and revised every two-three years). This does *not* mean, however, that the establishment is predominantly frequented by German clients; what Michael and Gabi always seek out is the place with a personal touch, whatever the price category or clientele. Just log on to some of the hundreds of web addresses they provide with their recommendations!

Dean was a find; he has lived in Turkey for over 20 years and helped research and implement the famous 'Lycian Way'. He has been involved in conservation for many years and now runs his own company organising activity, nature and cultural/historical tours from his base at Kayaköyü, near Fethiye. If you want to explore the area east of Bodrum and Marmaris in depth, contact Dean at Seven Capes Sea Kayak Centre, www.sevencapes.com; ✆ 0252 6180390 or ✆ 0537 4033779.

One common thread binds all the authors: a shared love of Turkey's ancient history, landscapes and traditional hospitality. This shines through all the pages of the book — from the humorous boxed asides about mythological characters to their determination to retrace ancient walking routes despite the bulldozers and overgrown paths.

Key to the maps and plans

touring map
- motorway
- trunk road
- secondary road
- minor road
- track
- mountain peak
- viewpoint
- campsite
- ancient site
- location of walks

town plans
- parking
- beach
- museum
- mosque
- tourist office
- post office
- bus stop
- taxi rank
- car hire
- hospital, clinic

walking maps
- dual carriageway/trunk road
- secondary road/motorable track
- jeep track/path or old trail
- main walk and direction
- alternative route and direction
- bus, *dolmuş* stop/petrol station
- *sarniç*/tank, tap, water source
- mosque/ancient site
- windmill/viewpoint
- building/castle, fort or tower

Country and people of the crescent moon — Turkey in facts and figures

Official name: Türkiye Cumhuriyeti (Republic of Turkey)

Geography: With a surface area of 779,452 square kilometres, Turkey is more than three times the area of the United Kingdom. Just three percent of the area is on the continent of Europe, with the remainder (generally called Anatolia) being in Asia. Turkey's highest mountain is Mount Ararat (5165m) in the easternmost part of the country. Turkey is one of the most seismically active continental regions of the world, with a long history of earthquakes due to tectonic activities in the fault line and the drifting together of the Eurasian and Arabian tectonic plates.

Political system: Turkey is a parliamentary democracy. The president holds office for a period of five years; the current incumbent (since 2007) is Abdullah Gül. From 2012 the president will be elected by popular vote; a one-term re-election is possible. The National Assembly (Parliament) is the law-making body and has 550 seats. For a seat in the National Assembly a party needs at least 10% of the national vote.
In June 2011 the reigning conservative AK party, headed by Prime Minister Recep Tayyip Erdoğan, won a third term, with just under 50% of the vote. Erdoğan is the only Turkish Prime Minister to have won three consecutive elections with an increasing majority each time. The AK party now has 327 seats. The second-largest party is the CHP (the Republican People's Party), with 26% of the vote. The legislative session lasts four years. Laicism (separation of church and state) is guaranteed in the constitution.

Economy: After several boom years, with economic growth of 5-10%, Turkey has also been affected by the global economic crisis. As of press date, however, things were looking more positive for the future. According to the OECD, Turkey is one of the world's 20 largest economies. Its industrial sector, based mostly in western Turkey (textiles, chemicals, electronicals, motor vehicles and heavy machinery) accounts for 30% of GDP; agriculture (which employs a third of the total workforce) only 10% of GDP. The service sector contributes most — about 60% of GDP. The per capita GDP is just above Bulgaria's. But the overstretched budget is worrying, and the national debt could be more quickly reduced if more than only one out of ten people in employment paid tax.
Annual income (depending on the source consulted) ranges between £4000-£9000, but true figures are hard to come by on account of the black market economy. There are strong contrasts between western Turkey and the poor eastern provinces. At press date the minimum monthly wage was 760TL (about £320).

Population structure: In 2011 Turkey had approximately 74 million inhabitants (1960: 28 million); the average age is 28 (UK: 39.5). The population density is very varied. The administrative district of Istanbul with 1330 inhabitants per sq km is

clearly the most dense. The lowest population density is in the underdeveloped provinces in eastern Anatolia with only 16 inhabitants per sq km.

Sub-populations: 85.7% Turks, 10.6% Kurd, 1.6% Arab, and 2.1% mixed (Armenians, Greeks, Laz, Circassian, Georgians and Muslim Bulgarians).

Health/social: one doctor per 723 inhabitants. The average life expectancy for women is 73 years and for men about 68 years. Old-age pensions do not exist, nor are there any unemployment benefits.

Education: Eight years' schooling is compulsory. A third of all graduates go on to further studies at one of the 83 universities. The estimated illiteracy rate for women is approximately 18%, for men about 6%. However there is a strong contrast between east and west: in the western part, illiteracy is mostly confined to the older generation, whereas in the east (where child labour is still common) the figures include children as well.

Religion: 99% of the Turkish population are Muslims. The remainder are Jewish and either Syrian or Greek Orthodox Christians.

Military: The armed forces number 515,000 men and therefore are among the largest in the world (the second-largest in NATO). Military expenditure as a proportion of GDP is about 5% (about double that of the UK). This as come about because of ongoing conflicts with the Kurds in the east of the country and the power struggle with Greece. Soldiers are highly respected by the Turkish people.

Introduction

This book covers the Bodrum and Marmaris peninsulas and the area around the Gulf of Gökova — as well as three of the most popular excursion sites in southern Turkey: Pamukkale/Hierapolis, Aphrodisias and Ephesus. Most people using this book will be arriving at/departing from Bodrum's airport or Dalaman east of Marmaris. If you plan a longer stay, there is the option of moving east with *Turkish Coast: Kaş to Dalyan,* which covers the ground from here to Kaş and the Kekova/Simena area.

When to go

The Taurus mountain range (with heights of over 3000 m) prevents the cool air mass from off the Anatolian highlands penetrating to the south coast until late autumn. Thus long, hot summers alternate with short, mild winters. The hot season experiences low rainfall, while the winter months are wet.

The bathing season around the Aegean lasts from Easter until mid-October, and outside this period many hotels are closed. April, May, September and October are the best months to visit, when the daily maximum temperatures only rarely exceed 30 °C.

Getting to Bodrum and Marmaris

By air

Most people reach the area on **charter flights** — either into Milas-Bodrum Airport 35km northeast of Bodrum or Dalaman Airport 100km east of Marmaris. The area is so popular that at time of writing there were (charter) flights to both airports from Belfast International, Birmingham, Bristol, Cardiff, Doncaster Sheffield, East Midlands, Edinburgh, Exeter, Glasgow, Humberside, London Gatwick, London Luton, London Stansted, Manchester, Newcastle and Norwich. Additionally, there are flights to Bodrum from Bournemouth and to Dalaman from Leeds Bradford, Liverpool and Teeside.

Scheduled flights (with Turkish Airlines or BA) necessitate a changeover in Instanbul. From the United States it's rather a long haul, with flights by Turkish Airlines in cooperation with American Airlines and BA, stopping over in the UK.

Flight-only options are ideal for anyone who wants to make their own accommodation arrangements — or fly into Bodrum and return from Dalaman (or even Antalya). It's very easy to make your own arrangements on the internet, and perhaps book a **fly-drive** as well.

Prices are highest between April and October, when there are also more flights: expect to pay around £270 *including taxes*. But in 'off-season' there are some very economical deals — around £130 return or less *including taxes*. Obviously, booking well ahead (or at the last minute!) you may well be able to better these prices.

The **travel documents** you'll need are listed on page 50 in the 'A-Z' section; for information about Milas-Bodrum Airport, transfers, etc, see page 61.

Package tours to the Bodrum/ Marmaris area are offered by a huge number of companies and are perhaps the easiest option if you just want to stay in one place and haven't the time to make your own arrangements. All the major UK tour operators offer both resorts, but there are also specialists for Turkey. For a list of specialist Turkish tour operators, visit www.gototurkey.co.uk and click on 'Specialist Tour Operators' (in the USA/Canada see www.tourismturkey.org and click on 'Tour Operators'). The most popular resorts with the main tour operators in the area covered by this book are Bodrum itself, Bitez, Gümbet, Gündoğan, Ortakent, Torba, Turgutreis and Yalıkavak on the Bodrum Peninsula; Marmaris itself, and nearby İçmeler, Turunç and Hisarönü just to the south.

Naturally all tour operators will be only too happy to book you excursions to tourist sights outside the region, *gulet* trips along the coast, or even hiking tours. Often these excursions are offered at time of booking, or you can ask your tour rep about them.

The **baggage** allowance is usually limited to 20kg on flights, but if you are flying with a Business Class or other seat upgrade, or are staying longer than 28 days, you may be able to get this lifted to 30kg. Otherwise you are likely to have to pay about £3-7 per kilo for excess baggage (although if you're just a few kilos over they are likely to turn a blind eye). For **sports equipment** the rules vary between airlines: golf clubs and diving equipment are usually carried free, but sometimes they are classed as extra baggage for a flat rate of between £20-40. Bicycles, paragliders and surfboards can be charged at anything between £20-£100. Naturally you will want to check all this in advance — in any case you are legally bound to give the airlines advance notice of oversize baggage.

By car

Driving to Bodrum/Marmaris is *possible* for those who have plenty of time (allow 4-5 days), especially if you want to tour and camp (campsite details are listed under 'Accommodation'). You will need an international driving licence, the vehicle's registration documents and valid Third Party insurance. On arrival, details of the vehicle will be logged in your passport, and you won't be able to leave the country without it. After crossing the Channel, you would make for one of the Italian ports: *Ancona* or *Brindisi* for ferries to Çeşme in western Turkey (Marmara Lines; www. marmaralines. com) or *Ancona* or *Venice* for ferries to Igoumenitsa in Greece (Anek Lines, www. anek.gr). The option via Greece is cheaper, but it's another 1000km to the Turkish south coast.

By train

This option is only for those really keen on rail travel; it is far more expensive than air. There are daily departures from London via Brussels or Paris to *Istanbul* (several routes, each taking three nights and with multiple changes of train). For details of these trips, see www.seat61.com. At the same web site there are links for onward travel in Turkey itself but, since no trains serve the coast, at some point you have to change to a bus.

Driving on the Reşadiye Peninsula

Getting around Bodrum and Marmaris

By car or motorcycle

Having your own wheels makes travelling around the peninsulas uncomplicated, but some caution is required. Once warrior-like Turks hunted on their steppe horses; today their great-great-great-grandchildren handle themselves with equal prowess in traffic — the combat cry has simply been replaced by the horn. For many drivers there is only one lane — the middle of the road. Overtaking on blind corners, driving the wrong way on a one-way traffic lane or street, not stopping for red lights: these things happen all too frequently. You will see all this for yourself in time, but it pays to be aware of it from the start. If this is your first visit to Turkey or this area, consider renting a car once you get acclimatised at your base, rather than picking it up at the airport — especially if you are arriving at night.

You can **rent a car** in the tourist centres on nearly every corner whereas, in comparison, the number of places offering **mopeds, motorcycles** and **bicycles** is pretty modest. If you are interested in renting any sort of vehicle, you must of course have your driving licence and passport or ID card. Some rental companies require that the driver is at least 21 or even 23 years old and has had their driving licence for at least one year. The large international rental companies usually forbid you from leaving asphalt roads so that, strictly speaking, you would not be allowed to drive to any bays or ancient sites only accessible via tracks. If you plan to do a lot of driving, look for a car that uses less expensive diesel.

Prices are usually substantially lower from local hire companies than from the large international chains. Depending on the season, you'll pay between £15-30 per day with the smaller companies. They offer this price advantage by having an older and usually less well-maintained fleet of vehicles. The prices of the better-known hire firms differ little — again, depending on the season, they charge about £35-55 per day for the cheaper models. Whichever you choose, the mileage is usually free. The best value is to book by the week before leaving home, and can be cheaper still if booked straight away as a **fly/drive**. Prices for motorcycles begin at approximately £20/day, scooters start at £15/day.

Do read the **small print**: make a note of the **insurance cover** specified in the contract, and particularly personal liability in the event of a claim. Note for instance that even with fully comprehensive insurance, underbody damage and flat tyres are not covered. Various rental companies accept credit card payment; gold cards usually offer an additional insurance protection/cover, which makes it

Special advice for motorists

- *Avoid driving at night if at all possible. Badly lit lorries and cars will be on the roads — to say nothing of people on completely unlit bicycles and farmers in dark clothing on their way back from work. The risks of an accident are also higher at night because you can't see the potholes and building works ahead, and they may only be marked off with some stones.*
- *If you are in the first row at a red light when it changes to green, look right and left before going ahead — not all your fellow road-users are interested in the colour play of traffic lights…*
- *In Turkey it is common practice to sound your horn before a blind bend. If the oncoming traffic does not hear anything, they assume the road is free. It is also common practice to sound your horn when overtaking!*
- *Exercise special caution on loose chippings, particularly on newly built stretches of road. Thousands of windscreens are broken every year. Keep well back from lorries!*
- *Take care after rain, especially if it hasn't rained for a long time; the roads may be like ice rinks.*
- *In order to curtail speeding, frequent radar controls are in place (minimum fine £35), and speed bumps have been added in recent years at the entrances to built-up and populated areas. For those who don't yet know their way around, these speed bumps can be treacherous, because there are usually no signs to make you aware of them, nor are they marked in colour (apart from large oil marks!).*

Traffic signs — what's what?

Bozuk satıh — bad stretch of road
Dikkat — be careful; caution
Dur — stop
Düşük banket — unfinished road
Kaygan yol — slippery surface
Park (yeri) — car park
Park yapılmaz — no parking
Şehir merkezi — city centre
Tamirat — roadworks
Taşıt geçemez — road closed (driving through prohibited)
Yavaş — drive slowly
Yasak — forbidden/no entry

unnecessary to take out passenger insurance or the like. If in doubt, ask your insurance broker.

Should you be unfortunate enough to be involved in an **accident**, you must ***not*** move the vehicle, but summon the police, no matter how remote your situation or seemingly minor the damage. A police report is mandatory for any insurance claim. *Do not sign any report which you cannot read* — or else make a note on the report that you could not read it. There are a few scare stories around about accidents involving personal injury to the effect that it's better to put your foot down and drive to the nearest police station as quickly as possible, lest you meet with summary justice at the scene. However well meant, this is totally irresponsible advice. You would be charged both for hit and run and for not giving aid, with far worse consequences than any possible reprisals at the scene of the accident.

Keep the following **traffic regulations** in mind: the **maximum speed** in built-up areas is 50km/h, outside 90km/h (with a caravan or motorcycle 70km/h, in a camper van 80km/h). On divided highways cars 110km/h, camper vans 90km/h. On motorways cars 120km/h (with a caravan or motorcycle 80km/h, in a camper van 100km/h). The **blood alcohol limit** for drivers of *cars without trailers* is 0.5mg/l, for everyone else (including motorcyclists) there is *zero tolerance*, no alcohol permitted at all. **Mobile telephones** may only be used with a hands-free device.

Petrol stations are frequent along the main roads and open seven days a week. Lead-free *(kurşunsuz)* petrol is readily available. Petrol prices in Turkey are higher than those in Britain at time of writing, with a litre of normal unleaded costing approximately £1.35 (diesel £1.20).

Don't worry if you have a **puncture**; the Turks are very helpful. Ask for the nearest *Oto Sanayi* — a group of workshops, usually on minor roads at the entrance to or exit from the larger communities.

By bus

The bus is the king of cross-country travel. The number of companies with networks serving the whole country is incredible, and the price differences are small.

The busiest companies use modern Mercedes or Mitsubishi buses, which are manufactured in Turkey under licence. Air-conditioning (take a jumper with you on the bus!) and video are standard; the majority of the buses also have toilets, tinted windows, special seat cushions, etc. Well-known companies are Metro, Ulusoy, Kamil Koç, Pamukkale and Varan. The better bus companies give you a token for your stowed luggage, so it's easily retrieved at the end of the trip. During the journey passengers are usually catered for by a young steward. Biscuits and drinks are distributed free of charge, as well as a Turkish eau de cologne *(kolonya)* for sticky and sweaty palms.

All the buses are non-smoking (but they stop for breaks approximately every two hours). The departure times listed in this book serve only as a rough indication and refer to data from the larger bus companies. Journeys with the smaller (predominantly local) bus companies invariably take longer, since they make so many stops along the route. Further information about bus travel can be found with introductory details about the towns and villages covered.

Bus fares vary little; on average one pays 3-4 pence/km, with the up-market companies charging somewhat more. So a trip from Marmaris to Datça would cost about £2.45. Booking a ticket also includes a **seat reservation**, and you can choose your seat from a plan. Naturally the front seats are usually the best and most coveted, but wait: you may be exposed to the driver's cigarette smoke — unlike the passengers, the drivers *are* allowed to smoke on the bus!

Arrive well in advance of **departure time!** Buses leave punctually — and often up to five minutes early!

Turkish **bus stations** *(otogar, terminal* or *garaj)* are very like British and continental *railway* stations, with toilets, waiting rooms, kiosks, restaurants and shops. If there is no official 'left luggage', you can usually leave your things at the counter of your bus company. Bus stations are usually located several kilometres outside the city centres, so to get to them you often first have to take a service bus or *dolmuş*. But the well-known companies and local bus companies normally offer a feeder service with mini-buses from the centre of town. Smaller towns frequently only have a collection of simple bus company offices near the market, and the buses either leave from just outside the office or stop briefly on the town bypass.

At larger bus stations, **touts** working for different bus companies will try to persuade you to one ticket counter or other. Just ignore them, so that you can compare departure times and prices in peace.

By Fez Bus

The 'Fez Bus' (www.fezbus.co.uk) is a hop on-hop off service aimed at backpackers and independent travellers. From the beginning of June until the end of October a Fez Bus leaves Istanbul every two days and makes a circuit round half of Turkey before going back to the Bosphorus. With just one pass (which is valid for the whole season), you can get on and off as often as you want on whichever route you've booked, and you do not have to start at Istanbul. The basic route (Istanbul — Gallipoli — Selçuk — Köyceğiz —

Gulets *anchor in crystal-clear coves during the 'blue cruises'.*

Fethiye/Ölüdeniz — Olympos — Antalya — Cappadocia — Ankara — Istanbul) is called the 'Turkish Delight Pass' and costs about £175, including an English-speaking tour guide. There are a great many add-ons, too — from detour routes on the mainland to *gulet* cruises and trips to Greece and its islands.

By *dolmuş* (shared taxi)

Shared taxis are one of the most popular ways to get around in Turkey. *Dolmuş* means 'full up'; in practice, this means that they do not operate to a strict timetable, but instead set off when the driver is happy that he has enough people on board. A *dolmuş* (usually a mini-bus seating from 14-20 people) can be recognised by a sign on the roof or hanging in the window indicating the destination. In cities there are special *dolmuş* stations for connections to outlying parts of the region, otherwise they leave from the town markets. In large connurbations some routes will have intermediate stops. Moreover, you can stop a *dolmuş* anywhere along its route by waving it down. The *dolmuş* is a boon for walkers!

Dolmuş **prices** (specified by the city councils) are somewhat higher than bus prices in city traffic, but a bit less once outside the built-up areas. The fare is usually collected once you are underway. A new law demands that prices for different distances must be shown, but this is not always adhered to — in which case take note of what your fellow (Turkish) travellers are paying, or you may end up paying an additional 'tourist fare'. The longer routes are broken down into sections, and you only pay for the stretch you travel.

By taxi

In the tourist centres you can find a taxi on every corner. The fares for longer journeys (for instance to some tourist attraction, site, etc.) are usually posted in the taxi in various currencies. For trips within the cities it's best to take a taxi with a meter or negotiate the price in advance. *Caution:* sometimes taxi drivers 'inadvertently' press their meter button, so as to make the fare higher. During the day *gündüz* must appear on the display (*gün* = day, *gündüz* = daytime; *gece* = night).

By train

Railways are not, so far, a significant element in Turkey's transportation network, and there are no trains operating in the Bodrum/Marmaris area.

By ferry

There are ferries from Bodrum to Rhodes and the Gulf of Gokóva (for Marmaris): www.bodrumexpresslines.com. In high summer there are two ferries a day to Datça: www.bodrum-ferryboat.com. Both have offices at the ferry quay near the castle.

By chartered boat

The Lycian coast and the southern Aegean are among the most popular sailing waters of the Mediterranean, as you can tell from just one look at all the top yachting magazines on sale in the area. Boats can be chartered locally, with or without a skipper. Bodrum and Marmaris are both major yachting centres. Or you can anchor in many secluded ports and bays.

By organised tour

Take a helicopter to Pamukkale, a bus to Ephesus or a boat to one of the offshore islands: whether by air, land or sea, all the tourist centres offer innumerable half-day, full-day and two- or three-day excursions to local and surrounding sights. If you

'Blue cruises'

The 'blue cruise' business is booming on the Turkish coast. A blue cruise is an all-inclusive holiday on a gulet, *a beautiful, broad-beamed wooden yacht. While they do have masts and sails, they are usually motor-powered, and the only sail which is always raised is the protective awning.* Gulets *are usually very comfortably equipped, since blue cruises don't cater for yachtsmen but for tourists who enjoy seeing the coast from the water, bathing in isolated coves … and sharing the 'on-board' experience with others. The only disadvantage is that, once the initial excitement has worn off, sharing a confined space with strangers can be trying. Backpackers will be used to this kind of accommodation and have the right attitude, but for more mature travellers it's a good idea to book as a group and charter your own* gulet.

Blue cruises are named after trips made by a famous circle of philosopher friends who gathered round the bohemian journalist Cevat Şakir Kabaağaçlı. This 'Turkish Jean-Paul Sartre' published his work under the alias 'Fisherman of Halicarnassus', after he had been exiled to Bodrum because of his anti-militaristic stance. He fell in love with the area and stayed on. In the early 1960s a group of his disciples joined him in Bodrum, where they all sailed along the Aegean coast on sponge-diving boats, trying to live as close to nature as possible and surviving primarily on fish and rakı. *They called their soul-cleansing travels 'mavi yolculuk', or 'blue journeys'.*

Tetrapylon at Aphrodisias, a popular destination on organised tours

haven't time to plan an independent excursion or you prefer not to travel on your own, these organised trips are an enjoyable way to learn more about Turkey. From the price point of view, they are most economical for those travelling on their own, since a couple could probably hire a car for the same money. Even better value are the boat trips to secluded bays which you cannot reach by car.

The big catch with many bus tours and boat trips, of course, is that most of the routes are nearly identical, so many bays and tourist attractions are inundated with huge crowds for a just few hours of the day. What's on offer, and where, is listed for each area in the section 'Practicalities A-Z' under 'Boat trips' and 'Organised tours'.

Prices for these excursions do not vary greatly between tour operators. If you *do* find a tour that is substantially cheaper than that offered by the majority of operators … then you can expect far more shopping breaks for carpets than are normally in the programme! The tour guides of course earn commission on everything you buy.

By bicycle

It's rare to find bicyles for hire — and when you do, they are usually poor quality. Cycling here is still in its infancy so, if you want to tour this area by bicycle, take your own bike — and a helmet as well (you must wear one by law). Combined moped/bicycle workshops offer help with punctures and repairs — provided no exotic spare parts are needed.

By hitchhiking

It's not common to hitchhike in Turkey, since public transport is so inexpensive, but in principle it's possible everywhere and once in a while is the best option at the end of a walk. But unaccompanied female travellers should *not* hitchhike on their own.

Walking

In recent years the development of the Lycian Way, Turkey's first long-distance trail, has been widely publicised. If you hadn't read that this is one of the world's top walks, you might never have thought of Turkey as a destination for walkers.

But you are in for a pleasant surprise! While you won't be following any of the Lycian Way (it ends well to the east of Marmaris and is covered in the *Kaş to Dalyan* and *Antalya to Demre* guides), in spring and autumn there is no more beautiful way to discover the Bodrum/Marmaris area than on foot. The countryside around each offers spectacular and unexpected walking opportunities. The scenic variety is awe-inspiring in the rugged open volcanic regions near Bodrum, while the green-cloaked hills of Marmaris rolling into an azure-blue sea present images certain to stop you in your tracks. This book describes **20 *day* walks**, with many variations, using local transport — or a car if suitable. There are walks for all ages and abilities, and all are graded.

Seasons: The best months for walking in this part of Turkey are those either side of summer: **April, May, September and October** (although early September can still be hot). The two walking seasons, spring and autumn, present different opportunities, but **spring** is loveliest, with a freshness in the air and flowers at their best.

By April the temperature is rising and, given average conditions, sunny days are plentiful, but there can still be showers around or short unsettled periods. (Equally, temperatures can rise to 30° and more.) May sees a steady transition to the hotter, drier conditions of summer. As the temperatures continue to climb throughout June, the walking season ends. In high **summer** walking is *not* advisable, owing to the constant dangers of heat exhaustion and dehydration.

At some time in September, a short unsettled spell brings a change and, although the fine weather usually continues well into the **autumn** and often to the end of the year, the temperatures fall back into the 20s°C. This autumn rain brings on a new spring: cyclamen suddenly brighten the woodlands and olive groves, the crocus are persuaded into flower, and it is a delight to walk again.

Winter rains can be heavy, but there are many fine days, and the cool, clear conditions are ideal for walking. February is the earliest month that can be considered, although March is a better choice, with the real possibility of some gently warm weather.

Guidelines: The **time checks** given at certain points always refer to the total walking time from the starting point, based on an average walking rate of 4km per hour and allowing an extra 20 minutes for each 100m/330ft of ascent. These time checks are not intended to pre-determine your own pace but are meant to be useful reference points. Do bear in mind that they do not include any protracted breaks. Before tackling one of the longer hikes, compare your pace with the authors' on one of the shorter walks. Depending on your level of fitness, you may also consider some of their 'easy' walks to be 'easy-moderate' — or even 'moderate'.

Please accept some words of caution: keep to the routes described and do not try to make your own way in this vast, rugged and difficult terrain. Points that may look close can sometimes take many hours to reach. There is hardly any sign-posting or waymarking, and

Walk 20 begins and ends here at Datça.

there are no accurate large-scale topographical maps. For any walks except those graded 'easy', it will help to have some walking experience, a good sense of direction, perseverance, stamina *and a little good will!* This last is particularly true for Bodrum and Marmaris, where there is so much ongoing building work. New developments spring up overnight, and walks which were checked just a few months before press date change substantially. Be sure to add extra time for this kind of problem and *check the online Update for the book before travelling!*

If you are an **beginner walker** or you are just looking for a gentle ramble, look for walks graded 'easy', and be sure to check all the short and alternative walks. Where there is some point of interest part-way along a walk, it is suggested as a turning-back point, but there is no reason why you shouldn't turn back even sooner.

Experienced walkers should be able to tackle all the walks in this book, taking into account the season and weather conditions of course. Quite a few are very long, so be sure of your fitness before you attempt them.

It is never advisable to walk alone, and this is especially true for women. If you must go alone, carry a mobile and a loud whistle to use as a distress signal in case of an accident. Whether you are alone or in a group, *do* inform a responsible person where you are going and what time you plan to be back.

Maps: The **maps** in this book have been drawn up from a wide variety of base maps — all very different, none of them accurate. Detailed large-scale maps for Turkey are not yet available, and it remains an area of some sensitivity. (Do *not* try to obtain large-scale maps in Turkey; at the very least you will be regarded with suspicion.) If anyone sends in GPS tracks for these routes, we will post them on our web site and use them to improve our maps (if a reliable government map becomes available).

Equipment: Give careful thought to **basic gear** before you go. Many footpaths are steep and stony; comfortable **walking boots** with ankle protection and good grip are strongly recommended. Long (and fairly thick) **trousers**, tucked into **long socks**, will help you avoid being scratched by prickly bushes and will keep ticks at bay too. **Sun protection** is crucial: sunhat, suncream, sunglasses, and a long-sleeved shirt. Always carry **plenty of fluid and food**: depending on the length of the walk you will need 1-3 litres of liquid per person. Your day **rucksack** should of course contain a **first-aid kit**, small **torch** and **mobile phone** (see page 48 for emergency numbers). You may also want to take an **anti-venom kit** (available from specialist camping stockists); see 'snakes' below. Between October and May, you should also take a **windcheat** and **waterproofs**; in winter a **fleece** or two, **woollen hat** and **gloves**. In summer, don't forget **swimming things** where appropriate. Any other special gear will be listed under 'Equipment' at the top of each walk (Walk 18, for example, suggests **secateurs!**).

Nuisances: Most pet **dogs**, and even strays, are harmless, but take care around shepherds' dogs, which may be aggressive. (If dogs worry you, take a 'Dog Dazer', an ultrasonic device which persuades aggressive dogs to back off; they are available from the Sunflower website, www.sunflowerbooks.co.uk.)
But you will have to be on your guard against **snakes**. Most are harmless and will move out of your way rapidly but, if they don't, the best advice is to quietly move out of their way. There are **vipers** around and, since it would be dangerous to step on a viper, it is ***imperative*** that you do not walk in the countryside in open sandals. Always have your feet and ankles well covered and, as a sensible precaution, wear your long trousers tucked into your long socks. Take special care near water, when you are about to sit down, or when you rest your hand, so unthinkingly, on a drystone wall. If you do have the misfortune to be bitten by a snake, seek medical help urgently — and if you cannot identify the species, kill it and take it with you!
In comparison with snakebite, the sting of the **scorpion** is painful, but not dangerous to most people. Again, as a precaution, don't leave any of your clothes on the ground.
Wild boar forage for food in the mountains, but they are nocturnal creatures, and unlikely to be seen.
You can avoid **ticks** by keeping your body covered. If a tick does get to your skin, it is necessary to make it withdraw before taking it off; an easy way to do this is to touch them with a solvent such as methylated spirits or alcohol.
Bees and **wasps** are around in summer, so make sure you carry the necessary medications if you are allergic to insect bites. In any case, always give beehives a wide berth!

Accommodation

Accommodation in the area varies from up-market resorts where you will be handed cocktails in the jacuzzi down to places where you wouldn't go into the toilets without shoes. Most hotels and guest houses are located along the coast. There is a very welcome increase in the number of '**boutique hotels**' — small stylish places to stay (some marketed as guest houses), which are often housed in old, restored natural stone buildings. *This book places particular emphasis on this type of accommodation.*
The standard of most hotels is in direct relation to the price, but the best value for money will be found out of season (September to June). The growing Turkish middle class all want to spend their July/August holidays by the sea. While Turkey is still a relatively inexpensive destination, during high season not only are prices higher, but it can be difficult to find a room — reserving in advance is essential. ***All recommendations in this book mention facilities like air-conditioning or telephones only in establishments where you would not expect to find them. Average prices are quoted for high season, and include breakfast and private bathroom (unless stated otherwise).***

All-inclusive resorts

The bulk of all-inclusive resorts in the area is clustered around Bodrum and Marmaris. These places, often behind high-security fences and with up to 2500 beds, are not geared up to receive individual travellers at short notice, so booking is either impossible or very difficult. If you do manage it, the walk-in rate is often well above double the normal rate that you would have paid booking through a brochure.

Note, too, that the term 'all-inclusive' is not clearly defined, and some hotels give themselves this accolade without actually earning it. So make sure in advance whether for example the drinks or the sports facilities on offer are included in the price. And even where everything *is* 'all-inclusive', it may not mean the same thing in different establishments. Is the orange juice freshly squeezed or out of a bottle? The greed of many holidaymakers is contributing to ever-diminishing standards of quality.

Prices for the all-inclusive resorts depend on equipment, service, size of the buffet, sports facilities, number of hosts and hostesses, etc. and range from £60-£205 per night for a double room.

Hotels

All hotels are registered with the Ministry for Culture and Tourism and are assigned categories. If you choose your accommodation depending on the number of stars, be aware that the classification is based on *equipment* (mini-bar, television, lift, restaurant, air-conditioning, etc.); criteria like location, architecture, friendliness of the staff, and the like are not considered. Moreover the rating is often out of date, because many Turkish hotels were built 'on the cheap', so the equipment often wears out quickly. This applies particularly to three-star hotels. Luxury **boutique** hotels are not categorised by stars. In hotels at the bottom end of the market and in many guest houses you will just have to accept the fact that there isn't always hot water and the amenities are often unreliable.

Prices: The larger, sophisticated hotels charge from £65 for a double in peak season. In simpler places (where private bath and air-conditioning are nevertheless standard), you can get a double for half that and a single for about £25. Prices are up to 50% lower between mid-September and mid-June. A room in really cheap accommodation, without bath or WC, starts from £8 per person.

Getting ready for the sunbathers at Marmaris

Bodrum: view from the old harbour to the new one

Pansiyonlar (guest houses)

When comparing simpler hotels and small *pansiyonlar*, the latter are usually the better choice, since their operators usually care more about the well-being of their guests. Even when compared with some of the top hotels, the *pansiyon* may be preferable, because the friendliness of the owners makes up for the (rarely missed) luxuries. Air-conditioning and private baths are standard almost everywhere. *Aile pansiyonları* (guest houses for families) aren't everyone's cup of tea; these are often very simple places where everyone eats together — and you may not want to share your evening meal with people with whom you have little in common.

Many campsites (see below) also let rooms; equipment is spartan, but the rooms (often in bungalows) are usually very well done.

Prices for *pansiyonlar:* a double room with shower/WC/AC starts about £25 in high season. Singles are usually given a double room at a reduced price.

Aparthotels

The number of aparthotels has been rising constantly in recent years. Basic equipment includes a kitchenette or small kitchen, a living room with a sofabed and TV and — depending on size — one or more bedrooms.

Prices vary substantially, depending on size, equipment and location. You should be able to get a good apartment for 4 people for about £290/week in high season.

Youth hostels

In the whole of Turkey there are very few youth hostels, not least because many private *pansiyonlar* (see page 24) offer inexpensive rooms. There are *no* hostels in the area covered by this book.

Campsites

The **official, licenced campsites** are, like the hotels, under the control of the Ministry for Culture and Tourism. The normal amenities include showers (not always warm), camper kitchens and power sockets, restaurants and (usually) supermarkets. Prices here are commonly around double the price of **unlicenced campsites**, where the ameneties leave something to be desired. Many campsites also let bungalows and parking bays for tents and camper vans. The 'bungalows' are usually simple wooden huts without much in the way of creature comforts, but they usually have tiled floors, bath and WC, terrace, etc.
'**Wild camping**' isn't a problem in Turkey's mountains (where there is no other option), but not otherwise recommended: between curious villagers and police checks it can be a very unnerving experience.
Prices: For two people and a tent or caravan, reckon on paying £5-17; bungalows cost £12-£45, depending on equipment.
Opening times: Many campsites are only open from May to October. They are only crowded in high summer. By the end of September you may be the only guest on the site … and find that the bar and restaurant have closed.

Food and drink

'The Iman fainted', when asked to taste 'women's thighs' and the 'lady's navel'. 'The ruler was pleased' when served the 'vizier's finger'… Whole dramas can be performed based on the names of Turkish dishes! They also hint at which tradition the recipe falls back on and how much fantasy the chef puts into his creations.
'Life comes from the stomach' is a Turkish proverb. And in fact Turkish cuisine can claim to be one of the best in the world. The basis for the dishes is usually fresh vegetables, including some that are either unknown or seldom used in Britain and Europe (like chick peas, broad beans, okra and purslane). It's different with herbs and spices: they virtually never use Eastern exotica, but rather trusted classics like pepper, paprika or parsley. Garlic is also used, but not as much as you might imagine.

Where to eat

In Bodrum and Marmaris you can of course find anything from Chinese restaurants to Italian pizzerias, Bavarian beer gardens, and cuisine from around the world. For Turkish specialities the choice is primarily between *lokantas* and *restorans.* Smoking is prohibited everywhere; you can only smoke on outside terraces.
Lokanta: You eat in a *lokanta* to get a meal under your belt rather than to enjoy the 'dining out' experience. *Lokantas* are found on on every street corner; they are simple, good and cheap (prices start at £3.50). The décor — tiled walls and cold neon lighting — is spartan to say the least. The pre-cooked meals are kept warm in glass cases, and you select from meat and vegetable dishes, soups and stews. The busier the *lokanta,* the fresher the meals usually are. There are many

A bit like Disneyland — an evening at Bodrum's Moonlight Bar

variations on the *lokanta,* too: depending on what the speciality of the house is, it may be called a *kebapçı, köfteci* or *pideci.* At an *işkembeci* they serve soup with entrails and other innards. Most *lokantas* do not have an alcohol licence.

Restoran: Restaurants normally have an alcohol licence, more tasteful décor, better service and of course higher prices. But the menu does not always differ from that of the simpler *lokantas;* this applies in particular to mid-range restaurants. A full meal with a beverage starts at about £6.50. For the better restaurants there is no set limit: if you want to enjoy a candlelit dinner at an elegant restaurant by the water's edge, expect to pay £20 or so per person (without wine).

Fish restaurants — those that serve netted or line-caught rather than farmed fish — rank price-wise with the more expensive restaurants, and for a three-course set menu you can expect to pay £17-26 per person.

Tipping

*In simple lokantas no tip is expected, but in restaurants it is. If the service is **not** included in the total (note that quite often it **is** included), about 10% of the total bill is expected (15% in more expensive restaurants). In restaurants where they have no menus and prices on boards, it is advisable to enquire about the prices before ordering — some waiters are sly foxes...*

Breakfast

In the larger tourist hotels, an 'international' breakfast is nearly always served as a buffet; how sumptuous or otherwise depends on the grade of hotel. If you want something 'local', go to a *pastane* (pastry shop also serving hearty snacks).

Do try a traditional Turkish breakfast *(kahvaltı)!* You will be served fresh white bread, jam, eggs (usually hard boiled), olives, cucumbers/gherkins, tomatoes, butter and sheeps' cheese. Turks enjoy sheeps' cheese on bread with honey. With all this, tea is the drink of choice. Filter coffee is not usually available; those who want it will have to settle for *neskafe* or something similar. Turks also eat *pekmez* (thickened grape juice) as a spread with *tahini* (sesame paste) on bread for breakfast — and it's delicious!

Starters

You can choose from things like piquant creamy yogurt *(haydari),* spicy vegetable purée *(ezme),* cold vegetables in plenty of olive oil *(zeytinyağlı),* stuffed vine leaves *(yaprak dolması),* melon with sheeps' cheese *(peynirli karpuz)* and similar delicacies. The Turks call such starters ***meze,*** and display them in glass cabinets for you to take your pick. In the better restaurants, cold meats like chicken salad *(tavuk salatası),* as well as fish and seafood like *tarama* (pink roe with lemon) or prawns *(karides)* may be part of the *meze.* It's also fairly common to do without the main course altogether and select only starters; in many restaurants it's no problem. Fresh white bread *(ekmek)* is always served on the side.
Turks rarely choose **soup** as a starter. They have soup as a replacement for breakfast, occasionally in between meals ... or to nurse a hangover. Many Turks swear by the Alka Seltzer effect of entrail soup *(işkembe çorbası)* ... but this may not be to your taste! If you would like some hot soup as starter, try the hearty lentil soup *(merçimek çorbası)* — another speciality.

Meat

The most popular meat dishes are *kebaps* and *köfte.* ***Kebap*** is the generic term for meat dishes of any kind (usually lamb, sometimes calf or poultry), which can be baked, grilled, or roasted. There is probably no need to dwell on *döner kebaps. Şiş kebap* is a tender meat dish roasted on charcoal, served with rice or bulgar (cracked wheat). *Patlıcan kebaps* are skewered minced meat with aubergine. If the meat is arranged with yogurt and tomato sauce on roasted round flat bread it's known as a *bursa kebap* (or *ıskender kebap*). A *tandır kebap* consists of pieces of mutton braised in a sealed clay pot. Try, too, the *adana kebap,* a strongly peppered mince meat kebab. Or *güveç,* a tender pot roast with vegetables cooked in a clay pot.
Köfte are essentially meat patties or meatballs made from minced mutton, lamb or beef; they can be roasted or grilled. The tasty 'women's thighs' *(kadınbudu),* with added rice and a coating of breadcrumbs, get their name from the elongated shape of the meatball.
Turks love offal — like roasted liver *(ciğer)* or kidneys *(böbrek). Kokoreç* is a snack on offer at many street corners — grilled intestines with onions and tomato in bread. There are many, many other curiosities to try, like grilled sheep testicles *(koç yumurtası),* stewed sheep heads *(kelle)* or feet *(paça).*

Vegetables

Vegetables *(sebze)* are used as the base of Turkish dishes rather than as a supplement to a meal. The choice of pot-roasted, baked, and stewed vegetables is enormous. A particularly popular dish is *dolma:* this consists of stuffed vegetables, like zucchini *(kabak dolması)* or aubergines *(karnıyarık)* filled with minced meat or bite-sized pieces of lamb. It is usually eaten with yogurt. Various stews are also tasty; try *kıymalı ıspanak* (spinach with minced meat). Chick peas *(etli nohut)* or okra with lamb *(etli bamya)* are also delicious. ***Caution:*** Take it easy, at least to start. The food is often swimming in olive oil — on stomachs unaccustomed to this diet, this can have the same effect as a dose of castor oil.

Turkey for vegetarians

A tired smile is all that most Turks can offer a vegetarian — because those who voluntarily choose to do without delicacies like şiş kebap, köfte or entrail soup must be either ill or mad. Don't worry: even without meat one can enjoy delicacies in Turkey. The bulk of the starters are purely vegetarian, and there are plenty of tasty vegetable stews, creamy soups, salads and filled pastry dishes awaiting discovery. In order to avoid any nasty surprises, make sure by asking 'Etsiz mi?' ('Is it without meat?', *pronounced* 'Aytsis mee?') *and follow this up by saying* 'Et yemiyorum' ('I do not eat meat', *pronounced* 'Ayt yaymeeyorum').

Fish

Salt-water fish frequently on offer are sea perch *(levrek)* and gilthead sea bream *(çupra* or *çipura)* — both usually farmed and so relatively inexpensive. Among the more pricey fresh fish are turbot *(kalkan),* Mediterranean mackerel *(kolyos),* mackerel *(uskumru)* and sardines *(sardalya).* These are usually priced by weight. Tuna *(palamut)* features on many menus, too, prepared in several different ways. Octopus *(ahtapot)* and squid *(kalamar)* are often on the starters menu. Trout is a particular fresh-water favourite, and there are several trout restaurants in the countryside.

'Bio': *Turkey is one of the world's largest exporters of 'bio' products. Organic foods are popular with Turkish young people, who find them cool. But when you see 'bio' or 'organik' on the menu in a coastal restaurant, it's just vegetables from their own garden!*

Sweets and fruit

One of the most popular **sweets** *(tatlı)* is *baklava,* a pastry made from several layers of dough, interspersed with almonds and pistachios. The small rectangles have a syrup of sugar, lemon juice and honey poured over them. *Helva* is just as sweet and sticky, a calorific 'bomb' made of white flour, sesame oil, honey and sugar. Easier perhaps on the British stomach (and conscience) are almond pudding *(keşkül)* or rice pudding *(sütlaç).*

Those who enjoy experimenting should try *aşure* at least once — a jelly-like dessert: when prepared properly in a top-quality restaurant, this contains more than 40 ingredients, including

Aphrodisias is one of the most popular excursion sites.

rose water, nuts, cinnamon and even beans! It was inspired by the legend of Noah's ark — you mix all the left-overs together and boil them up.
The recipe for *tavuk göğüsü* is equally unusual — a mixture of chicken breast chopped into small pieces, rice flour, milk and sugar. All these and many others are on offer at the *muhallebici*, snack bars specialising in sweets.
If you are happiest ending your meal with **fruit** *(meyve)*, there is a wide choice. Depending on the season, melons, figs, grapes, peaches, cherries, strawberries, pomegranates or citrus fruits are available. Washing all fruit thoroughly is good, but peeling it is better!

Soft drinks

Pepsi, Coke and all well-known brands are on sale everywhere. Water *(su)* is often placed on the table with the meal. If it comes from the tap, you should *avoid* drinking it. Freshly squeezed fruit juices *(meyve suyu)* are recommended. Delicious fruit juices are also sold everywhere in cans. *Ayran* is a refreshing drink made from yogurt, salt and cold water — a little like buttermilk.

Hot drinks

The Turkish national drink is *çay*. This good black tea from plantations on the Black Sea coast is drunk at every opportunity. Whether at breakfast, business meetings, in carpet shops or at the hairdressers, the small bulbous glasses are found everywhere. Tourists seem to have taken a shine to *elma çayı*, apple tea. Turkish mocha *(Türk kahvesi)*, which can de ordered either sweet *(şekerli)*, slightly sweet *(orta şekerli)* or without sugar *(sade)*, is usually taken after a rich meal. Those who

Making a Turkish pizza (top) and döner kebab (bottom)

don't mind grit in their teeth order *neskafe*. In chic cafés you can of course also get cappuccinos, espressos or macchiatos.

Alcohol

Rakı is the favoured tipple — about 45 percent aniseed liquor — and tasting rather like the Greek *ouzo*. The Turks prefer to drink it diluted with ice and water from high, narrow 0.2 litre glasses. It then takes on a milky colouring and so is also called 'lion's-milk'. *Rakı* counts as a digestive and medicinal aid against all possible ailments, and 70 million litres are consumed each year in the interests of keeping the population healthy. You can tell good quality *rakı* from inferior brands because it makes a film on the glass (the brand most highly prized is 'Tekirda').

Beer *(bira)* is popular with meals, the Efes brand being the most common. Danish Tuborg (brewed in Turkey) is available; it's somewhat drier than Efes.

Less known are Turkish wines *(şarap)*. The better varieties are normally excellent — especially the Dolucas and Kavaklideres. Turkish wines are stomach-friendly due to their modest acid content. But as wine is fairly pricey, even in supermarkets, Turks usually only drink it on special occasions.

Snacks

Snacking is an art form in Turkey, and *börek* can almost replace a complete meal; this speciality is a filo dough triangle filled with minced meat, spinach or sheeps' cheese. Similarly delicious fillings are hidden in *pide*, a crispy flat bread. Also worth sampling is *lahmacun*, the Turkish pizza topped with minced meat and herbs.

Mantı is known as the Turkish ravioli — so small that 30 fit on a single spoon; you eat it with garlic-flavoured yogurt, melted paprika butter and mint.

Simit salesmen are always around; their sesame rings are at their crispiest early in the morning. One often sees women in traditional dress as well, preparing *gözleme*, a kind of pancake filled with different kinds of sweet or hearty ingredients. And try *kumpir*, if you get the chance, giant stuffed potatoes.

Ancient sites — the most important terms

Acropolis: castle hill, also the upper part of town
Agora: market and meeting place in ancient Greece; the major part of a colonnade, surrounded by shops
Architrave: a main beam (usually stone) resting across the top of columns
Basilica: central Roman hall, in which the side aisles are lower than the main aisle (only later was the term used for churches)
Bouleuterion: council hall of the senate in Greek and Roman times
Cavea: auditorium of an ancient theatre, in Roman times usually semi-circular, in Greek times usually facing outwards
Cella: main hall of a temple, usually with one or several religious statues
Gymnasium: centre for athletic training, originally part of a school
Heroon: religious building in honour of a hero or dignitary
Capital: uppermost end of a column
Necropolis: graveyard
Nymphaeum: fountain
Odeon: theatre-like building for small cultural events
Orchestra: performance area of the theatre
Pantheon: a temple for all gods
Peristyle: a space surrounded by columns
Propylon: gate building
Stoa: roofed colonnade or portico

Beaches

The search for sun, sand and sea attracts millions to the Bodrum/Marmaris area every year. Some of the most beautiful and best-known beaches lie along the coast, but there is a multitude of idyllic 'hidden' bays as well. **Naturism** is forbidden in Turkey (although it is quite usual to see Turkish men bathing in their underpants). There have been quite a few police raids on beaches frequented by naturists.

The local young people prefer this sort of scene to the isolated cove.

Average water temperatures

January	15°C	July	24°C
February	14°C	August	25°C
March	15°C	September	24°C
April	16°C	October	22°C
May	18°C	November	19°C
June	21°C	December	17°C

Books for background reading

John Julius Norwich, *A Short History of Byzantium* (Penguin, 1998)

Louis de Bernières, *Birds without Wings* (Vintage, 2005)

George E Bean, *Turkey Beyond the Maeander* (John Murray, 1989), available from Amazon

Freya Stark, *Ionia, a Quest* (John Murray, 1954)

Chemists

Turkish pharmacies (*eczane;* open Mon.-Sat. 09.00-19.00) have more or less everything you would find at home. Many medicines are called by a different name, however, and are often available without prescription (for instance, antibiotics) — and they are cheaper too.

The nearest **24-hour chemist** *(nöbetçi)* will be shown in the window of the *eczane*.

Children

Turkey is paradise for those travelling with children. If your offspring plays sailboats with plates in the restaurant or cries on a long bus trip, nobody will get worked up over it, the pieces of broken glass will be removed with a smile, your child will even be comforted and probably given sweets. You will be welcomed with children wherever you stay — whether in a simple *pansiyon* or a luxury hotel. The latter often provide babysitters who arrange an interesting children's programme, the former will welcome you with unbelievable warmth — with the host even taking the little ones fishing on his boat. For alternatives to building sand castles there are

Camel Beach

camel rides on the beach, aquaparks with giant water slides, etc.

For nappies, Ultra Prima have the best reputation, and for baby foods Ülker and Mılupa (both are available in pharmacies and some supermarkets).

Climate and weather

See 'When to go' on page 10 and the detailed information for walkers on page 19. Below some statistics.

Monthly averages

	air temperature*	hours of sun	rainy days
Jan.	10°C (7/16)	5	11
Feb.	11°C (7/17)	6	10
Mar.	13°C (8/18)	7	7
Apr.	16°C (11/21)	8.5	4
May	20°C (15/25)	10	3
Jun.	25°C (19/30)	12	0
Jul.	28°C (23/34)	13	0
Aug.	28°C (23/34)	12	0
Sep.	25°C (19/31)	10	1
Oct.	20°C (15/26)	8.5	5
Nov.	15°C (11/21)	6	7
Dec.	12°C (8/18)	4.5	11

*followed by minimum/maximum

Consulates/embassies

Embassies for the English-speaking countries are located either in Istanbul (✆ prefix 0212) or Ankara (✆ prefix 0312).

UK ✆ 0312 455 3344
USA ✆ 0312 455 5555 (Ankara) and ✆ 0212 335 9000 (Istanbul)
Ireland ✆ 0212 246 6025
Australia ✆ 0312 459 9500
New Zealand ✆ 0312 467 9054

In case of emergencies, there are also British honorary consuls in Bodrum and Marmaris:

Bodrum
✆: 0252 313 0021
📠: 0252 313 0017

Marmaris
✆: 0252 412 6486 (ext. 36 or 39)
📠: 0252 412 4565

Crime

Thefts and robberies are relatively rare in Turkey. The country's worst crime is corruption, but that's another story and not a problem for tourists. Nevertheless, do be aware that, like everywhere else, there are cheats and con artists around — especially in the big cities and tourist centres. If you have a problem, contact the nearest police or tourist information office. They will help you because tourism is critical for the economy.

Of course it is a good idea to take the usual precautions of leaving valuables (including unneeded credit cards) in a hotel safe (*never* on view in a car or on the beach), carrying no more cash than you need, and keeping to well-lit streets at night. And make sure no one is 'spying' on you when you key in your PIN number!

Illegal drugs are on sale in Turkey: marijuana, hashish, opium and heroin. The punishments for bringing drugs into or out of the country, or drug use are severe — and Turkish prisons are known the world over for their dreadful conditions. *Never take a package out of the country without knowing what is in it.*

Currency

The currency is the Turkish lira (*Türk lirası* or TL). **Notes** to the value of 1, 5, 10, 20, 50, 100 and 200 TL are in circulation. One Turkish lira comprises 100 *kuruş* (KR), and **coins** have been issued for 1, 5, 10, 25 and 50 KR, as well as 1 TL. Inflation has fluctuated in the past few years at around 10%.

The prices quoted in this book were as accurate as possible at the time of writing (2010), but will no doubt differ greatly from the prices you find on the spot! This is partly due to the fact that prices in Turkey do not rise or fall in line with inflation, but remain stable for longish periods and then jump steeply. But of course the chief factor is the instability of all exchange rates at present. **At the time of writing £1 = 2.36 TL.**

Turkey's **foreign exchange control regulations** require you to declare cash amounts to the value of US $5000 (about £3250) or more on departure.

You can **exchange currency** at banks (normally open Mon.-Fri. from 09.00-12.00 and 13.30-18.00) or the many exchange bureaus in the area. The difference in rates between the two is generally small.

Cash machines (ATMs) are thick on the ground, too, and the exchange rate on withdrawals using a debit card *(Maestro)* is often better than in an exchange bureau. But always taking out small amounts may eat up any advantage gained, so it's better to 'tank up'. With *Maestro* cards you can take out up to 800TL a day (but some ATMs only allow 400-600TL a day).

Credit cards are accepted in all of the better restaurants, hotels and shops.

Not every branch of a bank is authorised to redeem **travellers' cheques**. American Express Travellers' Cheques can be cashed (as long as it's by the person who signed them) at branches of Akbank, Türkiye Bankası and Yapı ve Kredi Bankası.

Tipping: in restaurants the rule is generally 10% of the bill; hair-dressers, masseurs, chamber-maids (per day) around 2TL. You needn't tip taxi drivers, but rather round up the fare. In bars and cloakrooms just leave some small change.

Students reductions and other **concessionary prices** are shown with the relevant entry fees.

Dress

Away from the holiday centres in Turkey, great importance is attached to cleanliness and proper dress. For what to pack check the table of monthly averages on page 32. For a beach holiday on the coast, light clothes — preferably cotton — are enough, but remember that in spring a cool breeze blows off the water in the evening.

For visits to mosques see the panel 'Mosque etiquette' on page 41.

Shave ... or lose out

Whether bushy and magnificent or fine and delicate, they are always well trimmed: only a moustache makes a Turk a man — at least in Anatolia and in conservative circles. Even today village men who have worn moustaches for years keep an eye on the younger generation, to make sure that no young rascal grows a moustache before the 'proper' age.

But in many places on the south coast the young don't want to know about such antiquated traditions, so they are smoothly shaved or sport designer stubble. To them, the classical mousta-chioed male, with his standard grey department store jacket, has all the status of the village nincompoop from the Anatolian countryside. Even the young women see them as sleazy perverts with x-ray eyes. In some trendy clubs, the bouncers make sure that anyone with a moustache is barred.

Those who wear full beards also remain outsiders, at least when it comes to public offices and universities. In secular Turkey (see page 42) the full beard is seen as a symbol of the wearer's Islamic faith — the equivalent of women covering their heads.

Electricity

The power supply is 230 volts as in continental Europe, and two round-pin plugs are the norm, so take your continental or international adapter.

Festivals and holidays

The tourist centres on the coast have surprisingly little

information about national holidays — probably because it's always holiday time (but only for the tourist, not for them!).

1st January: New Year's Day

January or February: Kurban Bayramı (movable dates, four days); see page 41.

23 April: Independence Day, commemorating the first time the parliament sat in Ankara (on 23 April 1920). Is also celebrated today as 'Children's Day'.

1 May: Spring Festival (an unofficial holiday replacing the former Labour Day).

19 May: Youth and Sports Day; it marks the start of the Turkish War of Independence in 1919.

30 August: Victory Day, commemorating victory over the Greeks in 1922.

29 October: Republic Day; Turkey was proclaimed a republic on 29 April 1923. This festival is celebrated with parades.

October or November: Kadir Gecesi (movable dates); see page 41 and Şeker Bayramı (moveable dates); see page 41.

10 November: while not an official holiday, the day of Atatürk's death (1938) is 'semi-official', since a large part of the population stays away from work.

See also 'religious holidays' on page 41.

Flora and fauna

The coast is characterised by typical Mediterranean vegetation, with forests of pine and cypress as well as bushy macchia comprised of oleander, holly, kermes oaks, box trees, myrtles, lavender, carob trees, etc. On the

higher elevations, the prevailing tree is the Turkish pine *(Pinus brutia)*, but you will also find isolated firs and cedars.

Uncontrolled hunting of wild game has led to the decimation of animal numbers roaming free. Stags and roe deer once played in the forests; today one only sees them rarely. With a bit of luck, in the mountains you can still come across foxes, wild boar, badgers, polecats, tree martens, stone martens and the almost-extinct porcupines or rodents like the cute ground squirrel. Wolves and bears are found only in the most secluded parts of the Taurus.

Fauna with 'lower profiles' can be seen darting or waddling along on the ground — lizards, geckos and turtles. When you're out hiking, you will also see snakes once in a while. Most are not dangerous but, if you are going out walking, read more about snakes on page 22.

Of the birds, the storks (under protection in Turkey) are fascinating. There are also many birds of prey such as eagles, falcons and buzzards. Further

east (see the *Kaş to Dalyan* guide) ornithologists will be in their element on the beach at Patara and by the Dalyan Delta, where they can see grey and purple herons, kingfishers, white storks, songbirds, night swallows, and many more.
Finally, just another piece of advice regarding 'animal pests': mosquitoes, fleas and cockroaches don't only see the forests as their habitat!

Gays and lesbians

Behave discreetly! Homosexuality is frowned on in Turkey, where being outed leads to merciless discrimination. It's even one of the very few reasons accepted for avoiding military service. Turkish gays and lesbians can only avoid discrimination in the anonymity of very large cities like Bodrum and Marmaris. To find information about gay- and lesbian-friendly bars and hotels, see www.turkey-gay-travel.com.

Greeks and Turks

At the beginning of the 20th century the Greeks were the largest non-Muslim minority in the Ottoman Empire. Many places on the Mediterranean and Aegean coasts were in Greek hands. Over centuries they had lived together peacefully with the Turks; tensions were the exception, not the norm. But after the First World War and the attempt by Greece to seize Asia Minor, the situation changed. The Turkish War of Independence followed, at the end of which came the so-called 'population exchange' — a driving out and/or ethnical cleansing: some 1.4 million Greeks had to leave Turkey, while about 350,000 Turks moved back from Greece.
A Greek-Turkish 'Ice Age' began, which reached its peak with the Cyprus conflict. For many years NATO partners worried at the behaviour of its two warring 'allies'. The improvement in relations between the two nations has only come about in recent times with, for instance, each offering the other help with severe earthquakes and wildfires.

Import and export regulations

You are allowed the following **duty-frees** for personal consumption when entering Turkey:
200 cigarettes (400 if bought in a Turkish duty-free shop before going through customs)
50 cigars or 200g of tobacco
0.7 litre spirits
gifts to the value of £255.
If you come into the country with anything extremely valuable (a high-carat diamond for example), it must be registered in your passport by the Turkish customs on entry.
To **export antique objects** from Turkey, one needs the written permission of a museum director. This also applies to old seals, medals, carpets, etc. Offenders are threatened with harsh punishments. The export of **minerals** also needs written permission (from MTA in Ankara, ✆ 0312 2873430). To take or ship out **carpets**, you must produce a receipt.
When you leave the country, items bought for private use (clothing, for instance) up to a

value of £390 can be brought back into the UK tax free (at time of writing). Check with the airlines before leaving about the latest regulations on bringing back duty frees.

Information about Turkey

All the international branches of the Turkish Ministry of Tourism (www.gototurkey.co.uk or, in the USA, www.tourismturkey.org) have mouth-watering brochures that they will send on request (direct from their web sites). Otherwise you can contact:

UK
Turkish Culture and Tourism Office
29-30 St James's Street
London SW1A 1HB
☎ 020 7839 7778
Fax 020 7925 1388

USA (New York)
Turkish Government Tourism
821 United Nations Plaza
New York, NY 10017
☎ 212 687 2194/5/6
Fax 212 599 7568
ny@tourismturkey.org

Inoculations

No inoculations are *required,* but it is advisable to be vaccinated against tetanus, diphtheria, polio and hepatitis A before your trip. Double-check with your airline, tour operator or the Department of Health (www.dh.gov.uk), to see if there are any changes.
By the way, if you are plagued by a cold during your stay: blowing your nose in public is considered very unrefined in Turkey!

Internet access

Many hotels and *pansiyonlar* offer WIFI or internet access. There are also plenty of internet cafés. The more stylish the café, the more expensive it is to be on-line: half an hour costs £0.65-1.25. The addresses of internet cafés have *not* been given, because they change so frequently.

> **Tip on info**
> *Compared with many other destinations, there's relatively little information on Turkey's 'official' web pages, so it's worth surfing the names of places in this book — from hotels to sites. For practicalities, a brilliant site is www.turkeytravelplanner.com*

Invitations

The Turks are extremely hospitable. Those who enjoy mixing with the locals, whether on bus journeys or on visits to simple restaurants, are frequently spontaneously approached or even invited to tea. Invitations to their homes, on the other hand, for example for the evening meal, are much more rarely extended, because of the sanctity of the family.
If you are ever invited into anyone's home, you can take it as a sign of special esteem. Because of this, it is important to remember some of the host's customs and conventions (although small breaches of etiquette will obviously be forgiven).
Guests usually bring a **gift** — nothing lavish, just something simple that would please the host or family.
Shoes are removed at the entrance. If there are no indoor shoes ready, socks will do.
For a hearty welcome, one

traditionaly exchanges a double **kiss** (right cheek, then left cheek) — this is more common between people of the same gender than the opposite gender. If you are uncertain, just politely offer your hand and let your Turkish host take the initiative before committing a *faux pas.*

Speaking loudly in the presence of older people is considered poor manners. Seniors are treated very courteously. In traditional families it is even usual to stand when the head of the family appears.

To refuse something offered is impolite. The hosts have undoubtedle made a great effort to please you, possibly spending well beyond their means.

Islam

Islam (in English 'submission' or 'surrender') is the youngest of the major world religions. Like Judaism and Christianity, it is a strictly monotheistic religion; its followers believing in one omnipotent God. According to Islamic belief, Allah is the creator and guardian of all things and all life. He cares for, guides and judges human beings; on the day of the Last Judgement, 'the saved' enter paradise, while 'the condemned' descend to hell.

The religion's founder was Mohammed (around 570-632), who grew up as an orphan in Mecca. His religious and political work began around 610, after the Archangel Gabriel appeared to him in a vision, but his first sermons were received with scepticism in his home city. It was only when Mohammed moved to Medina in 622 (the start of the Islamic calendar) that he became established as a world and religious authority, generally accepted as a legislator and prophet. Some of Mohammed's messages were revolutionary for the times — for instance the condemnation of slavery in the name of God.

The role played by the Islamic faith in Turkey varies from region to region. For many inhabitants of the Westernised coastal towns, it means almost nothing. But just a few kilometres inland, things look very different. The swirling currents of Islam were a thorn in the side of pre-AKP governments, which chose the *imams* (who are government employees) and prescribed both what they were allowed to preach and what they could teach in theological lessons based on the Koran. With the coming to power of the pro-Islamist AKP, this strict control has changed to mutual agreement.

The Koran and *Sunna* are the fundamental teachings of the Islamic faith. The **Koran** (Holy Book of Islam), which consists of 114 *suren* (chapters), is believed to be the true word of God, as told to Mohammed by the Archangel Gabriel. This explains the infallibility attributed to the Koran. The Sunna ('Tradition') is a collection of 9th-century stories *(hadith)* about the life of Mohammed and his followers, giving an insight into how some of the Koran's more obscure chapters can be put into practice. In contrast to the Koran, the Sunna is *not* considered infallible.

Islam teaches that since human beings are morally weak and fallible, God sends **prophets** to

Koran, with translation into modern Turkish (see page 51).

The Five Pillars of Islam

The Koran dictates five obligations for all Muslims:

— profession of faith (kelimei şahadet): 'I testify that there is no God except Allah, and Mohammed is His prophet...')
— prayers (namaz) five times a day, washing before you pray
— extending charity to those in need (zekat)
— fasting during daylight hours during the month of Ramadan (oruç)
— a pilgrimage to Mecca (hac)

With some of the duties there is a bit of flexibility. Thus the Muslim need only make his pilgrimage to Mecca if he is healthy and can afford it; washing before prayer can be just done as a ritual, if no water is available; pregnant woman, the sick, and young children can postpone fasting.

them, who teach them how they should live. In Islam, Jesus also ranks among these prophets, beside Abraham and Moses. The Christian view, in which Jesus is seen as the son of God, is not shared by Islam. Muslims believe that the long line of prophets came to an end with Mohammed, and that the Koran is the final true word of God.

Disputes after Mohammed's death about who should succeed him led to **a splitting of Muslims into two main groups: Sunnis and Shiites**. Over 70 per cent of Turks are Sunni. The Sunni saw the caliph as Mohammed's legal successor and the head of the Muslim world. For the Shiites (the name comes from the Arabic word *schia, or* 'party'), however, only a blood relative of the prophet could stake their claim to leadership. Since Mohammed left no surviving sons, the Shiites saw Ali (Mohammed's cousin and son-in-law) and his descendants as the legitimate successors *(imams).*

Around 25 per cent of Turks (including many Kurds) are **Alevis**, who are Shias. But the only thing Alevis have in common with Iranian Shias is the belief in blood-line succession. For example Alevis reject the strict Islamic *Sharia* law: unchanged for more than 1000 years, this interpretation of the Koran and Sunna sets out the rights and obligations of individuals in the community and covers every conceivable aspect of life.

Mosques *(cami)* are not only intended for prayer; they are also used for community meetings, theological lessons, political

Laicism: separation of religion and state

'Islam will one day govern Turkey, the question is only whether the transition will be easy or hard, sweet or bloody.' Statements like this, from the former party chief Necmettin Erbakan, were one of the reasons for the banning of the Islamic Welfare Party (1998) and the Virtue Party that succeeded it (2001). From the broken pieces of the latter, the Party for Justice and Development (AKP) was formed, winner of the parliamentary elections in 2002. The banning of religious parties was justified on the grounds that Turkey had been a secular state, with a strict separation of state and religion, since Atatürk founded the republic ('any politician who needs the help of religion to run the government is an idiot').

For the revolutionary modernisers, supported by the military and Western-orientated politicians, Islam was the largest obstacle in the way of modernising the country. Atatürk rejected the Islamic calendar and withdrew Islam from its position as state religion. The Turkish experiment was the first and most successful example in the world of the secularisation of an Islamic state.

But even after all these years laicism is still exposed to many dangers, as was pointed out by the former Turkish President Süleyman Demirel (1993-2000): 'Our state is laical, but its population is not'. The secular way presents a constant potential for conflict, insofar as the basic Islamic social philosophy is the principle that all spheres of life form an inseparable unit, whether spiritual, social, political or economic. While radical forces militate for a religious state, moderates look for ways to preserve traditional Islamic values in today's secularised world and not play off one side against the other. A popular advocate of this approach is Yaşar Nuri Öztürk, Dean of the Islamic Faculty at Istanbul University. His publications rank among Turkish best-sellers.

meetings and temporary accommodation for pilgrims and the homeless.

Usually one enters a mosque via a forecourt *(avlu)*, where the ritual washing is done at the cleansing well *(şadırvan)* before prayer. The prayer hall, spread with carpets, consists of a prayer niche *(mihrab)* which always points toward Mecca, a pulpit for the Friday sermon *(minbar)* and a chair or kind of throne *(kürsü)*, from which the prayer leader *(imam)* reads out passages from the Koran.

Men and women pray separately, always however in the direction of Mecca. By kneeling and bending the head to the ground, one shows Allah humility and respect.

The muezzin calls followers to prayer five times a day from the mosque's minaret. Minarets were only introduced in the 8th century — before that the muezzins climbed onto the roof. But today the call to prayer, so alluring and 'Eastern-sounding' to the European ear, usually only comes from loudspeakers.

Mosque etiquette

Turkish mosques can be visited by non-Muslims at any time, but follow some simple guidelines:
— non-Muslims should not visit during prayers
— men should wear long trousers and long-sleeved shirts
— women should cover their heads and shoulders, and their skirts should be at least knee length
— shoes must be removed
— maintain a respectful silence
— those at prayer should not be photographed

The exact timing of **religious holidays** (see also 'Festivals and holidays' on page 35) is determined each year according to the Islamic moon calendar. In Islamic convention a holiday begins at sunset the evening before. When it comes to important holidays, all shops, offices, etc. will close at noon the day before. The following holidays are of particular importance.

Kadir Gecesi (Night of Power) falls on the 27th night of the fasting month of Ramadan. This holy night celebrates the Revelation of the Koran to Mohammed through the Archangel Gabriel. People believe that wishes and prayers expressed on this night will be granted.

Şeker Bayramı, the Sugar Festival, is the feast marking the end of Ramadan, the month of fasting. One visits relatives, and children go from house to house asking for sweets — hence the name. All businesses and public offices are closed for this three-day holiday.

Kurban Bayramı, the Sacrifice Festival, is the most important Islamic holy time and a four-day public holiday. This festival is rooted in the story of Abraham, who was willing to sacrifice his son Isaac, in order to prove his loyalty to God. At the last moment God provides a ram instead. The Turks follow in this tradition, with a lavish meal of newly slaughtered sheep for family and friends. All left-overs are donated to charity.

This is the time of year when pilgrims travel to Mecca, so that both domestic and international travel in Turkey is at a peak — be aware of this and try to avoid travelling on the first or last day. Remember, too, that banks will be closed and some ATMs will run out of money.

Ramazan

This is the name the Turks give the Islamic month of fasting, which is called Ramadan in most other Islamic countries. Followers may not eat, drink, smoke or have sexual intercourse between sunrise and sunset for 30 days. After darkness falls however … everything is possible. In conservative rural areas, you may find many restaurants closed during Ramadan, but of course In the holiday centres on the coast one hardly notices any difference.

Medical care

There is no reciprocal health agreement between Turkey and the UK (or any other English-speaking country); it is strongly recommended that you take out **private health insurance** and read the conditions carefully if

you intend to take part in any potentially dangerous sports like paragliding or rafting.
For minor ailments, it often suffices to visit one of the many chemists' shops and describe your symptoms to the pharmacist. Although they are very unlikely to speak English (use gestures), they have been dispensing remedies for the usual tourist problems for years. If by chance you are suffering from 'tourist tummy', straight away you might try drinking some black tea with a bit of salt in it.

Music and belly dance

To European ears, all Turkish music may sound the same, but there are different styles.
Folk music: In traditional Turkish folk music *(halk müziği* or *'Türkü')* a *saz* (Turkish lute, usually with three strings) takes pride of place. Soloists or small combos sing about the simple things of countryside life — birth, love, death. After decades of absence, Kurdish folk music is also making a come-back. One hears this music mostly in a cosy oriental tavern *(Türkü-bar).*
Classical (art) music: In contrast to folk music, *fasıl* or 'art music' is performed in restaurants. It had its origins in Ottoman palace music, but there are traces of more modern influences. The singers are usually accompanied by the *kanun* (zither), *darbuka* (hand drum), *tef* (tambourine) and *ud* (lute). One of the most successful interpreters on the Turkish art music scene is busty Bülent Ersoy: gaudily made up and clothed in mink and glitter, this corpulent 50-year-old Barbie Doll was a man until 1979.
Turkish **pop music** addresses the same topic as most English hits: love. 'Türkpop' mixes traditional Turkish melodies with modern influences, so the interpreter has a wide-ranging palette — from top songwriters like Sezen Aksu ('the Madonna of the Bosphorus') to trendy teen stars and even schmaltz.
Arabesque music, as the name suggests, has its roots in Arabian music: the topic is unrequited love. This rather monotonous oriental 'wailing' is often heard on the TRTint TV station ... or on the *dolmuş.* Top among performers is Müslüm Gürses, who comes across as a love-sick dachshund. There have been some notorious Arabesque concerts frequented by 50-year-olds (usually stoned) who fall about howling in ecstacy and cutting themselves with razor blades.
Many Europeans see **belly dancing** as the epitome of Turkish-oriental sensuality. But in Turkey itself, even today it is seen as somewhat indecent and is often attributed to other cultures. So for instance conservative Turks will tell you that these erotic shows originated in Egypt, whereas the Arabs are convinced that the dance was brought to Turkey by the Ottoman occupiers. Belly dance today is primarily put on for the tourist market.
Rock and electronic beats: Catchy guitar sounds are supplied by the female virtuosos Özlem Tekin and Şebnem Ferah, the soloist Teoman or the Duman Trio. Rashit's music is more punk. For grunge there's Mor ve Ötesi and for psychedelic Baba

Belly dancers' costumes on sale; below: catching up on the news

Zula. The percussionlist Burhan Öçal drummed his way into the international music scene, and the band Orient Expressions combined Anatolian folk music with electronic beats. For Turkish ska punk there's Athena. Among the country's most popular DJs are Emre and Murat Uncuoğlu. Arkın Allen, who lives between Montreal and Istanbul and is also known as Mercan Dede, pioneered links between Turkish Sufism and contemporary Western electronic music.

Newspapers and magazines

English newspapers and magazines are on sale in all the tourist centres on the coast, the papers usually available the day after publication. The English-language *Daily News & Economic Review* prints background information and current news — politics, economics, sport and culture. A new English-language daily newspaper, *Today's Zaman*, has appeared. It is very conservative (Islamic) editorially; if any Western-thinking Turks see you reading it, you will be shunned.

Opening times

The Islamic day of rest is Friday, but the legal day of rest in Turkey has been **Sunday** since Atatürk's reforms.

Banks: see 'Currency', page 33.

Government offices: Mon.-Fri. 08.30-12.00 and 13.00-17.30; closed Sat./Sun.

Shops: The retail trade has no standard opening times; usually shops open Mon.-Fri. from 09.00-13.00 and from 14.00-19.00 and on Sat. from 09.00-13.00 only. But in tourist centres every day is shopping day. Large shopping centres are also usually open every day until late in the evening.

Post office: Open Mon.-Fri. 08.00-12.00 and 13.00-17.00; closed Sat./Sun.

Museums: 08.30-17.00; usually closed Mon., but see individual entries.

Restaurants: Usually open daily from 11.00 until at least 23.00. But small *lokantas* often close early in the evening.

Everything from scarves to seeds is on sale at the weekly pazar.

Police

You'll see a lot of police about. Since they are very badly paid, they are usually bad tempered — except in their dealings with tourists, when they are generally very pleasant and courteous. The *jandarma* is another police force — a military unit in green uniforms, who ensure public order and security.

Post offices

Post offices (and post boxes) are instantly recognisable by their yellow signs with the three black letters PTT. The main post office *(merkez postane)* in larger cities is usually located near the main square or the bank and/or shopping district. A **postcard** takes about a week to arrive in the UK. Post offices usually have **telephones** (see page 48).

Prices

Compared with the UK, Turkey is an inexpensive destination, even if prices in the tourist centres are higher than in the rest of the country. What a holiday will cost you depends on your requirements, but there is something for virtually every budget. Living very simply, for instance in a *pansiyon* with breakfast provided, picnic lunch and one restaurant meal, you could get by on well under £35 a day, including bus or *dolmuş* travel.

What Turkish names can mean

Imagine your butcher being called Etyemez ('he does not eat meat') or the drinks salesman Eck Suiçmez ('he does not drink water'). This can happen in Turkey.

The many strange, composite surnames go back to a law passed in 1934. In the course of Atatürk's reforms the Turks, who until that time had no surnames, had to give themselves one. Some could select a name, others were appointed one. Some made perhaps a suitable choice for their circumstances at that time, but didn't consider the legacy that would be left to their sons and daughters. And so the piano player at the hotel bar may be called Parmaksız ('without fingers')...

Unfortunately, today only the choice of first names remains. But these are in no way lacking in imagination either: the joy felt at the birth of a first child may be expressed by the name Devletgeldi ('the luck came') or Gündoğu ('the sun rose'). On the other hand, sometimes when the family is too large, they hope to be able to stop by naming the last-born (whether a boy or girl) Yeter ('this one's enough') or Dursun ('it ought to stop').

Shopping and bargaining

Leather goods, carpets, gold jewellery, ceramics, tea, spices, onyx, and all the other purchases that hint of the Orient are among the most popular souvenirs. Not forgetting T-shirts, jackets and trousers from the top designer labels — these are all imitations of course, but at least they fulfil their purpose: one can wear them. On the other hand, take care with the deceptively packaged top-name perfumes, which are just ghastly.

It's best to buy from boutiques and shopping centres in the larger cities, where items are priced and you can compare prices.

Where there are **no fixed prices**, you must **bargain**. To bargain well, you must be able to estimate value and authenticity. Without wishing to get the better of you, unfortunately just about all Turkish dealers are sly as foxes (like the waiters mentioned earlier). So don't let them sell you artificial leather as fine napa lambskin and only believe a fraction of what you are told. If you know, when you first plan your trip to Turkey, that you will be interested in buying gold jewellery or carpets, check the value of what you want to buy in your own country before you leave.

Turkish **weekly markets** with stalls selling everything from vegetables and cheese to clothing and shoes are called *pazar*; **fixed markets**, like those at the market quarters, with proper shops, are *çarşi*.

VAT: If you buy anything to the value of around £60 or more from shops or boutiques with a tax-free symbol in the shop window, you can get the VAT of 8% refunded in the airport departure lounge at so-called 'Cash Refund Offices' (the counters are usually in the airport check-in hall). To claim the refund you need a completed tax-free receipt from the seller.

Some tips for buying hand-knotted Turkish carpets are in the panel opposite … forewarned is forearmed.

Sites and museums

Some of the most famous ancient sites in the world are covered in this book and the *Kaş to Dalyan* and *Antalya to Demre* guides. You will also come upon a multitude of other sites, all indicated by brown signs. The most important of these are described, usually with accompanying site plans. Any site not described here is not worth the visit, unless you are a fanatic willing to walk a long, sweaty way through brambles just to stand next to a couple of weathered stones.

The **entrance prices** for ancient sites and museums are not uniform and are updated annually. Once in a while you find extreme jumps in price of 30-50% (up or down). However, as a rule of thumb, an entrance fee of up to £9 applies at the major sites. At time of writing only rarely were **concessions** available for students (with ISC) or seniors — this may change in future.

Photography or filming (video) occasionally costs extra and then usually *quite a bit extra* (up to £8!). On the other hand there are many sites with free entry.

A word to the wise: often self-appointed 'guides' try to take money from tourists. Don't let yourself be taken in; only officially-authorised guides can hand over an entrance ticket!

Sport and leisure

The Turks are becoming more sports-orientated. Joggers, walkers and hikers will no longer find themselves conspicuous! But in places where the Turks themselves holiday, the sports on offer are meagre — after all, the precious holiday weeks are taken for recovery, which means lazing about. In the international tourist centres however, the trend is

Buying Turkish carpets

Turkey is well known for its low-priced carpets. But you have to know what you're doing and exactly what you want. Most tourists are talked into buying something on the spot — usually overpriced, too large, too small, or in unsuitable colours.

To negotiate a good price you must be able to distinguish high-quality workmanship from inferior goods. Forget everything you've ever heard about settling on one-third the asking price to guarantee a bargain; everyone gets two-thirds off after the tenth tea. The dealers know all about this rule of thumb, so who's to say that they don't start with a price magnified a hundredfold?

If you know next to nothing about carpets, by all means buy a small, cheap one as a souvenir (when you consign it to the loft the moths will be happy) — or go to a specialist back home, put up some security, and take a carpet home to try out.

If you must *buy a carpet in Turkey, go with the advice of an expert: check the thickness of the knots and the number of knots per sq cm. Flex the carpet in natural light, dividing the pile with your fingers to make sure the colour goes straight through. Be careful not to burn a hole in the carpet with the infamous cigarette lighter test, or you'll fall straight through. Be sure to ask if the carpet can fly and, if not, immediately ask for a 50% discount. If you heed all this advice, the dealer won't take you for a fool. One more thing:* never *accept a dealer's offer to post your carpet home for you!*

towards European-style active holidays. More and more tour operators offer leisure and sports programmes in addition to the obligatory excursions to touristic highlights. Naturally water sports dominate along the coast.

Diving: You can snorkel with mask and fins almost anywhere along the coast, but underwater hunting with tanks is forbidden — as is removing any historical and/or antique articles.

Golf: There is a 5-hole course on the Bodrum Peninsula (www.golfclubbodrum.com) and another near the airport; despite what their web site (www.vitaparkgolfresort.com) says, it has 12 holes, not 18. A course is planned for Marmaris (date unknown). But Belek, about 45km east of Antalya, is the golfing centre of Turkey, with championship courses.

Paragliding: The flying centre is Kocadağ (640m) between Bodrum and Marmaris; see under 'Ören' on page 107.

Riding: There are riding stables at Bodrum offering treks in the highlands; you can usually book through local tour companies.

Sailing: see page 17.

Surfing: Bodrum is one of Turkey's top places to surf; the surfing schools also rent boards.

Tennis: Many of the larger hotels have tennis courts, at which non-guests can also pay to play.

Water sports: In the international resorts on the coast, various water-based activities are offered. Reckon on paying £20-£25 for 15 minutes on water skis, £25-£30 for 10 min. parasailing, £20-£25 for 10 min. jetskiing, £8 for 15 min. banana-boating, £60-£70 per hour in a speedboat with a 50 HP engine or £90-£100 for a 115 HP engine. The organisers are usually on the beaches.

Telephone

Making calls with a mobile is problem-free in nearly the entire area, but the roaming charges are expensive. If you make *a lot* of calls, or if you plan to stay in Turkey beyond a couple of weeks, it would pay to buy a SIM card from a Turkish network operator. But you will have to buy a new or used Turkish mobile as well (they're available everywhere), since Turkish SIM cards tend not to work in foreign mobiles after a week or so.

Those who don't have a mobile or want to save money should make calls using a card phone. **Telephone cards** *(telefon kartı)* are available from post offices, kiosks and small roadside stands. A good choice for international calls is the Arakart: 100 units for example (about £2.70) allows you to phone the UK for 15 minutes.

International dialling codes: for the UK first dial 00 44, for the USA 00 1, for the Irish Republic 00 353. This is followed by the local code (without the initial zero, if there is one), then the number.

Calls to Turkey: From outside the country dial 00-90, then the local code (without the initial zero), then the number.

Internet: Many hotels and guest houses now offer WIFI, whereby you can call free using Skype (www.skype.com).

Beware of making calls from your hotel room; these are often charged at extremely high rates. Better to make a brief call and ask to be called back (directly to your hotel room).

Emergency numbers

Police ☎ 155

Traffic police ☎ 154

Ambulance ☎ 112

Fire brigade ☎ 110

Time

Turkey is on Eastern European Time, two hours ahead of Greenwich Mean Time, in both summer and winter (clocks go forward or back on the same days). At noon in Turkey, it's 10am in the UK, 5am in New York.

Günnücek Milli Parklar is a lovely green park bordering the sea about 1km east of Marmaris's bus station — a pleasant place to stretch your legs.

The *hamam* — cleansing body and soul

The saying goes that the Ottoman past lives on in the hamams, the traditional Turkish communal steam baths which cater for all classes. Once inside, you're in a different world … enveloped by hot, moist air and the smell of soap, relaxing under the spell of splashing water and the murmurings of shining naked bodies lying on a huge marble slab.

The hamam *is divided into three areas. The entrance hall (camekân), usually with a decorative fountain, is surrounded by the reception and changing rooms. On entering, you will be given a small robe (peştamal) and sandals. While it's usual for men to wear a towel around the loins and for women to bathe naked, you can bring a swimsuit if you prefer.*

After changing you move through a passageway (soğukluk) into the main part of the hamam, *the steam room (hararet). The huge marble slab in the centre, which is warmed from below, is the* göbek taşı *(navel stone).*

First you are expected to wash all over at the basins along the wall, then rise thoroughly (taking care to leave no suds behind, in case the water is used for ritual washing at the mosque). Then you lie on the marble slab, first to sweat for 15 minutes or so, and then to be massaged.

Women are usually massaged by a hefty masseuse, men by wiry muscle-men. Before the massage begins, the tellaks *soap you down, then use a very rough flannel for exfoliation (a procedure called the* kese*). By this time your limbs are soft and rubbery, ready for the massage. Be warned: you will be pulled, twisted, kneaded and pummelled like a lump of dough; the massage is intended to loosen tight muscles and joints. Afterwards you will feel totally drained, totally relaxed.*

Most hamams *have separate sections for men (erkekler) and women (kadınlar). At smaller baths men and women bathe at different times or on different days, but in tourist centres mixed bathing is sometimes offered.*

Toilets

Men's toilets have the label 'Bay', women's 'Bayan'. In tourist centres the facilities are usually up to European standards; otherwise is it not uncommon to find the stand-up 'hole in the floor', and *no* paper. *Take your own!* If a small bucket is provided in the toilet cubicle, please throw any paper in there and do not try to flush it away — the old-style thin sewage pipes simply cannot cope (and besides, toilet paper in the cesspits delays decomposition).

Naturally there are toilets in museums and at sites (small charge), and in restaurants. Otherwise you can usually find public toilets near a mosque.

Travel documents

Travelling from the UK or any English-speaking country you will need a **passport** and a **visa**. Package tour operators will arrange visas for you, otherwise you can buy one on the spot *for cash* at the airport or border when you enter Turkey.

While not strictly required, it is suggested that you also have a **ticket** for return or onward travel.

At time of writing you do not need any **inoculations**, but see page 37. Private **health insurance** is strongly recommended; see page 42; **travel insurance** is mandatory.

If you plan to hire a car, you must have your **driver's licence**; if you are driving to Turkey in your own car, see pages 11-12.

Visiting or business cards

Turks seem to love them, and will sometimes honour you by handing you their card, or will ask for yours. Before a Turk hands you his card, he will usually make a squiggle on the back, thus 'invalidating' the card. This is because in the past people could go into a restaurant or shop, and it was understood that the bill would be settled by the person named on the card.

Turkish

In all the tourist centres you should be able to communicate in English with no difficulty. But in the countryside you may have problems if you don't know at least a few words of Turkish, since many schools there teach no foreign languages at all.

Turkish is a very logical language and, once you have mastered a few of the rules you can progress quite rapidly, especially with pronunciation. A number of the letters in the Turkish language are unfamiliar to English speakers, but are easy to pronounce; one or two 'normal' letters are pronounced differently. **In Turkish, *usually* the first syllable is stressed.**

C/c	pronounced like the 'j' in 'jet'; *cami* (mosque) is pronounced **dja**mee
Ç/ç	pronunced 'ch'; *çam* (pine) is pronounced **cha**m
Ğ/ğ	just elongates the previous vowel; *dağ* (mountain) is pronounced **daah**
İ/i	pronounced 'ee'; *iki* (two) is pronounced ee**kee**
I/ı	pronounced 'eh'; *altı* (six) is pronounced al**teh**
Ö/ö	pronounced like the 'ea' in 'learn'; *köprü* (bridge) is pronounced kurh**prew**
Ş/ş	pronounced 'sh'; *şeker* (sugar) is pronounced **she**ker
Ü/ü	pronounced like the 'u' in 'lure'; *köprü* (bridge) is pronounced kurh**prew**

Basic words and phrases

Evet/hayır	Yes/No
Lütfen	Please
Teşekkür ederim	Thank you
Affedersiniz	Excuse me
Merhaba	Hello
Allaha ısmarladık (said by the person leaving)	Goodbye
Güle güle (said by the person staying)	Goodbye
Hoşça kal	So long, cheers
Günaydın	Good morning
İyi günler (as a greeting or when leaving)	Good day
İyi akşamlar	Good evening
İyi geceler	Good night
Nasılsın?	How are you (singular)?
Nasılsınız?	How are you (plural)?

İyiyim	I'm fine.
... var mı?	Do you have...?
Saat kaç?	What time is it?
Büyük/küçük	Big/little
İyi/kötü	Good/bad

In towns

Tren istasyonu	Railway station
Garaj/otogar	Bus station
Havalimanı/ havaalanı	Airport
İskele	Ferry dock
Saray	Palace
Sokak	Alley
Cadde	Road
Meydan	Square
Cami	Mosque
Hisar	Fort
Kule	Tower
Kilise	Church
Müze	Museum
Banka	Bank
Hastane	Hospital
Köprü	Bridge
Ada	Island
Kütüphane	Library
Kitabevi	Bookshop
Eczane	Chemist
Bakkal	Grocer
Süpermarket	Supermarket
Pazar	Weekly market
Çarşı	Market
Postane	Post
Seyahat acentası	Travel agency

Modern Turkish

Originally Turkish contained many Arabic and Persian words written in Arabic script. Despite Atatürk's language reforms (the Roman alphabet has been used since 1928), these influences remain. In his attempts to make the language more 'Turkish', the old words had to be transliterated into the Roman alphabet, leading to some inconsistencies that remain today.

Directions/getting around

Nerede ... ?	Where is ... ?
Ne zaman?	When?
Sağ/sol	Right/left
Doğru	Straight ahead
Otobüs	Bus
Tren	Train
Araba	Car
Taksi	Taxi
Vapur	Ferry
Yaya	On foot
Bilet	Ticket
Varış	Arrival
Kalkıs	Departure
Giriş	Entrance
Çıkış	Exit
Tuvalet	Toilets
Bay/Bayan	Men's/Ladies'
Açık/kapalı	Open/closed
Polis	Police
Girilmez	No entry

Numbers

Bir	1	*On sekiz*	18
İki	2	*On dokuz*	19
Üç	3	*Yirmi*	20
Dört	4	*Yirmi bir*	21
Beş	5	*Otuz*	30
Altı	6	*Kırk*	40
Yedi	7	*Elli*	50
Sekiz	8	*Altmış*	60
Dokuz	9	*Yetmiş*	70
On	10	*Seksen*	80
On bir	11	*Doksan*	90
On iki	12	*Yüz*	100
On üç	13	*Iki yüz*	200
On dört	14	*Bin*	1,000
On beş	15	*On bin*	10,000
On altı	16	*Bir milyon*	1,000,000

Eating and drinking — general

Şerefe!	Cheers!
Yemek listesi	Menu
Bunu ısmarlamadım	I didn't order that
Hesap, lütfen	The bill, please
Kahvaltı	Breakfast
Öğle yemeği	Lunch
Akşam yemeği	Dinner

Tabak/çatal	Plate/fork
Bıçak/kaşık	Knife/spoon

Breakfast

Beyaz peynir	Sheep's cheese
Bal	Honey
Reçel	Marmalade
Ekmek/tereyağı	Bread/butter
Yumurta	Egg
Seker/tuz	Sugar/salt

Drinks

Çay/kahve	Tea/coffee
Türk kahvesi	Turkish mocca
Neskafe	Instant coffee
Süt	Milk
Meşrubat	Non-alcoholic
Su	Water
Soda	Sparkling water
Meyve suyu	Fruit juice
Ayran	Drink made of yogurt, water and salt
İçki	Alcoholic drink
Bira	Beer
Fıçı bira	Draught beer
Şarap	Wine
Beyaz şarap	White wine
Kırmızı şarap	red wine
Viski/votka	Whisky/vodka

Starters

Meze	Turkish starters
Ezme	Vegetable or yogurt cream
Haydari	Yogurt dip with mint and garlic
Humus	Hummus
Patlıcan salatası	Aubergine salad
Zeytinyağlılar	Cold vegetables in olive oil (various types)
Piyaz	Salad of beans, olive oil and lemon
Sigara böreği	Elongated fried pastry filled with sheep's cheese
Çerkes tavuğu	Chicken in walnut sauce
Beyin salatası	Salad of calves brains
Çiğ köfte	raw meatballs
Çorba	soup
Mercimek çorbası	Lentil soup
Yayla çorbası	Yogurt soup with mint and lemon
Domates çorbası	Tomato soup
Tavuk çorbası	Chicken soup
İşkembe çorbası	Entrail soup

Main courses

Dolma	Stuffed vegetables
Yaprak dolması	— vine leaves
Biber dolması	— peppers
Patlıcan dolması	— aubergines
Kabak dolması	— zucchini
İmam bayıldı (literally 'the Iman fainted')	Baked aubergine with onions and tomatoes
Güveç	Braised vegetables, often with bits of meat
Köfte	Meatballs
Hindi	Turkey
Tavuk	Chicken
Piliç	Small chicken
Sığır/dana	Beef/veal
Kuzu	Lamb
Pirzola	Cutlet
Karışık izgara	Mixed grill
Şiş kebap	Skewer
Adana kebap	Peppered mince kebab
Bursa kebap	Doner kebab/tomato sauce and yogurt
Tas kebap	Braised lamb
Arnavut ciğeri	Pieces of liver

Fish and seafood

Alabalık	Trout
Balık	Fish
Barbunya	Mullet
Levrek	Sea bass
Lüfer	Blue bass
Kılıç	Swordfish

Sardalya	Sardines
Kalkan	Turbot
Hamsi	Anchovy
Uskumru	Mackerel
Dil balığı	Sole
Midye/yengeç	Mussels/crabs

Vegetables and side dishes

Sebze	Vegetables
Bamya	Okra
Kuru fazulye	Dried beans
Taze fazulye	Green beans
Bezelye	Peas
Havuç	Carrots
Ispanak	Spinach
Karnıbahar	Cauliflower
Lahana	Cabbage
Domates	Tomatoes
Zeytin	Olives
Soğan	Onions
Salatalık	Cucumbers
Sarmısak	Garlic
Salata	Salad
Çoban salatası	Mixed salad with sheep's cheese
Yeşil salata	Green salad
Cacık	Yogurt/cucumber/garlic
Makarna	Noodles
Patates/pilav	Potatoes/rice
Bulgur	Cracked wheat
Yoğurt	Yogurt

Fruit

Meyve	Fruit
Armut/elma	Pear/apple
Karpuz	Watermelon
Kavun	Honeydew
Üzüm/muz	Grapes, banana
Portakal/limon	Orange/lemon
Çilek	Strawberries
İncir/kiraz	Figs/cherries
Şeftali/kayısı	Peach/apricots
Nar	Pomegranate

Desserts, sweet

Tatlı	Any sweet
Sütlaç	Rice pudding
Lokum	Turkish delight
Dondurma	Ice cream
Kek/pasta	Cake/gâteau

Snacks

Börek	Stuffed filo pastry
Gözleme	'Turkish pancake' (filled)
Lahmacun	Turkish pizza
Simit	Sesame rings
Turşu	Pickled vegetables

Women

Thanks to the reforms of Atatürk in the 1920s (and Turkey's ambitions to join the EU), the position of women is nothing like that in most Islamic countries. Nevertheless there is a large discrepancy between their legal rights and reality in a country so long dominated by men. Naturally the divide is greatest between town and country. The increased literacy rate is mainly due to the education of women. On the Mediterranean coast and in the towns, over 50% of the female workforce are educated beyond the compulsory eight years, but in the countryside the figure falls to 5%, and one woman in three is illiterate. On the other hand, more women are in managerial positions than in many other European countries: a third of the doctors are women, a quarter of the lawyers and a fifth of the judges. **Women travelling alone** won't be treated any differently in the tourist areas than would be the case in, for instance, Italy or Spain. To avoid problems, it's sensible to dress decently and even wear a 'wedding ring' and carry photos of your 'husband' and 'children' (all can be fake). If you're approached, speak formally and avoid eye contact. Should you be out at night, it's best to get a taxi back to base.

From about 150,000 BC (palaeolithic): Nomadic hunter/gatherers roam across the Turkish Mediterranean coast according to finds from caves near Antalya; cave finds on the Aegean coast date from about 80,000 BC.

8,000-5500 BC (neolithic): In what is now southeastern Turkey town-like settlements spring up, which today rank among the oldest 'cities' in the world. Loam is used in the building of dwellings. With the establishing of settlements, agriculture and cattle breeding also begin. Pottery is developed at about the same time — during excavations close to Konya (about 150km northeast of Antalya as the crow flies), archaeologists discovered small sculptures of full-breasted goddesses, symbols of fertility.

5500-3200 BC (chalcolithic): More finely-worked pottery and simple tools come into use, wrought from copper. The first settlements on Turkey's west coast date from the end of this period.

3200-2000 BC: The Early Bronze Age sees the spread of spinning and weaving mills, as well as bronze jewellery work. Troy is founded, the oldest city on the Turkish coast. Traders from Assur (on the Tigris in what is today northern Iraq) meet with the central and eastern Anatolians, bringing them into contact with writing.

2000-1200 BC: The Hittites cross the Caucasus, and central Anatolia becomes part of the 'Old Kingdom', from which the 'Great Kingdom' is later formed. Hattussas (some 170km east of Ankara) is made the capital. At the same time Mycenaeans expand their rule over the Aegean as far as Minoan Crete. Troy develops into a prosperous trading centre.

Around 1200 BC: The so-called 'Sea People', about whom little is known, invade from the north via Thrace. Among them are the Phrygians, who play a substantial role in the destruction of Troy and also put an end to the supremacy of the Hittites and Mycenaeans.

1200-700 BC: There is an increase in Greek colonisation (Aeolian, Ionian and Dorian) on the Mediterranean coast of Asia Minor. They come into direct competition with the local tribes (Lelegians, Carians, Lycians, and Lydians). By the 9th century BC many of these Greek settlements have grown into substantial ports.

690-550 BC: The Lydians found a large kingdom in the west of Asia Minor, with Sardis as its capital (about 90km east of İzmir); their king, Croesus, becomes legendary. They also conquer further parts of the south and west coasts. Art, culture and science begin to flourish in the cities.

From 545 BC: Under Cyrus the Great, the Persians penetrate as far as western Anatolia and destroy the Lydian Kingdom. They use satraps (colonial governors) for the administration of Asia Minor. Regular rebellions against the Persians follow.

From 479 BC: The Persians withdraw from the Aegean coast.

Cities and small towns come and go.

334-333 BC. Alexander the Great conquers Asia Minor. This is the beginning of the Hellenistic period, which lasts until the era of the Roman Caesars and brings enormous cultural development.

From 323 BC: After Alexander's death the Macedonian Kingdom disintegrates; its army leaders divide it among themselves. The most important of these Diadochian realms are those of Ptolemy (in Egypt), incorporating Lycia and other parts of the south coast, the Attalid Kingdom of Pergamon in western Anatolia, and the Seleucid Empire — the largest part of Alexander's former kingdom, with Antioch (modern Antakya) as the capital.

From 133 BC: On the death of Attalus III, Pergamon passes to Rome and becomes the first capital of the new province of Asia; the capital later moves to Ephesus.

42 BC: With Caesar's murder, the eastern part of the Roman Empire falls to Mark Antony.

31 BC: Octavian (later Emperor Augustus) is victorious over Mark Antony's fleet in the battle of Actium. Beginning of the 'Pax Romana', lasting nearly 250

Hardly anything remains of the Artemision of Ephesus, one of the Seven Wonders of the Ancient World.

years. Roman culture penetrates all cities in Asia Minor. Temples, boulevards, theatres, aqueducts and the like still bear witness today to the glory of the age.

45-60 AD: St. Paul the Apostle stops off at Ephesus and visits different cities on the Lycian coast during his missionary journeys. The first Christian communities are formed.

330: Emperor Constantine (the Great) names the former Byzantium (Istanbul today) Nea Roma (New Rome) and makes it the new capital of the Roman Empire. Soon after his death, Constantinople becomes the generally accepted name.

380: Christianity becomes the state religion; all pagan cults are forbidden.

395: The final division of the Roman Empire into west and east. The latter, later known as the Byzantine Empire, becomes the heartland of Christianity, with Roman law and Greek as the language.

527-565: Under Emperor Justinian I, Byzantium expands and blooms. It extends from southern Italy over the Balkan Peninsula and the whole of Asia Minor to the edge of the Iranian highlands. All building activity is concentrated in Constantinople. The coastal towns play a subordinate role from now on, even though many of them are made diocesan towns.

622: Mohammed and his followers emigrate to Medina (the *Hijra*, or 'Flight'); this is later designated the first year of the Islamic calendar.

From 636: Eastern Byzantium is conquered by the Arabs. Trained by Syrian sailors, seaborne invaders plunder the Byzantine coastal towns. Coastal fortresses are rebuilt or strengthened for protection — often using ancient stonework for the building materials.

1054: Schism of the Roman Catholic and the Greek Orthodox churches.

From 1071: Seljuk Muslims penetrate west from the Kirgistan steppes and attack Byzantine troops in the battle of Manzikert. They bring Islam with them, and spread throughout central Anatolia, making Konya their capital and holding the remnants of the Byzantine Empire in fear.

From 1096: Help comes to Byzantium from the Occident: the Crusades begin, to free the lost holy cities from Islamic rule.

1204-1261: The Fourth Crusade is organised against Constantinople itself, with the intention of reviving the Roman Catholic faith. After taking the city, the Knights establish a Latin (Roman Catholic) Empire. The Greek Byzantines withdraw to Nicea (İznik); it is not until 1261 that, under Michael VIII Palaeologos, the Greeks take Constantinople back from the Latins.

1226: The Seljuks conquer further parts of the coastal region. Venetians and Genoese receive permission to establish future trade.

From 1243: The Seljuk Sultanate is crushed by the Mongols. In its place several small principalities are established in Anatolia by Turkmen dynasties.

From 1309: The Order of Knights of St. John found a sovereign state on Rhodes; in the following years they establish various fortresses in the Aegean.

1326: Osman I (1281-1326), army leader and chieftain of a Turkmen tribe, conquers the west Anatolian city of Bursa, later called the cradle of the Ottoman Empire. Since Mongolian armies control the east, Osman's successors look to the north and west.

1354: Gallipoli is conquered by the Ottomans, providing them with their first foothold in Europe.

1402-1406: The Mongolian ruler Timur Lenk (1365-1405; also known as Tamerlane) makes a short and bloody appearance in Anatolia, devastating many cities. This however has little effect on the ascent of the Ottoman Empire.

1453: The Ottomans conquer Constantinople, the only remaining stronghold of the Byzantine Empire, thereby wiping it off the map. From now on Constantiniya (Istanbul since 1930), is capital of the Ottoman Empire, and its sphere of influence grows steadily. Less than 20 years later the Ottomans take the Turkish south coast.

1517: Selim I (1512-1520) conquers Syria and Egypt, thus bringing the Caliphate to the Bosphorus.

1520-1566: Süleyman I, known as the Magnificent, conquers

Sultanate of Women

Süleyman the Magnificent (1520-1566) and his main wife Roxelane initiated the so-called 'Sultanate of Women' — a transfer of power from men to women and an explanation for the slow decline of the Ottoman Empire lasting over three centuries.

With her intrigues and murderous plots, Roxelane brought her own son Selim II (1566-1574) to the throne. He went down in history as 'Selim the Sot'. Even before he slipped and drowned in the bathtub, the Ottoman Empire lost its entire fleet.

Selim II had five sons, four of whom were murdered by his wife Nurbanu, so that her own offspring could be crowned Sultan Murat III (1574-1595). Like so many sultans, he proved to be more active in the harem than in politics. This rewarded him with over 100 children, of whom his wife Safiye contrived to have 19 murdered, so that their son took the throne as Sultan Mehmet III (1595-1603)…

One could go on and on about the history of female influence on the successors to the Ottoman throne. And the fact that the budding sultans grew up in the harems, pampered and spoilt, in a world completely out of touch with reality. Flattered by courtiers scheming to see their own interests satisfied, the regents were for the most part incapable of acting for themselves. Many were not even strong enough to govern to the natural end of their lives. They were either strangled, poisoned or so weak-willed that they were driven out of office.

Bagdad, Belgrade, Rhodes, Hungary, Georgia, Azerbajan and parts of North Africa. In 1529 he besieges Vienna for the first time. He leads the Ottomans to the zenith of their powers, when it takes 75 minutes for the sun to set over their Empire. Süleyman and his successors have little interest in the development of Asia Minor's coastal towns.

From 1683: Defeat after the second siege of Vienna means the end of expansion and heralds the gradual decline of the Ottoman Empire. There are repeated flashes of unrest on the domestic front.

From 1808: Under Mahmut II (1808-1839) the first attempts take place to gradually reform the Empire. He eliminates the Janissaries (an elite military unit who resist all progressive currents), probably by the ruse of inciting them to revolt, leading to their massacre or exile. He outlaws the turban and introduces the fez in its place.

1853-1856: The Crimean War; Russian-occupied territories are recaptured. Florence Nightingale gains fame for her nursing work in Istanbul.

1875: The 'Sick Man of the Bosphorus' receives the bill for its failure to join the Industrial Revolution and its many expensive wars: the consequence is national bankruptcy.

1876-1909: During the reign of Abdül Hamit II the Muslim population instigate pogroms against the Christian Armenians. At the start of the Young Turk movement, officers force the resignation of the sultan. True power now lies in the hands of the military.

1912-13: The First Balkan War; the Ottoman Empire loses its remaining European territories.

1914-1918: During the First World War the Turks side with Germany and lose. The winners divide the spoils: Greek troops march on Ankara; Italy occupies the coastal strip around Antalya; France occupies Cilicia; English troops control the Bosphorus. The Ottoman Empire now only consists of central Anatolia.

1919-20: Istanbul is forced to accept the Treaty of Sèvres on behalf of the Ottoman Empire, however the nationalists do not. April 1920 sees the first meeting of the Grand National Assembly in Ankara and the formation of a new government under Mustafa Kemal, later Atatürk (see panel opposite). Military resistance is organised.

1921-22: Kemal's troops strike the Greek army at the Sakarya River. The Italians and French retreat.

1923: With the Treaty of Lausanne the Allies recognise the independence and sovereignty of the new Turkey. In Ankara, the new capital, the National Assembly proclaims the Republic and selects Mustafa Kemal as President. In the same year, the Norwegian Fritjof Nansen, working on behalf of the League of Nations, suggests a population exchange between Greeks and Turks. Ankara agrees immediately. This effectively ends the 3000 years' history of the Greeks in Asia Minor.

1924: A new constitution comes into force, which among other

Atatürk, father of the Turks

Atatürk's likeness greets you in every office, shop and restaurant; he bids you goodbye from every lira you hand out. He excites the imagination of Turkish sculptors, too — because with the exception of Atatürk, public statues are rarely commissioned. Hardly any other statesman is assigned such cult status.

As Mustafa Kemal (born around 1881) he was elected the first President of the new Republic of Turkey in 1923. He secularised and Europeanised the new state in an enormous act of will. For his services to the country, in 1934 Parliament gave him the name Atatürk, 'Father of the Turks'. Four years later he died in Istanbul from cirrhosis of the liver. His remains rest in the Atatürk Mausoleum in Ankara.

things incorporates the separation of state and religion. Islamic Sharia law is replaced by Swiss civil law, Italian criminal law and German commercial law.

1925-1938: Up until Atatürk's death numerous reforms are brought in to Europeanise Turkey: education and writing reform (transition from Arabic script to the Roman alphabet), the introduction of surnames, changing of the rest day from Friday to Sunday, etc.

1945: Having remained neutral for most of the Second World War, Turkey declares war on Germany. In the same year it becomes a founding member of the United Nations.

1950: Atatürk's former political party loses the first free elections.

1952: Turkey joins NATO.

1960: Kemalistic officers stage a *coup d'état* and allow the execution of the Prime Minister Adnan Menderes. The military sees itself as the guardian of Laicism (see page 40) and of Atatürk's legacy. It stands in clear opposition to Islamic fundamentalism and radical left-wing groups.

1971: Social unrest and strikes. The cabinet is forced to resign. But the following government is also faced with unemployment, inflation, foreign exchange debts and the rising militancy of left versus right, Kurds and Turks, Alevites and Sunnis.

1974: Turkish troops occupy northern Cyprus.

1980: The military take power again and dissolve Parliament.

1984-1999: The Kurdish fight for autonomy claims roughly 25,000 victims in the east and southeast. The situation eases in February 1999 with the arrest of Kurdish Workers' Party boss Abdullah Öcalan; a truce is agreed.

1995-1998: The pro-Islamic Welfare Party (RP) led by Necmettin Erbakan wins the forced elections, thus becoming the first Muslim overall winner in the 72 years since a republic was established. But the party is banned as anti-constitutional in 1998, and Erbakan himself is forced from the political arena.

1999: A devastating earthquake in northwest Turkey kills 18,000.

From 2002: The AKP are clear winners in the elections; many small parties lose seats due to a clause requiring a 10% minimum threshhold for a party to gain entry to Parliament. Party leader Recep Tayyip Erdoğan becomes the head of government a year later, and there is a full-on push for much-needed reforms. Laws are passed to meet the Copenhagen criteria for EU membership. But Islamic extremists do not want to see a successful democracy in an Islamic land: to destabilise the country and make Europe fear Turkish EU membership, a Turkish terrorist cell with supposed Al-Qaida connections commits several atrocities. The bloodiest shake Istanbul in November 2003: explosions at two synagogues, the HSBC Bank and the British Consulate kill 64 (including the Consul) and wound 750.

From 2005: Having ended their five-year armistice in 2004, the PKK brings more terror. Splinter groups cause atrocities in several resorts, including Marmaris.

2006: The long-awaited EU negotiations begin. But any joy in finally getting to the table is quickly swept aside by the unwelcoming attitude of the EU member states. EU euphoria in Turkey decreases correspondingly: in 2004, 70% of the population were in favour of joining, by 2006 the figure is down to only 30%. Orhan Pamuk becomes the first Turk to win a Nobel Prize; his novels typically deal with the clashes of identity between East and West.

2007: Gül, a member of the conservative AKP, becomes President. The fact that his wife wears a headscarf almost precipitates a military coup

2008-2012: The international financial crisis hits Turkey. In six months the Turkish lira loses 30% of its value. National bankruptcy can't be ruled out. By the first quarter of 2010 the Turkish economy had bounced back, with growth of over 11%. In the list of the world's largest economies, Turkey ranks 17th.

1 BODRUM

History • Accommodation/camping • Food and drink • Nightlife • Beaches and diving • Sights • Practicalities A-Z

Area code: 0252
Information: Tourist Office at the port in front of the castle. In high season open daily from 08.00-12.00 and 13.00-19.00, otherwise shorter hours and closed Sat./Sun. ☎ 3161091, www.bodrum-guide.org. There's another info kiosk at the bus station.
Connections: The international airport, **DHMI Milas-Bodrum Hava Limanı,** lies about 35km northeast of Bodrum on the road to Milas. It has both domestic and international terminals. In 2010 a new international terminal was being built; the old international terminal will become the new domestic one. In the international arrivals terminal there are cash machines, a post office, tourist office (☎ 5230066, ℡ 5230288; officially open daily 08.00-20.00 from May to end Oct., but don't count on it!), and a car rental kiosk.
Transfers to and from the airport are by **Havaş buses**; 8-15 departures a day (tickets £7.50; very good connections between 07.00-19.00). Departures in Bodrum are from the bus station. Info at ☎ 5230040, www.havas.com.tr, at the THY main office (see 'Travel agents' on page 73) or at the many travel offices in the centre. By **taxi** the trip costs £38. It's about 2.5km from the airport to the main Milas/Bodrum road, where there are *dolmuşes.*
Bus and *dolmuş:* The bus station is on Cevat Şakir Cad., just a couple of minutes on foot from the centre. Several buses every day to Kuşadası (change in Soke; 2h; £8), İzmir (3-4h; £10.50) and Pamukkale (4h; £10.50), as well as to all the holiday resorts along the coast and the major towns in western Turkey. *Dolmuşes* also operate out of this bus station, with good connections to all the places on the Bodrum Peninsula and Milas (45min.).

Bodrum has St. Tropez's glamour and Ibiza's nightlife. The small white 'sugar cube' town with its large marina ranks among the most popular motifs for photos of the Aegean. The city's main landmark is a castle built by the Knights of St. John on a peninsula in the middle of the picturesque twin bays.

Bodrum is the pearl of the Turkish west coast and much finer than its reputation suggests. The largely intact and well-kept centre, with its serried ranks of whitewashed houses and palm-lined promenades gives the place its charm. Winding alleyways with bougainvillea-draped mansions and magical gardens remind one of when Bodrum was still Greek. Fortunately it was recognised in time that building large hotels here would damage the image and attractiveness.

But this small town of 40,000 inhabitants is only tranquil in the shoulder seasons. Between June and September high-life prevails around the clock, and the population swells to 250,000. Tourists from all over join the hip Turkish youth to take part in the hottest parties of the year here. Even Istanbulites, with all the nightlife they are accustomed to, swarm to the Bodrum Peninsula during summer. Nowhere else in Turkey can you find more love of life, liberal attitudes and an 'anything goes' atmosphere.

Bodrum's popularity as a resort and place for a second home has resulted in the city expanding more and more: it has already merged with the neighbouring towns of İçmeler to the south and Gümbet to the west. Gümbet offers what Bodrum unfortunately (or fortunately?) lacks — a long sandy beach. As a result Bodrum itself is more often a destination for day trippers from the local resorts and the nearby Greek island of Kos than a holiday base.

History

It is assumed that ancient Halicarnassus, in what is today the Bay of Bodrum, goes back to a Dorian settlement from the 11th century BC. The city's first famous personality was Artemisia I, who in 480 BC fought so courageously on the side of the Persian King Xerxes that he is supposed to have commented 'My men have turned into women and my women into men!' Her compatriot Herodotus (about 485-425 BC), known as the 'Father of History', also features strongly in the city's past.

In the 4th century BC, the Persian satrap Mausolus (376-353 BC) moved the seat of government from Milas to Halicarnassus, and it blossomed into one of the most outstanding cities in the region. His monumental mausoleum, one of the Seven Wonders of the Ancient World, gave the city immortality (see under 'Sights').

In 334 BC Alexander the Great met with heavy resistance during the conquest of Halicarnassus. During the first half of the Hellenistic age, the city came under the control of several short-term foreign rulers, but it still maintained its position as an important centre. Only when Rome took control of Caria in 190 BC, did the city's star begin to sink. And once Gaius Verres, the governor of Cilicia, had robbed all the city's works of art, Halicarnassus slipped into obscurity.

The situation changed again in 1402, when the Ottomans were occupied with Timur Lenk. This gave the Knights of St. John of Rhodes the opportunity to move into Bodrum unimpaired and develop a fortress. Their rule lasted approximately 120 years before the Ottomans conquered Bodrum, and the small town once again disappeared from the history books.

At the beginning of the 20th century, Muslim refugees from Crete brought boat-building and sponge-diving to Bodrum. And in 1923 the Greek inhabitants (the majority) were forced to abandon their homes during the population exchange, with a second

wave of Muslim refugees from Greece taking over those houses that had become free.
People lived modestly here from traditional trades. The only 'visitors' were exiled dissident artists and journalists (see 'Blue cruises' on page 17). All that changed however in the 1980s, when tourism discovered Bodrum and the local peninsula. Within a few years, it went from being a simple fishing village to the most exclusive holiday destination in Turkey.

Accommodation/camping

(see plan overleaf)
Bodrum has approximately 60,000 hotel beds and accommodation in all categories. If you decide to stay in the centre, be prepared to share in the nightlife — there's little peace and quiet. From July until the end of August reservations are recommended, and even the shabbiest rooms will be expensive. In the shoulder seasons prices tumble. Several inexpensive pensions can be found in the alleys off Atatürk Cad. The choice of lovely small boutique hotels is much greater on the peninsula than in Bodrum itself.

Marina Vista Hotel (15), by the port. 84 rooms divided among several buildings set around the pool. A 4-star hotel, classical-modern building; unfortunately rather small windows. Very chic, bright lobby. Fitness area, sauna, 'pillow menu'! The reception could be friendlier. Doubles £126; singles £100. Neyzen Tevfik Cad. 226, ☎ 3130356, ℻ 3162347, www.hotelmarinavista.com.

Antik Tiyatro Oteli (1), 19 comfortable rooms and 1 suite, set among several terraces full of greenery. All rooms with superb view over the city. Pool. First-class restaurant (see 'Food and drink' on page 67). One bitter note is its location on the noisy ring road, but all rooms are on the far side from the road. Doubles £100. Kıbrıs Şehitlerı Cad. 243, ☎ 3166053, ℻ 3160825, www.antiquetheatrehotel.com.

Su Hotel (2), idyllic, colourful little place only a short way from the centre and yet totally tranquil. 25 comfortable rooms with nice small design touches, laid out around a small pool dripping with bougainvillea. All the rooms decorated with great attention to detail. 'Simply charming' say readers. Doubles £71, singles £55. Turgutreis Cad. 1201 Sok., ☎ 3166906, ℻ 3167391, www.suhotel.net.

Gözen Hotel (23), one street back from Kumbahçe Bay. 10 freshly renovated rooms (great at the front, nothing special at the back). Roof terrace for breakfast. Like the Baç Pansiyon a few doors further on (same prices, but Bac's breakfasts aren't as good and sometimes the staff are unfriendly). Doubles with sea view £70, at the back cheaper. Cumhuriyet Cad. 18 (*not* accessible by car), ☎ 3162079, ℻ 3161227, www.gozenbutikhotel.com.

Hotel Güleç (16), a clean little guest house some way back off Kumbahçe Bay. 18 well equipped rooms with climate control, most with new baths and tiled floors; not all with balcony. Breakfast in a lovely garden under orange trees with twittering birds. Doubles £59. Üçkuyular Cad. 22, ☎ 3165222, www.hotelgulec.com.

Gurup Otel (19), You couldn't find a more central location, on the harbour road above a clothes shop. 12 small, simply furnished rooms with carpeted floors. Narrow balconies from where you can watch the comings and goings down at the port. Doubles £37, singles £25. Karantina Cad., ✆ 3161140, ℻ 3133151.

Sevin Otel/Pension (13), pleasant accommodation near the promenade with international guests. 38 rooms in three versions: 'Standard' (narrow, plain baths), 'Lüx' (somewhat larger baths with shower cubicles) and 'Super' (even larger, but not *that* large, newer furniture), all with climate control and tiled floors. Restaurant, courtyard with hammocks, friendly staff. OK value for money. Doubles (depending on

fittings £29-33. Türkkuyusu Cad. 5, ☎ 3167682, 📠 3134919, www. sevinpension.com.

Yenilmez Pansiyon (5), 9 simple, clean rooms of varying sizes (some family rooms), all with private bath, some with balcony. Friendly, reserved, family-run. A big advantage: some parking places! Doubles £29. Menekşe Çıkmazı 30, ☎ 3162520.

Şenlik Pansiyon (4), apleasant central address. 20 plain, clean rooms with tiled floors (several for up to 4 people); nice balcony; roof terrace. Heating if needed. Doubles £25. Türkkuyusu Cad. 1045 Sok., ☎ 3166382, www. senlikpansiyon.com

Bodrum Backpacker (18), the local backpackers' meeting place. Amply large rooms with dark furniture, baths with shower cubicles. Also a dormitory.

Nothing special, but OK for young people — travel info, book exchange, etc — and an adjacent 'English pub'. Bed in the dorm £8.50; double with bath £25. Atatürk Cad. 31 B, ✆ 3132762, www. bodrumbackpackers.com.
Camping: The nearest campsite is in **Gümbet** (see page 74); another place is at Yahşi Beach (page 76).

Food and drink

(see plan on pages 64-65)
Being hungry in Bodrum is expensive. Every evening in the summer Bodrum's waterfront esplanade transforms itself into an enticing display for the wealthy 'beautiful people'. There are top-class Italian, Chinese and, exquisite fish restaurants; with the exception of Istanbul or Ankara, nowhere else in Turkey is the gastronomic palette broader or the prices for a cosy dinner higher. The really snobby places are those right on the water at the marina. Travellers with thinner purses should make for the simple *lokantas* on the way out of town (for instance on Artemis or Atatürk Cad.).
Tips: Try out some restaurants on the peninsula. Bodrum is also well known for sole, but it's largest and best in winter.
Antik Tiyatro Oteli (1). To have dinner at this hotel (see 'Accommodation' on page 63) can be a wonderful memory of your visit to Bodrum. There is fantastic Turkish/international cooking and an equally fantastic view, with wonderful service. Only open for dinner; prices are high.
Kocadon Restaurant (8), another of Bodrum's long-established gastronomic highlights, especially popular with foreigners who live in the city. Idyllic garden with decent lighting (!), A1 service. Specialises in refined fish and seafood dishes (good sole). Mains £8.50-15. Saray Sok. 1, ✆ 3163705.
Liman Köftecisi (12), a good value-for-money address for anyone who wants to eat on the promenade. *Meze* and meatballs in various versions; the speciality, *Liman köfte*, is delicious (meatballs with yogurt, tomato sauce and butter on *pide*. White/blue seating gives the place a Grecian flair. Mains £3-6.50. Neyzen Tevfik Cad. 172, ✆ 3165060.
Balıkçılar Çarşısı (Fischmarkt), in the bustling alleys west of Cevat Şakir Cad. There are few fishmongers here these days, but more restaurants: *meze*, fish, sometimes live music and always a good atmosphere. Have a look around.
Alin's (17), on Belediye Maydanı, a well-kept, high-class fast-food café and restaurant with very tasty dishes; part of a chain. Terrace.
Berk (29), although right on the front with other tourist places, visitors don't seem to come to this simple fish restaurant. There are only a couple of plastic chairs downstairs, but upstairs is a nice terrace decorated with fish nets. Fair prices: *meze* £2.50, fish from £6.50. Cumhuriyet Cad. 167, ✆ 3136878.
Nazik Ana (14), a low-budget tip. Large self-service *lokanta* with top-quality home cooking. The dishes change daily. Friendly young staff and decent music; no rip-offs. A really satisfying meal middasy meal for £3. Eski Hükümet Sok. (a small side-alley

between Türkkuyusu Cad. und Cevat Şakir Cad.).

Café: Bodrum Belediyesi Bodrumspor (11) is the covered terrace café of the town's sports association. Almost all the clientele are locals. Breakfasts, snacks, filter coffee (!) and very reasonable prices. *No* alcohol. On the port promenade by the mosque.

Sweets: Özsüt (6), part of a countrywide chain that is very popular for its huge variety of tasty cakes, rice and other puddings, etc. With terrace. Neyzen Tevfik Cad. 198.

Yunuslar Karadeniz (20), one of the city's best bakeries/pastry shops. Delicious fruitcakes, braided yeast buns, muffins, and other snacks. Only to take away, but there is a tiny place to stand. Cumhuriyet Cad. 13.

Nightlife

(see the plan on pages 64-65)

Bodrum nights are long — not for nothing is it called the Ibiza of Turkey. Put on heavy make-up, take a fat wallet and off you go. But the dancing doesn't start till 1am. Until then you spend your time at the chic bar scene in Neyzen Tevfik Cad., at Salmakis Bay or in various locations on Cumhuriyet and Dr. Alim Bey Cad. in Kumbahçe Bay — where you will find all sorts of cafés and bars. The change is enormous and what's 'in' today is 'out' by tomorrow (or has a completely different name) — so discover them for yourself! The most lighthearted drinking places are the many pubs in Meyhaneler Sok. (also called Banka Sok., a side lane off Kale Sok.).

Kumbahçe Bay: Halikarnas (30), an open-air night club for over 5000 people, in business for over 20 years. It ranks among the largest and (self-proclaimed) best discos in the world — in any case it could stick most large European city discos in its pocket. Various stages, many different music genres, laser show, parties, roof terrace and huge dance area. Music between techno and Turkpop. Open till dawn. Entry £15.50-21, depending on day of the week (includes a free drink). www.halikarnas.com.tr.

Bodrum Marine Club (25), on a catamaran moored at the foot of the castle, which then sails out into the harbour. Apart from Halikarnas, *the* in place in the city — with room for 1700 night owls. Huge dance floor with a glass bottom (!), several bars. Entry £12.50 weekdays, £17 Fri./Sat. (includes a free drink). Again, Turkpop, house and chart-toppers played constantly. Themed parties, with a lot of tourist groups. Dress code! Boat service for those who want to leave before the catamaran reberths. Also open till dawn. www.clubbodrum.com.

Club Hadigari (28), room for 2000. One of the forerunners of Bodrum's hot club scene, in business since 1974. Mostly standard music, sometimes live performances. VIP lounge right on the water. Near the castle. Somewhat cheaper than the other two. www.hadigari.com.

Fora Bar (26), small place only a few steps from the Bodrum Marine Club. DJs playing the range of Turkish music; some dancing (small dance floor). Cosy terrace. Dr. Alim Bey Cad.

Moonlight Bar (24) will appeal to

anyone looking for somewhere romantic. A lovely place to have a drink at sunset. A couple of tables right on the beach, with sea spray and a view of the boats anchored in the bay and the illuminated castle. Somewhat hidden, at Cumhuriyet Cad. 60. **Café del Mar (27)**, about 200m past the Moonlight Bar. Also a couple of tables on the beach, this time with lounge music, really good coffee and all kinds of drinks. This place is less full at sunset than at sunrise, since it's a good 'after hours' bar, open 24 hours a day. Cumhuriyet Cad.

Salmakis Bay: There are several classy lounges and clubs on Neyzen Tevfik Cad. which runs along Salmakis Bay. Most have cosy gardens in front of old Greek houses. Without doubt the most chic is **Fink (10)**, with cool electro music and a lot of 'beautiful people'. Without the right gear (and what might that be?), you've no chance of getting in. **Küba Bar (7)**, a bit further along, also has a good ambience.

Beaches and diving

Bodrum's local beach, the small Halk Plajı right at the southern end of Kumbahçe Bay, is not all that attractive. For swimming, the wonderful bays on the Gulf of Gökova (east of the city, see page 105) or the beaches on the Bodrum Peninsula (see page 74) are far better — especially Gümüşlük. Or you could take a boat trip with stops for swimming.

Diving: There are several options. They speak English at The Aegean Pro Dive Centre in Bitez (diploma courses). Day trip with two dives ££31, including lunch (with loan of equipment £40). Four-day beginners' PADI open-water beginners' course £224. Kavaklısarniç Sok. Asarlık Sitesi 30, ✆ 3160737, www.aegeanprodive.com.

Aquapark: Dedeman Bodrum, an enormous aquapark with 'Kamikaze tube', 'Hydro-tube', etc. — a jamboree for families with children. Entrance fee: adults £17, children £12.50. On the Ortakent road; *dolmuşes* stop right in front.

Sights

There is no longer much to remind one of ancient Halicarnassus, and what *does* remain scattered around the city is hardly spectacular. On Mars Mabedi Caddesi above Salmakis Bay there are the meagre remains of a **Mars Temple**; the **Myndos Gate**, which was once part of the city defences, is near Büyük İskender Caddesi on the way to Gümbet; the 3rd century BC **theatre** (*Antik Tiyatro,* still used for events today) is on busy Kıbrıs Şehitlerı Caddesi high above Bodrum. It's nothing special *(in summer open daily from 08.00-19.00, in winter till 17.00; entry free).* In any case, the most important legacy from Halicarnassus is the mausoleum.

Mausoleum: The mausoleum of Halicarnassus, a monumental tomb, was considered one of the Seven Wonders of the Ancient World and gave its name to all burial places of this kind. During his lifetime (4th century BC) Prince Mausolus commissioned the architect Pytheos to do drawings for a tomb which he later had built from white marble; the work was completed after his death by Artemisia II, his sister and wife. It stood on a terrace 105 x 242 metres in size and was over 50 m high. A step-pyramid formed the top, at the apex of which was a statue of Artemisia and Mausolus riding a *quadriga* (a two-wheeled chariot drawn by two pairs of horses). The best artists and craftsman of the time took part in the decoration of the tomb. Earthquakes — and plundering of the stonework for the building of the castle — account for the fact that only the foundation walls remain today. Fortunately a few diagrams help one form a mental picture. The first excavations of the mausoleum were undertaken in the 19th century by Sir Charles Newton. Precious finds such as reliefs and tableaux were sent on to the British Museum, so only a few column bases remain for visitors today.

Address/opening times: Turgutreis Cad. In summer open daily (except Mon.) from 08.00-19.00, in winter till 17.00; entry fee £3.50.

Bodrum Castle/Museum of Underwater Archaeology: Also called the **Castle of St. Peter**, this powerful building was established on the foundations of an older Byzantine fortress by the Order of the Knights of St. John of Jerusalem during the first half of the 15th century. At that time the Order, which had founded a sovereign Knights' State on the island of Rhodes, possessed an enormous fleet, with which it plundered Islamic trading vessels. The Order was divided into several sections, known as 'tongues' (due to the different languages spoken). Each tongue had its own lodgings, and in the event of an attack had a section of the fortress to defend. The designation of the towers by nationality originates from that time.

In 1523 the knights were driven out of the Aegean, and a few years later established themselves on Malta. During the Ottoman era, the castle lost its importance, and at the end of the 19th century it was transformed into a prison. It came under attack for the last time during the First World War, when the French warship Dubleix sailed into the Bay of Bodrum. Today the castle accommodates a museum for underwater archaeology, the largest of its kind in the world — but you do need to have an overwhelming interest in amphorae…

The **entrance** to the castle is in Salmakis Bay. Just behind the ticket office you pass a small courtyard with a shady café. From there you walk along one of the outer bastions to a courtyard with a mulberry tree in the centre. On the right is a small **chapel** from 1406, which has a minaret added by the Ottomans in 1523. Today the chapel houses the replica prow of a Byzantine ship which sank off the Bodrum Peninsula in 626. To the left in the courtyard is a large exhibition of **amphorae** (it is estimated that the oldest dates from 1400 BC).

Beside the chapel, steps lead to an upper courtyard. Here you pass the **Glass Hall**. Inside are small vases, glasses, and bowls which sank to the seabed between the 14th century BC and the 11th century AD. Diagonally opposite the Glass Hall is the entrance to the **Glass Shipwreck Hall** (with a separate admission fee and an exit in the lower courtyard). On view here is the skeleton of a trading vessel which sank close to Marmaris in the year 1025. Also on display are finds from the hold and personal possessions belonging to the crew.

The upper courtyard resembles a small park, with a fountain and a couple of peacocks strutting about. Behind the gate to the courtyard, on the left, is the **Spanish Tower**, which our circuit passes later. Instead, climb the steps on the right to the highest towers — the **Italian Tower** on the right and the **French Tower** on the left. In the space between them, and in the French Tower itself is a small display about the recovery of a Greek merchant ship that sank in the 5th century BC off Cape Tektaş south of Çeşme and was found in 1996. It took about 5000 dives for the archaeologists to recover the hull.

Behind the next terrace is the **Carian Princess Hall** (which also demands a separate admission fee). Inside are the bones of the Carian 'princess' Ada from the 4th century BC. Her sarcophagus was found by construction workers close to Bodrum in 1989. On show are burial objects (including golden bracelets, a chain and a laurel ring) and — the pride of the museum — a life-size model of the lady herself. This was created at the University of Manchester with the help of pathological knowledge (pity that science does not cheat a bit in favour of beauty).

If you climb the steps near the Carian Princess Hall, you come to a terrace between the **Italian and French towers**, from where there's a splendid view over Bodrum. From this terraces you also have access to the displays on the upper floors of both towers. One houses a small collection of coins and decorations, the other medieval weapons (but neither display is currently open to the public).

Green arrows point the way to the **English Tower**, which marks the southeastern part of the castle. Inside are a couple of exhibits evoking the Order of the Knights of St. John of Jerusalem — armour, flags, coats of arms and two ship models.

If you keep walking along the outer, eastern fortress wall, you pass a low building housing the remains of the **Ulu Burun Shipwreck** from the late Bronze Age. A somewhat kitsch model shows the ship with a tableau. The ship sank about 3400 years ago off the eponymous coast off Kaş and is the oldest known shipwreck in the world. Only about 3% of the hull has been recovered, but much more from the cargo: amphorae, ceramics, jewellery, weapons and the like. In a side-room there's a film about the salvage operation involving about 22,000 dives.

A few steps further along, a sign enquires: 'Do you have a strong heart to walk into the dungeon?' Maybe the question refers to the many steps down to the **dungeon** (a dead end), because there is nothing shocking inside: what you see is a gloomy red colour and what you hear is some indistinct tape-recorded groaning.

If you decline the pleasures of the dungeon and head left, you find yourself in front of two toilets from Ottoman times. In the display room opposite are the skeletons of slaves who were condemned to row on the galleys. Their bones, still in iron chains, were not discovered until 1993 near the English Tower. Some 15m further on is the **German Tower** (more amphorae and some furniture in German Renaissance style), but it was closed at time of writing. The next tower, about 30m further on, is the **Spanish Tower** — also known as the Snake Tower, since a relief of a snake is carved into the stone at the left of the entrance. If you enter at this point you will find a display of … amphorae. If you go in via the upper entrance, there's a small exhibition about 'birth, life and death', displaying medical instruments, statues, phallus-like mortar and pestle, as well as grave- and votive-stones.

At the left of the Snake Tower you can gain access to the outside fortifications again and stroll to the **Commando Tower** enjoying lovely views over the port. This tower has a small display about the shelling of the castle by the French warship Dubleix (see page 70); this display was also closed during our last visit.

Opening times: daily from 08.30-18.30 (in winter till 16.30). Entry fee £4.20. Carian Princess Hall and Glass Shipwreck Hall (only Tue.-Fri. 10.00-12.00 and 14.00-16.00) £2.30 extra for each attraction.

Zeki Müren Museum: Zeki Müren

Bodrum Castle

is hardly known outside the country, but in Turkey he had cult status (only surpassed by that of Atatürk) due to his many films and hit records. The rise of this charismatic singer and composer began in the 1950s, unhindered (even then) by his gay/transsexual appearance. In 1955 he received Turkey's first golden record. Up until his death in 1996 (when he had a heart attack during a live performance), he had brought millions to tears. He was buried in his hometown of Bursa. Müren's house in Bodrum is now open as a little museum, with fan letters, records, costumes full of fantasy … and his American roadster in a glass case.

Address/opening times: Zeki Müren Cad. Daily (except Mon.) 09.00-12.00 and 13.00-17.00; entry £1.25.

Practicalities A-Z

Boat trips: Several day trips are on offer to various places where boats lay anchor — for example to Karaada (Black Island) with hot springs, to Ortakent Beach (see page 76) or to the so-called 'Aquarium', a crystal-clear snorkelling bay. These boats leave from Salmakis Bay west of the castle, usually around 11.00, and return around 17.00. Per person with lunch £13.00. It's best to book at the last minute, so you can see how full (or overloaded) the boat is.

Car hire: Available everywhere. The cheapest car with the internationals costs about £51/day in high season; local firms are less expensive. **Avis**, Neyzen Tevfik Cad. 66/A, ☎ 3165632; www.avis.com.tr.; **Europcar**, Hamam Sok. 1, ☎ 3130885, www.europcar.com.tr.

Consulate: see page 33.

Doctors and dentists, English-speaking: Universal Hospital Bodrum on Kavaklı Sarnıç Cad. high above Gümbet Bay, ☎ 3191515.

Events: In summer various events are held in the ancient **theatre**, from ballet festivals to pop concerts and in the open-air theatre by the castle. Every year there is a *gulet* regatta at the end of October, the **Bodrum Cup**. In January there are **camel fights** in Bodrum and various places on the peninsula; these bloodless spectacles have a long tradition in the Aegean.

Ferries: There are ferries to **Kos** all year round (daily from mid-May to mid-Oct.; in winter Mon./Wed./Fri.); departures at about 09.30, returns 16.30, sailing time 1h; day return £24, open ticket £48, motorbikes one-way £33, cars £83.

In high season there are two daily ferry services to **Datça** (see page 154 under 'Boat trips'); in winter this ferry sails three times a week. Datça is not a good idea for a day trip, as the journey each way takes about 2 hours.

From mid-Jun. to mid-Sep. a hydrofoil runs twice a week (Thu./Sun.) to Gelibolu on the Gulf of Gokova, from where a bus goes on to **Marmaris** (sailing time about 1h30min, day return £25, open ticket £50).

There's a twice-weekly hydrofoil to **Rhodes** from Jun.-Sep. (Mon./Fri.; sailing time 2h30min, day return £50; open ticket £100). In summer the crossings to the Greek islands are usually expanded; information from the tourist offices. Tickets and information about the ferries to Rhodes and Marmaris are available from **Bodrum Express Lines** at the departure point by the castle (☎ 3161087, www.bodrumexpresslines.com), and for Datça and Kos from the **Bodrum Ferryboat Association** one door away (☎ 3160882, www.bodrumferryboat.com). The hydrofoils to Rhodes and Marmaris currently start from the same place, but may move to the new cruise ship port at the south-east end of Kumbahçe Bay. The small car ferries to Datça and Kos leave from near the marina.

Golf: see Ortakent, page 76. Also: Vita Park Golf Resort, about 35km northeast of Bodrum (sign-posted off the airport road). 18-hole course opened in 2008 (par 71) with 7 lakes. Green fee £63. An adjacent resort hotel is planned. ☎ 5245333, www.vitaparkgolfresort.com.

Launderette: There are many, for instance **Nesli Laundry** at Türkkuyusu Cad. 27. Machine wash and dry £2.25.

Money: **Cash dispensers** are everywhere in the centre. **Exchange bureaus** are mostly

located on Cevat Şakir Cad.
Newspapers and magazines in English: These are available at almost all kiosks in the centre.
Organised tours: The dozens of tour operators arrange trips to the hinterland as well as boat trips. Choice and prices vary little. For an excursion to Pamukkale or Ephesus including lunch expect to pay £25; two-day tour to Ephesus and Pamukkale with overnight accommodation £50; trip to the Tuesday market at Milas £8.50; jeep safaris along the Gulf of Gökova around £21.
Parking: Out of season there's no problem. In high season you can use the garage under the *dolmuş* station (access via Cevat Şakir Cad., £1.70/h, £6.50 for 24h). There is also an underground garage opposite the post office (same access, same prices).
Police: near the Tourist Office, ☎ 155.
Post: on Cevat Şakir Cad.
Riding: Horse-riding is on offer at **Turgutreis Countryranch** near İslamhaneleri between Gürece und Bağla. ☎ 3825654, www.countryranch. net.
Shopping: If you can afford it, the chic goods (Tommy Hilfinger, Diesel, Paul & Shark Yachting, etc.) are all on sale in the open-air **Shopping Center at the Marina**. Another modern shopping centre is the **Oasis** on Kıbrıs Şehitleri Cad., the ring road north of the centre. This has many clothing shops and all kinds of economical and good restaurants. **Markets** are held on Tuesdays (clothing) and Fridays (food) at the bus station. The large **Migros Supermarket (3)** is on the way out of town, between Turgutreis Cad. and Myndos Cad. Finally, Bodrum is well known for handmade leather sandals, and the best craftsman was Ali Güven, who died in 2010 — even Mick Jagger shopped there. Now a good choice can be found at **Arkadaş Sandalet (21)**, run by Mehmet und Türker Dikan (Uslu Sok. 4; near the Moonlight Bar).
Travel agents: **Elele Turizm** for Atlasjet, Onur Air tickets, etc (Neyzen Tevfik Cad. 66A; ☎ 3165632). **THY** main office in the Oasis Shopping Centre (see 'Shopping'; ☎ 3171203, www. turkisairline.com).
Turkish Bath *(hamam)*: **Bardakçı Hamamı**, over 250 years old (but newly restored), lies on Omurca Dere Sok. at Kumbahçe Bay east of the castle. Mixed bathing possible. Entry with massage £17. Open daily 07.00-24.00. The newer **Bodrum Hamamı** (similar prices/opening times) is on Cevat Şakir Cad. opposite the bus station. Separate sections for men and women.
Two-wheel hire: There are one or two firms near the bus station. Scooters from 50cc (about £13/day) to 125cc (£19/day), as well as 250cc Enduros (£25/day). Bike rental is rare: there's too much aggro for too little profit.
Yacht charter: The coastal waters around Bodrum are just perfect for yachting trips lasting several days, and there is a correspondingly good choice of boats available for charter. You can deal direct with the captains at the marina or go to an agency like **Aegean Yacht** at the marina, (☎ 3138631, www.aegeanyacht. com). Reckon on £42-83 per person per day.

2 BODRUM PENSINSULA

Gümbet • Bitez • Ortakent and Yahşi • Kargıkoyu • Akyarlar • Turgutreis • Gümüşlük • Yalıkavak • Gündoğan • Türkbükü • Gölköy • Torba

Area code: ✆ 0252
Connections: The *dolmuş* connections between Bodrum and the places on the peninsula are very good, but connections between the villages themselves are not. To tour the whole peninsula, it's best to have your own transport.
Walks: 1-10

It's quite a long time now since the Bodrum Peninsula has been an idyll of undisturbed nature. Holiday villages and resort hotels dominate most bays, and the 'Lego'-style, cloned low-level building continues apace. It seems only a question of time before the entire coast of the peninsula is forested with houses. Many once-romantic little places have been robbed of their charm — although not in the eyes of the country's better-off. For them the Bodrum Peninsula in summer is still *the* place to be. So much so that many areas are very well-kept and ritzy-looking. From mid-June till the end of August the peninsula is choc-a-bloc, whereas in spring and autumn many restaurants and hotels have not yet opened or have closed.

At sunset, the views from the inland hills over the coastline full of bays are lovely, especially with the silhouettes of the offshore islands adding a charming lattice-work backdrop. In the villages you will often see windmills and large white, semi-circular cisterns called *sarnıçlar* (singular: *sarnıç*). These feature on several walks (see photograph on page 87). Rainwater was once stored inside them in winter, for watering thirsty cattle and dry fields in the summer. Today they are usually functionless.

Below is a tour of the peninsula in a clockwise direction.

Gümbet

This bay, 5km west of Bodrum, has been taken over by package holidaymakers, primarily from Britain. The narrow beach gets a new set of clothes in the spring, when several truckloads of sand are brought in. In the high season you can easily read the latest papers by glancing over at the next beach chair. But there are a couple of pleasant beach clubs. Just behind the beach there's a row of bars, restaurants, souvenir shops and well-maintained club resorts. In addition, all the usual fun water sport activities are on offer.

***Accommodation/camping*:** For individual travellers (campers excluded) it's not a good scene. The guest houses only start three or four streets back from the beach, and better accommodation can be found elsewhere for the same price.

Zetaş Camping, two streets back from the beach behind a club (with loudspeaker music and several restaurants). Plenty of

shade, antiquated but OK sanitary facilities, campers' kitchen. £6.20 per person, tent £2.25, camper van £5.25, incl. electricity. Apr. to the end of Nov. ☎ 3192231, www.zetastourism.com.

Bitez

In the next bay is Bitez, the calmer continuation of Gümbet. The crush of people on the narrow beach (in places more shingle than sand), with a mosque right by the sea, is manageable most of the time, and the water sports on offer are similarly good. There's a large flea market above the beach in the old part of town every Sunday (ask for *Bit Pazarı*).

Accommodation: Most accommodation is right on the beach, including a few guest houses. **Çömez Motel**, pleasant inn a short way back from the beach. 14 very clean, well-kept rooms with dark furniture, climate control, tiled floors, and good baths, 3 with balcony. 4 apartments for up to 4 people. The big plus point is having breakfast served on the terrace, with a wonderful view over the whole bay. Family-run and friendly. Doubles £50. ☎ 3638181, www.comezmotel.com.

Diving: The **Aegean Pro Dive Centre** is in Bitez: see page 68.

Ortakent and Yahşi

The villages of Ortakent and Yahşi lie inland. From here the road to the coast leads past citrus trees, whitewashed little houses and elegant mansions with manicured gardens. The two beaches, named after these two adjoining villages, are separated by a small port. Behind is an accumulation of hotels, guest houses, and holiday settlements which are predominantly occupied by Turks. During the Turkish school holidays, the scattered beach village is quite busy, before and after it's like a ghost town. The most popular places to stay are at the western end of Yahşi Beach.

Accommodation/camping: All places arel well signposted. **Kaktüs Motel**, at the eastern end of Yahşi Beach. A row of 16 rooms with green furniture, tiled floors, telephones, TV and climate control, all with balcony overlooking the shore promenade. Behind the motel is a garden-like area with cacti, palms, pool, cosy nooks for relaxation and a bar — where you can also **camp** (good sanitary facilities). Open Jun.-end Sep./Oct. Good value for money. Doubles £38; 2 people camping £14.50. ☎ 3483004, ☎ 3483276. www. kaktusmotel.com.

Aras Pansiyon, a family-run guest house behind the eponymous shop. Two minutes from Yahşi Beach. 40 clean rooms with balcony or terrace, some with kitchen. Try to get a room at the back; rooms at the front get the noise from the garden of the hotel opposite. Doubles £25, no breakfast. ☎ 3483140, cafer.aras@hotmail.com.

Food and drink: Palavra Balık Restaurant, on Ortakent Beach, signposted. One of the best on the peninsula. Tables right on the beach, good choice of Turkish wines. Very fresh fish, unusual *meze* (a lot of fish and seafood). außergewöhnli-che Meze (viel Mid-to-high price range. Helpful service. ☎ 3586290.

Golf: Bodrum Golf Club, signposted in Ortakent. Small 5-hole course (par 16). Green fee £25. You can rent equipment. ☎ 3587280, www.golfclub bodrum.com.

Kargıkoyu/Kargı Plajı ('Camel Beach')

Camel rides on the lovely hot sands of Kargı Beach are a very popular tourist attraction, hence the nickname. It's also a popular destination for boat trips. The resorts here are well camouflaged in the green woods along the undeveloped shoreline, whereas holiday settlements stud the surrounding slopes. **Bağla** and **Karaincir**, two bays further south, look similar. Between them is the '**Aspat Termera Resort Solida Beach**', which has a whole beach to itself (www. aspat.com.tr).

Akyarlar

This one-time fishing and sponge-diving settlement is one of the more peaceful places on the peninsula. The narrow beach is not intoxicating, but does have some flair, being lined by a few old Greek houses. The cosy fish restaurants are among the least expensive on the peninsula. The east and west ends of the beach are edged by large resorts, which unfortunately spoil the panorama from the beach. Further along the road towards Turgutreis, the beaches have completely lost their attraction now, due to the building of monotonous holiday settlements.

Accommodation: Babadan Motel, right on the beach. 20 restored rooms with white furniture and fridge, but with only 3 facing the sea. Adjacent restaurant with seaside terrace. Friendly service. Doubles £46. ☎ 3936002, 📠 3937987.

Motel Kılavuz, only a few steps on from Babadan, behind the restaurants. 27 simple rooms, some with private terrace. Own parking area. Jun. to mid-Oct. Doubles £42. ☎ 3936006, www.kilavuzmotel.com.

Turgutreis

Not too long ago, this town, named after the famous 16th-century Ottoman sailor Turgut Reis, was still a sleepy fishing village. But now its population of 18,500 inhabitants swells to some 300,000 or so in summer (!), and it has become the second largest town on the peninsula after Bodrum, completely given over to tourism. But Turgutreis doesn't have Bodrum's charm. Fishing boats are rarely seen in the port now; in their place are yachts of various sizes in the newly built marina with its chic small mall and pricey restaurants. Apart from the marina, much of Turgutreis looks sadly makeshift. The people tanning themselves on the long sandy beach are predominantly holidaymakers from Britain, and the local businesses appreciate their custom — virtually every restaurant offers 'bacon and eggs' for breakfast.

North of Turgutreis is the Bay of Kadıkalesi, popular with surfers. A few old Greek houses keep the resorts company here, while the few square metres of public beach in between is hardly worth a mention.

Getting there: Turgutreis has its own bus station on the road to Gümüşlük, with good connections during the summer to all the larger cities in western Anatolia. In addition there are regular connections by dolmuş *to Akyarlar and Gümüşlük.*

Accommodation: There's a wide range of places to stay, from simple pensions in the centre to aparthotels and resorts. Here's just one address, in case you're stranded in Turgutreis.

Kumsal Motel: walk north along the beach about 200m from the main square, then it's on the right. 14 clean rooms, some really narrow. Two terraces, one of them on the roof, the other at ground level and with very pleasant oriental seating nooks. Doubles £33. Sahil 2. Sok., 16, ☎ 3822854, 📠 3824848.

Food and drink/nightlife: The reasanably prices places, where the locals eat, are between Migros and the port.

Nights are quieter than in Bodrum. Among the most popular places for a beer is **Tash's Bar** (everybody knows it) and the nearby **Radio Bar** and **Brothers Bar**. All the bars have Sky Sports.

Practicalities A-Z

Boat trips: Boat trips to Kos start at 09.30 each morning in summer, returning around 16.30. Travel time is just 45 min. Day return tickets cost £23.50, open double! No cars. Information in the brochures from the **Bodrum Ferryboat Association** close to the marina, ✆ 3829441, www.bodrumferryboat.com. There are also daily tours to bays south and north of the town, as well as the offshore islands: £13 per person including lunch.

Shopping: large **Saturday market** in the centre.

Gümüşlük

Gümüşlük is by far the most tranquil place on the Bodrum Peninsula. There are plenty of restaurants lined up alongside the quay in an idyllic setting. Anyone who knows Bodrum well will tell you that an extravagant meal in one of the Gümüşlük fish restaurants is a must.

Gümüşlük consists of little more than the restaurants and a few guest houses behind the narrow, mostly pebble beach. Let's hope things don't change, but the current stop on all building remains highly contentious. On the small offshore island of **Tavşan Adası** (to which you can wade through the shallow water), rabbits jump around between the meagre remnants of ancient **Myndos**, which in earlier times gave its name to what is now the Bodrum Peninsula. They've been excavating here since 2004. So far they've unearthed the ruins of a church with mosaic floors and nearby graves containing skeletons. Most of Myndos lies under water today, the 'Sunken City'.

Every evening in spring and late summer, the Bay of Gümüşlük offers one of the most beautiful sunsets on the entire west coast — most romantic.

From Gümüşlük there's a lovely walk to Karakaya, a picturesque village (see Walk 2).

Accommodation/camping: Mostly simple guest houses or apart-hotels. In summer best to reserve in advance.

Liman Motel, 5 small rooms with white furniture and good views over the bay and port (but only tiny, stand-up balconies). 2 suites with galley kitchens at the back. Large roof terrace, where breakfast is served. On the front, by the fish restaurants, above the Liman Restaurant (but ask about a room in the coffee house at the back). Doubles £66; suites £92. ✆ 3943747, ✆ 3943747, www.limanmotelrestaurant.com.

Paradise Garden (apart-hotel), 12 conveniently equipped studios in 3-storey blue and white buildings around a well-kept pool. Ground floor studios with terraces, upper floors with air-conditioning. £54 for 2 people. One road back from the beach, behind the Arriba Apart Otel. ✆ 394141, www.paradisegardenapart.com.

Özak Pansiyon, right on the beach. Under new management from 2010 and at the time of our research a building site. They are planning 14 simple rooms without air-conditioning, but with a covered area and shower for tents (not caravans), volleyball field, and oriental seating nooks. Friendly young personnel. Doubles £50, rooms for 3 people £63, camping for 2 with tent £8.50. ✆ 3944443, www.ozakpansiyon.com.

Arriba Apart Otel, on the beach. 4 large, simple, clean apartments (for up to 4 people), with balconies overlooking the sea or terrace. Also 5 cosy wooden cabins in the garden behind, with fridges and terraces. Friendly service, restaurant, garden with hammocks. Apartments £63 (without breakfast), doubles £50. ✆ 3943654, www.arribaapart.com.

Sysyphos Pansiyon, long-established pension at the south end of the bay. Lovely old stone building, restaurant with seaside terrace, idyllic little courtyard garden. Very cosy. 20 simple clean rooms with bath, all with balcony or terrace, 8 with sea view. Plus 2 apartments for 4 people maximum. Praised by readers, despite the sometimes sluggish service. Doubles £33, apartments £50 (without breakfast). ✆ 3943016, ✆ 3943656, www.sysyphos-gumusluk.net.

Food and drink: All the restaurants are pleasant and serve good fresh fish — the *meze* displays provide the competition. For a complete meal with wine reckon on about £15 per person; it's usual to bargain! **Important:** In summer the last *dolmuş* back to Bodrum leaves around midnight, but *double-check* with the tourist office!

Mimoza Restaurant, away from the hubub (walk past all the fish restaurants towards the bay) is the best in Gümüşlük. Terrace with white furniture, lovingly decorated, fresh flowers on the tables. The best fish and the best *meze*, refined clientele, very popular. *Meze* £3-£6.50, mains £6.50-£12.50. ✆ 3943139.

There is a particularly beautiful view (fantastic at sunset) from the **Café-Restaurant Limon** near the road to Yalıkavak, about 20 minutes on foot from the centre. If you take a good book, you could spend all afternoon here lounging around on the ultra-comfy cushions.

Practicalities A-Z

Information: The Tourist Office is in the centre near the fish restaurants. Very friendly and helpful staff. In the high season open daily from 08.00-16.00, reduced opening times in winter ✆ 3944487.

Diving/snorkelling: Officially, this is banned around the Sunken City. But since the most important finds have already been saved, a blind eye is *usually* turned to snorkelling. But whatever the Tourist Office says, the *jandarma* may think otherwise, so do enquire again!

Yalıkavak

This former sponge-diving centre is a dignified resort today. The village centre, where the old men meet to socialise, still looks pretty much as it must have done years ago. The small stretch of bazaar is straw-covered, no one pesters you, and there are no crowds. You can dine royally in the fish tavernas a few steps further along (the marina, with space for 450 yachts, provides them with plenty of up-market clientele). The narrow beach is admittedly not the most spectacular, but it's OK and not ruined by large hotel blocks. Similarly, at the only two attractions, there are none of the usual hassles: in the centre, changing art exhibitions are shown in a late 19th-century *sarnıç* (open sporadically, free entry); at the port there's an old restored windmill with sails. There are wonderful views on the road from Yalıkavak to Bodrum, as well as on Walks 3 and 4, which start at Yakıkavak.

Accommodation: **4reasons Hotel**, about 3km outside the centre. Gorgeous complex run by a Turkish/Canadian couple. 20 beautifully decoratedmodern rooms, readers say one of the best hotels in Turkey. Excellent service, restaurant with superb fusion cuisine. Lovely pool area. To get there, from the *dolmuş* station in the centre, take the road towards Bodrum, go left at the T-junction, then it's signposted. Early booking recommended! Open all year. Doubles from £125. Bakan Cad. 2. ☎ 3853212, 📠 3853229, www. 4reasonshotel.com.

Lavanta Hotel, another luxury inn, this one high on a hill with breathtaking view over Yalıka-vak. Extremely comfortable, individually decorated rooms (some with antiques, expensive carpets, wood floors, etc.). Superb pool area. Occasional dinner evenings. Signposted off the road to Gündoğan and Türkbükü. Doubles from £110. Papatya Sok. 32, ☎ 3852167, 📠 3852290, www. lavanta.com.

Adahan Hotel, about 100m from the marina, in a caravanserai-like building. 24 very tastefully decorated rooms. Antiques scattered throughout. Pool with classical music, library. Family-run. Open all year. Doubles from £110. ☎ 3854759, 📠 3853576, www.adahanotel.com.

Cüneydi Pansiyon, clean, well-kept family guest house with 15 plain rooms on the promenade. All rooms with stone floors and bath, nice little garden. Doubles £42. Plaj Cad. 14, ☎ 3854077, www.pansion.cuneydi.com.

Yalı Hotel, another simple place a few steps further along the promenade, this one right on the water. 7 rooms, 3 with sea view. Steak house. Doubles £42. Plaj Cad. 28, ☎/📠 2353987.

Food and drink: Of those on the port promenade, chic **Cumbalı** stands out. It's in a restored stone house, with a welcoming terrace in front. *Meze* £2-£4, mains £3.50-£11. ☎ 3854996. In the little centre, opposite the mosque by the cistern, **Gülten Abla** offers honest Turkish home-cooking (stuffed vegetables, *köfte*, soups). Mains about £3.50-5. Seating is under shady trees.

Practicalities A-Z

Boat trips: Swimming trips are on offer at the port for about £15 per person including lunch.

Shopping: There is a large **weekly market** on Thursdays near the Hotel Adahan.

Gündoğan

During the First World War the inhabitants of Gündoğan shifted their dwellings a few hundred metres inland from the coast, in order to avoid offering English warships a target to attack. Today the old inland village, still unspoilt, has merged with the mass of new buildings round the U-shaped bay. The noise level rising from local and foreign youngsters on the rough sand beach drowns out the pounding of the waves. But the water is crystal- clear, and there is a huge choice of water sports on offer. There are also take boat trips to nearby Apostle Island with the ruins of a Byzantine church.

Accommodation: Since value for money does not exist here, we offer *no* recomendations.

Food and drink: **Terzi Mustafa'nın Yeri**, a popular fish restaurant on a beach east of the port. Fresh flowers on the tables, some of which are right on the beach. The speciality is squid with dill sauce. When it's busy, service can be slow. ☎ 3877089.

Türkbükü

Türkbükü, in the north of the peninsula was still a fishing hide-away 20 year ago; today it's one of the most elite addresses in the country. But constant building works and the dusty roads between the villas and exclusive mini resorts detract from the charm. The small esplanade with its chic restaurants is where the rich and famous stroll. Rumour has it that you'll always meet some celebrity or other here. Since the narrow sand beach is unsuitable for sun-bathing, you get your tan lounging on wooden jetties over the sea, with rott-weilers and golden retrievers for company. When you're seeing and being seen, don't worry if your money runs out — there are ATMs right on the beach…

Getting there: Türkbükü and Gölköy are somewhat confusingly sign-posted as 'Göltürkbükü' from the Gündoğan/Torba road.

Accommodation: While we await all the new building work to end, the three best addresses at time of writing were (all signposted):

Ada Hotel, in a small fort, is one of the best hotels in Europe. Top-class luxury and service. Only 8 rooms and 6 suites with small private terraces, own *hamam*, 2 pools, relaxing garden, theatre, private yachts, etc. Double rooms from £580-1155. High above the bay. ☎ 3775915, 📠 3775379, www.adahotel.com.

Maki Hotel also attracts the beautiful people. At the north end of the bay, without direct access to the beach. Minimalist-functional décor. All rooms with balcony. Pool and terrace restaurant above the sea. Private yacht to take guests to various beaches. Doubles from £189-600. ☎ 3776105, 📠 3776056, www.makihotel.com.tr.

Kaktüs Çiceği Hotel, French-Turkish management. 18 modern, modestly sized rooms with lovely wallpaper. Good restaurant. Doubles at fair prices for Türkbükü: £100. ☎ 3775254, 📠 3775248, www.kaktuscicegi.com.tr.

Gölköy

Gölköy, which you pass on the way to Türkbükü from Bodrum, is a simpler variation of the latter. Gölköy's beach is no better than Türkbükü's, and you have to make do with bars instead of posh restaurants … because here in Gölköy you'll also find ordinary holidaymakers like Fred and Gladys sunning themselves. With all the holiday develop-ments, the beauty of this bay has been totally lost.

Getting there: see Türkbükü above.

Accommodation: Gölköy isn't cheap either. A double in a simple family-run pension well back from the beach will set you back about £42-50 in high season.

Torba

This last port of call on the peninsula is of little interest for individual travellers. There are chic resorts all along the bay and not a square metre of beach for the day visitor. But there is a nice fish restaurant, Gonca Balık, on the beach (Bodrum prices!).

Distance/time: 3h
Grade: easy-moderate, mainly over footpaths and tracks (often stony underfoot); initial ascent of about 275m
Equipment: see pages 21-22.
Travel: 🚐 *dolmuş* from Bodrum to Akçaalan mosque (Bodrum/ Turgutreis service, frequent departures, journey time 20min); return by 🚐 *dolmuş* from Akyarlar to Turgutreis, then 🚐 *dolmuş* back to Bodrum
Shorter walks
1 Akçaalan — Karabağ — Turgutreis (under 2h; easy; good shoes and sun protection are all you need). Follow the main walk as far as Karabağ. Return along the road by which you entered the village — or take the lower road, following it down to the main road. Turn left, down to the seafront at Turgutreis.
2 Akçaalan — windmills — Turgutreis (under 3h; grade as main walk). Follow the main walk to the windmills, walk back to Karabağ and on to Turgutreis, as in Shorter walk 1.

The dolmuş journey out to Akçaalan takes you westwards from Bodrum through the village of Ortakent, or 'middle town', to give it its English name. Once beyond Ortakent. notice how the scenery changes. The greenery-cloaked, rounded limestone hills, so familiar around Bodrum, are replaced by the open volcanic landscape that covers the whole of the western half of the peninsula. As if to emphasise the starkness of the landscape, a lone tree might find a foothold. The hollows at a lower level collect and hold the soils washed down from the mountainsides, sometimes forming areas large enough for cultivation. Imagine such a pocket of cultivation — an emerald green meadow, walled in brown stone; imagine it with a solitary white farmhouse built on the very edge, so that it takes up little or none of the valuable land for cultivation; picture the white farm with the luxury of a little shade from the single tall leafy green tree. See all this in your mind's eye against the brown barren hills rising steeply behind, and you have an image of the dramatic contrasts which are so typical of this intriguing landscape. This walk follows an old route between two lovely villages, passing some delightful old windmills which grace the skyline almost from the start. At the end of the walk lies Akyarlar (see page 76).

Start out in **Akçaalan** with the mosque on the right, by heading momentarily uphill. Turn right by a shop into Okul Sokak (School Street). After a short way the street ends. Continue more or less ahead (there is a small **tower house** on the right) and take the surfaced road to the right of the **Amiral Turgutreis Ilk Okul** (Infant School) and fountain. Once past the school, you pass a ***sarnıç*** (water cistern, see page 87) on the left and a **mosque** to the right. Looking ahead, you can see three windmills on the skyline. Keep along the road as it swings right and shortly becomes walled-in. There is a lovely pastoral feel to the walk, as you head past well-tended farmlands on your left. Viewpoints open up as you climb.
Shortly the road you are on joins a narrower road on a U-bend: turn left here. A minute up this road gives you your first view of Karabağ above; it is perched on a platform nestling into the hillside. Higher, to the right, are

the windmills. Continue up into the village of **Karabağ** (**45min**), to the Hawthorn Karaca Hotel. With your back to the hotel, you will see a small mosque beyond the Konak Apartments. Head for the **mosque** and follow the streets uphill through the village, always bearing slightly right and making for the windmills. The road becomes a track as you leave the village, swinging round the back of new holiday homes. Turn right at the next junction, then left at the junction 200m further on. Keep on the track to the crest of the hill. To inspect the **windmills** and enjoy some spectacular views, take the track uphill to the right. Looking at the craggy hilltop surrounded by pink-hued rocky terrain over to the east, the eye can just make out the remains of farm buildings which blend so well into this hostile environment. This may also have been the site of ancient Termera which is known to be in this region.

Head back from the windmills and turn right when you rejoin the track. Follow the track as it continues over the crest of the hill. As the track reaches its highest point, eye-catching splashes of yellow and green lichen decorate the rosy-hued rocks where, in autumn,

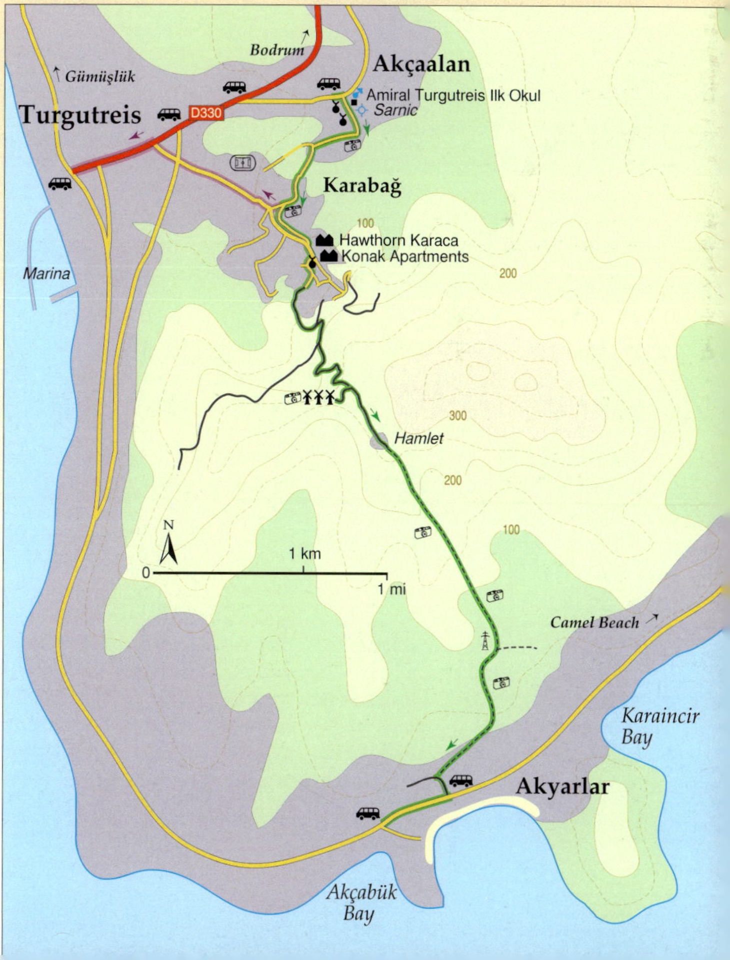

Unfortunately many of the peninsula's lovely old windmills have not only lost their sails — but their wooden frames as well (this photograph was taken on Walk 2 several years ago).

Cyclamen hederifolium shyly hide and the white *Narcissus serotinus* waft around in the breeze. You pass through a **deserted hamlet**, then the track ends. The route continues as a walled-in trail, with cactus lining the right side.The view opens out across to the Greek Island of Kos and the built-up coastline around Akyarlar.

Once into the descent towards Akyarlar, the trail becomes a path which is vague at times as it crosses the top of an open area of bedrock. Keep ahead, close to the wall on the right, to pass through a small rocky outcrop. In three minutes you reach a very wide walled-in trail, currently blocked by a barbed-wire fence. Clamber (easily) round the right-hand side of the fence, but beware of the deep hole, covered by brushwood, as you do so. Dull red waymarks may offer some guidance. Keep downhill, in the middle of the two walls initially, moving more to the wall on the left as the right-hand wall sweeps away. As the wall on the left angles left, about three minutes later, take the less likely route to the left, heading down a shallow depression. The path is unclear at times but, keeping the wall on your left, head along the hillside towards a **solitary pylon** at the end of the ridge, which lies to the left of the Akyarlar peninsula (130° southeast).

Pass to the left of the pylon and, a minute later, reach a junction of trails. Turn right here to descend a rocky walled-in trail (if you encounter a brushwood gate, replace it behind you). The trail eventually widens out and heads more to the right of the Akyarlar peninsula. Edge over to the right, where you meet a strong path. But as the wall on the right swings away, keep ahead to continue alongside another wall joining from the right. Turn right through a gap at a junction of walls a couple of minutes later. Continue on the path contouring the hill, with a wall on your right. Make for the corner of a track that you can see ahead. When you meet the track, turn left to the **main road**. You can catch the *dolmuş* here. Or else turn right and then left, to reach the shore at **Akyarlar (3h)**.

Walk 2: Karakaya circuit from Gümüşlük inland village

Time: 2h30min
Grade: easy, but the paths are very stony underfoot; ascent of about 150m
Equipment: see pages 21-22.
Travel: 🚌 *dolmuş* from Bodrum to Gümüşlük *inland main village*, frequent departures, journey time 25-30min; return by 🚌 *dolmuş* back to Bodrum, either from coastal Gümüşlük or from the main village. (Several villages on this peninsula are divided into two, with part of the village by the sea but the main village well inland. *Dolmuş* drivers expect all tourists to visit the coast, so may try to dissuade you: say 'tamam' ('OK'), to reassure them!)
Shorter walk: to the **windmill** and back (5.7km/3.5mi; 1h45min; grade as main walk). Follow the main walk to the windmill, retrace steps, then continue down to the coast as in the main walk.

Rickety wooden landing jetties in the unhurried sweep of the bay, waterside cafés and restaurants, a scattering of white buildings … and a peaceful unchanging life-style — this is Gümüşlük. This unspoilt fishing village (see page 78) has been denied growth because of the archaeological importance of nearby Myndos. And the local people prefer it that way. Traffic too is kept outside the village, but there is a car park. This short walk has been designed to leave you time to enjoy the peaceful ambience of Gümüşlük, perhaps to enjoy a meal at the water's edge and wander around the remains of Myndos (such as they are: most of the ruins are now under the sea). You might also visit 'rabbit island', which is joined to the mainland by a causeway. There is no problem if you want to go, but it does mean that you have to paddle across — and the water may be up to your knees in places. The walk itself takes you to one of the old windmills on the peninsula and, like Walk 1, explores the dramatic landscapes in this fascinating volcanic region. Gümüşlük takes its name from the Turkish word for silver, and there is evidence of old silver mines nearby.

Start the walk in **Gümüşlük** main village: with the **mosque** on your left, head seawards, but at the roundabout turn sharp right into narrow cobbled Sarnıç Sokak. After some 260m you pass a ***sarnıç*** (water cistern; see page 87) on the left. Keep right here for just 20m, then fork left (Samanlık Sokak). After about 140m the road loses its tarred surface and forks: go right on large rough cobbles and gravel (Degirmen Sokak), passing behind a farmhouse and winding steeply up a concrete section to some **housing**. Go to the right of the houses, to pick up the path heading left up the hillside. In a minute or two you pass just to

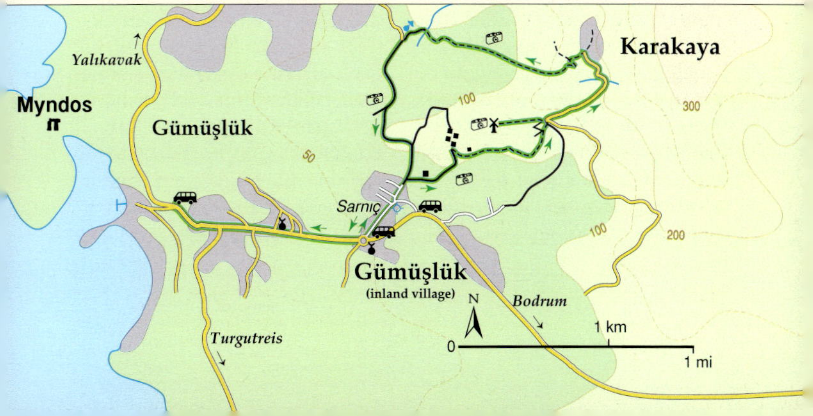

Restaurants line the harbour at Gümüşlük

the right of a white pump house. This is a good place to catch your breath and admire the views: a line of seven windmills on a hilltop to the east catches the eye, as do the offshore islands — of which Kos is the larger one. The three windmills silhouetted on the skyline to the south are visited in Walk 1.

Thorny burnett, *Sarcopoterium spinosum*, giving a realistic impression of wire-netting bushes, dot the way now along a stony, enclosed section of path. But the terrain opens up again as the path leads up left through a cutting, to give you a compelling view of Karakaya. The village clings to the hostile slopes of a rocky mountain, overlooking the green and fertile valley floor which this walk rounds.

Join the road which heads to Karakaya, but first go through a gap in the fence to the right of the lime-green **electricity substation**, to divert up to the windmill. Pass beneath the furthest pylon on the left and follow the path around the contour to the right of the hill. Below the third pylon, head up left to the top, then go right to the **windmill (45min)**. Flower-filled meadows in spring provide a perfect setting for this old mill (shown on page 84), which was once used to grind corn.

Return to the Karakaya road and follow it until it ends below the village. Continue along the path to the left which runs to a **junction of paths below Karakaya (1h05min)**. (If you explore Karakaya, return to this junction. Karakaya is a luxurious hide-away for both upper-class Turks and tourists who rent some of the exquisitely refurbished villas.)

Continue on this path below the village. It leads into a steeply-descending trail, quickly taking you out of sight of Karakaya and into an open rocky area. Descend here, generally following the line of the wall on the left, and keep left where the path divides a few minutes later. Swing right with the wall at the bottom to continue on the trail. There are some captivating views of rocky formations over to the right, as you cross a stream bed, and a new softness comes into the landscape — especially in spring, when you glimpse fields white with Greek chamomile, *Anthemis chia*. Beyond here the trail widens to a motorable track.

After passing a **fountain** in a large grassy area, you descend to the main track/road. Turn left, quickly passing a **fountain** on the left and a square **water tank** on the right. At a fork, the widened track veers off right; keep up left here, on the older track between walls. Follow this back to the *sarnıç* and **inland Gümüşlük (2h10min)**. Continue back to the mosque, turn right on the main road and descend to **coastal Gümüşlük (2h30min)**.

Time: 4h15min
Grade: moderate; many of the paths and trails are stony underfoot; ascent of of 300m
Equipment: see pages 21-22.
Travel: 🚌 *dolmuş* from Bodrum to/from Yalıkavak *dolmuş* station, departures fairly frequent, journey time 25min.
Short walk: Sandıma (under 2h; easy-moderate). Follow the main walk to Sandıma and retrace your steps.

An adequate supply of water, for crops, for animals and for man, has been one of the major problems of survival in the arid volcanic western region of the Bodrum peninsula. There is no shortage of rain in winter but, with no great depth of soil to hold or store the water, there is need for some other system, hence the sarnıç. *The* sarnıç, *or* gumbet, *is a lovely domed structure for storing water. It is often plastered and painted white.You will see many of these around the peninsula, but there is a particularly fine one along this walk (see below).*
Apart from some glorious coastal views which stay with you for a good length of time as you climb above Yalıkavak, there are also two villages en route which are captivating for quite different reasons. Sandıma is situated in a bowl, at the base of a ring of barren hills. It is almost deserted; most of the population having moved down to the valley. But at least one house has been newly renovated, and no doubt more will follow. Most surprising of all, there is a small art gallery with a café!
Friendly Geriş, in contrast, shines white and exudes vitality from its hilltop position — with the inevitable building sites. Yalıkavak (see page 79) is a tourist resort with a large marina, but is still relatively unspoilt.

Start the walk from the ***dolmuş* station** in **Yalıkavak**. Turn right out of the vehicle exit and then right again immediately. Then, facing the *belediye* (town hall), turn right. After 100m you come to a junction, where Kayacik Cad. is signposted straight ahead. Follow this concrete and cobbled road due south. Ignore all turn-offs for the next 20 minutes or so, until you leave Yalıkavak behind. Then take care: when the road bends left by a transformer mast (there may also be a sign for 'Ada Evleri' here), go straight ahead. After about 100m look left to see the ***sarnıç*** shown below. This dome-covered cistern was a dingy grey when last seen, and partly obscured by a bank of earth and rubble. But it's worth a stop to enjoy the views and setting.
The now-unsurfaced road takes

Rain falling on the outer dome of this sarnıç *below Sandıma is channelled to the excavated interior, where it is protected from the evaporating rays of the sun. A door and steps inside the dome give access to the water. Most* sarnıçlar *are unused today; the one in Yalikavak is used for art exhibitions.*

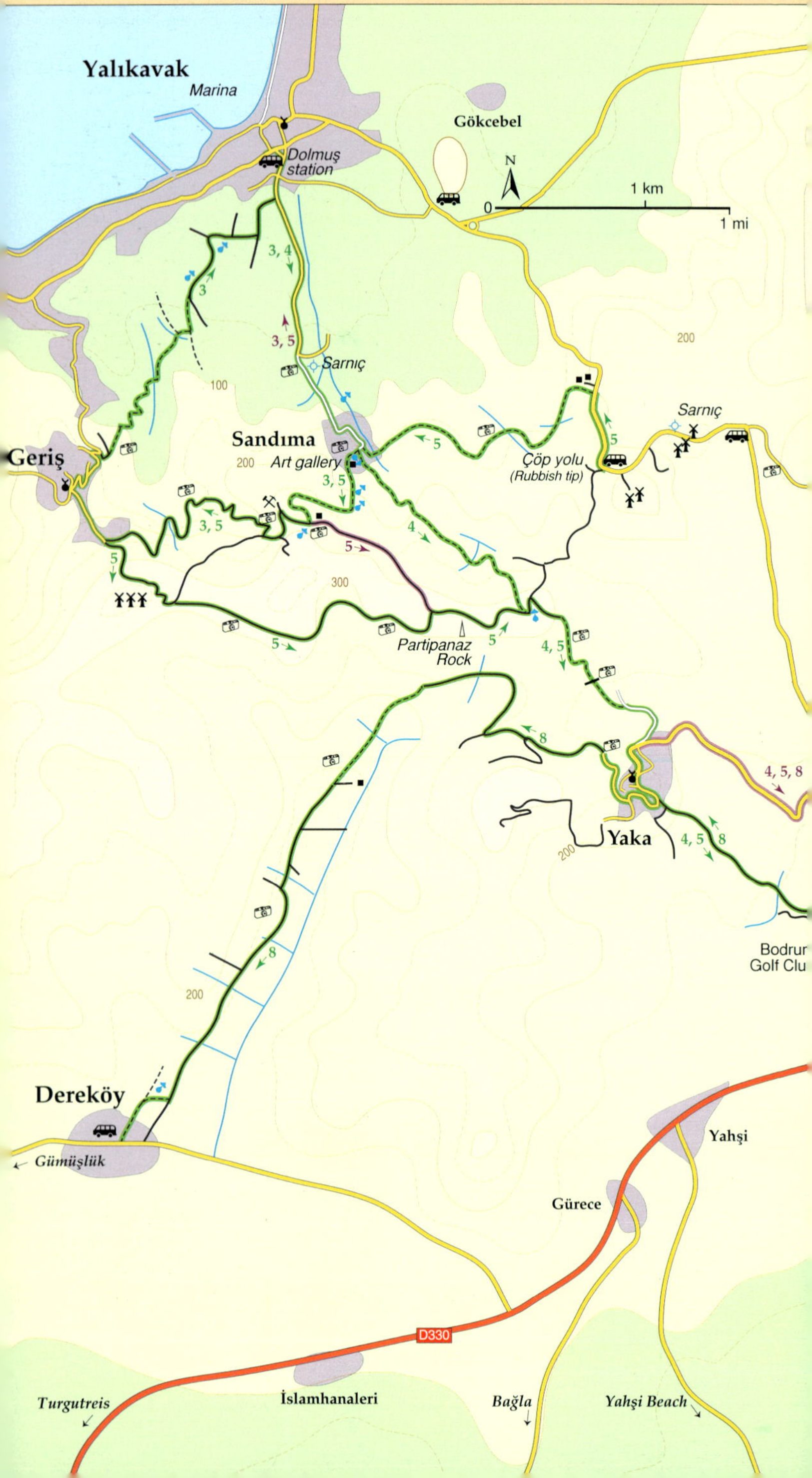
Yalıkavak
Marina
Dolmuş station
Gökcebel
N
0
1 km
1 mi
3, 4
3
3, 5
Sarnıç
100
200
Sandıma
Art gallery
3, 5
5
Sarnıç
Çöp yolu
(Rubbish tip)
Geriş
200
3, 5
5
4
300
5
5
Partipanaz Rock
5
4, 5
8
4, 5, 8
Yaka
4, 5
8
200
Bodrur
Golf Clu
8
200
Dereköy
Gümüşlük
Yahşi
Gürece
D330
Turgutreis
İslamhanaleri
Bağla
Yahşi Beach

you straight to **Sandıma (50min)**. As you first enter the village there is a **large grassy area** (Walk 5 comes in here from the left) and some tall eucalyptus trees over to the right — a delightful spot with fine views. After passing a first well with the date 2006, continue to a second well, where Alpine gardeners may well eat their hearts out at the sight of the delightfully-shaped stone troughs. Follow the yellow-painted sign on a rock to 'Sanat Evi' (Art House), the only inhabited building — an art gallery-café. Otherwise, silence still hangs heavily around this nearly-deserted village, creating an atmosphere of the unreal, as if you have just walked onto a huge film set. Photographic opportunities abound.

To continue, walk round the right-hand side of the house and pick up a small-bore **metal pipe** that will appear intermittently as you stay close to the wall on your right. Eventually, you are channelled into a walled-in trail. Head uphill, almost due south, through the right-hand side of the village. You will come to a **double ornamental fountain**, supplied by the metal pipe. Continue in a fairly steep ascent following the line of the pipe, in two minutes passing a running water source and a trough on the left. The path is somewhat indistinct over the hard rock, but keep the pipe and a wall on your left until you **cross the pipe** before it passes through the wall ahead. This a good place to catch your breath and take in the captivating views back over Sandıma. The climb becomes more gradual as you press on, keeping a wall on the right, and you find that you are being channelled into a walled-in trail. Some 50m after passing a **farmstead** on your left you reach a track (**1h20min**); turn right. *Cyclamen hederifolium* shelter beneath the spreading plane tree here in autumn. Follow the track, passing a water trough on the left, enjoying the superb coastal views as you go. Turn sharp left uphill before a small **quarry**. There is another fine view of Sandıma from this point and, above the village, you can see the rich meadow *(yayla)* which once sustained it. See also how the flat-topped houses are built on the naked rock to preserve the productive land. Continue to the **highest point of the walk** (**1h40min**). Up here you are likely to encounter barriers across the track — stones, brushwood, wire netting. They are there to keep animals *in*, not to keep walkers *out*. So just climb over them.

Ahead now is a beautiful fertile valley, where walled terraces weave their own patterns into the landscape. Geriş comes into view only moments later, glistening white in the sun from its hilltop position. About 10 minutes from the views of Geriş, at an ill-defined junction of tracks, be sure to turn sharp right, passing just to the left of a ruined building. Descend to the valley floor and cross a dry stream bed. Swing right here and head up towards Geriş. At a junction of tracks about 10 minutes later, turn right and keep ahead into Geriş on the cobbled road *(but turn left for Walk 5)*. You come into the **village square at Geriş (2h35min)**, with the mosque on your left.

Skirt round the pylon ahead and taking the cobbled track just beyond it, heading downhill to the right from the corner of the square. Keep down right at the junction, then down right again. Just over a minute later, as the track starts to rise up round a development on the left, turn right down a rough track. Less than a minute later, as the track turns sharply left, keep ahead, passing to the left of a rustic 'gate' (a few twigs nailed together!), to enter a narrow sunken path. Descend this stony path, enclosed by walls, to a stream in a small wooded valley splashed pink with oleander. Cross the stream bed and follow the path to the left. Shortly, pass through a shaded plant 'tunnel', as the path leads away from the stream past old, gnarled olive trees and back into a walled-in path.

Yalıkavak

Around eight minutes later, cross a stream bed; moments later, ignore a trail off left: keep ahead over bedrock. Almost immediately, meet a crossing of trails and go left (there may be waymarks). The countryside here announces its fertility with drifts of springtime colours.

Some 10-12 minutes beyond the stream bed, when you meet a track, keep round to the left. Pass a well on the left in a few minutes and then, as the track swings left, take the lesser track off to the right (by a fountain). Ignore the minor track off left in five minutes, but turn left two minutes later. The twin minarets of the mosque in Yalıkavak can be seen ahead.

You now enter new developments with a confusion of new roads and tracks. Just bear right and continue downhill, eventually arriving back in **Yalıkavak** on Kayacik Cad. (the road you started out on). Turn left and continue back to the **bus station (4h15min)**.

See map on pages 88-89.
Time: 4h
Grade: moderate; many of the paths and trails are stony; ascent of 300m
Equipment: see pages 21-22.
Travel: 🚐 *dolmuş* from Bodrum to Yalıkavak, departures fairly frequent, journey time 25min; return by 🚐 any *dolmuş* from Ortakent back to Bodrum.
Shorter walk: Yalıkavak to Yaka (just over 3h; grade as main walk). Follow the main walk until you reach the road at Yaka. Turn left here and walk on to the Yalıkavak road, where you can wait for a *dolmuş* back to Bodrum.

Apart from some dramatic scenery with weird rock formations, villages add considerable interest to this walk. The village of Yalıkavak (see page 79), where the walk starts, is famous for its sponges and still has a thriving fishing industry. Next along the route is the almost-deserted, but very photogenic village of Sandıma (described in Walk 3). Heading south from Sandıma, you cross over a hill to Yaka. If there is such a thing as a typical Turkish village hardly touched by tourism on this western part of the Bodrum peninsula, then it must be Yaka, which sits near the top of a hillside, looking down over the pastures which sustain it. If you are looking for shops or any other facilities, then wait until you reach Ortakent. Ortakent is another of those villages which exist in two parts, one inland and one by the sea. This walk ends at inland Ortakent. If you have time in hand, then it is worth having a look around to see some fine examples of old Turkish architecture, including the Mustafa Paşa tower house which dates from 1601. To reach the Ortakent beach from here requires a further journey by dolmuş.

Start the walk at **Yalıkavak** by following Walk 3 (page 87) to **Sandıma (50min)**. Walk 5 comes in here from the left, but keep ahead and enter the confines of a walled-in path for a short while. Although the path may be obscure at times, it basically follows the line of the gully over to the left, heading straight up the valley. The steep gully is brightened by pockets of pink oleander, prickly pear cactus *(Opuntia ficus-indica)* and the century plant *(Agave americana).* The latter's flower-spikes take several years to form and resemble a telegraph pole in height and thickness.

After you pass to the right of a ruined building above the gully, the route ahead can be seen more clearly. Cross the middle of bedrock about six minutes later, to be channelled back into a walled-in trail. On reaching a further area of bedrock a few minutes later, keep by the wall on the left initially, then head up more towards the wall on the right — to pass through a rocky outcrop.

Around eight minutes later, meet a dry stream bed and keep round to the left. Still ascending steadily, stay more or less beside the wall on the left as the path crosses an area of *Phrygana* and enters another walled-in section. Some four minutes later, at a junction of paths, go left along the stream bed, before rising up right onto the path alongside it. Shortly, before the path dips down to meet a confluence of

Yalıkavak's old harbour

streams, take the path uphill to the right; it becomes walled-in. You rise up onto a gravel **track, by a well (1h45min)**, where Walk 5 joins from the right. Turn left here and, almost immediately, go right, to continue up onto a saddle, from where there are new vistas down to the southern coastline.

The track soon becomes a path and snakes downhill at the left of a wall or barbed wire. Partipanaz Rock and the valley encountered in Walk 8 are over to your right. Where the route is overgrown, look for an alternative path over to your left. About 15 minutes from the high point, the path kinks to the left and runs parallel with a barbed wire fence to the left. Again, where the trail is overgrown, look for an alternative path, this time on your right, higher up. About 10 minutes from the kink to the left, you go through a gate and, 10 minutes later emerge on a motorable track. Keep right here, straight downhill.

The track swings right and **Yaka** lies before you (**2h30min**). The track soon acquires a tarred surface. On meeting the main village road (by a **bust of Ataturk** near a phone booth), keep right. *(But turn left here for the Shorter walk.)* A few minutes later, at a fork, ignore the cobbled road up to the right; take the little tarred lane down to the left. This runs below the new village mosque and forks in less than two minutes (by an electricity pole with lights). Keep left here too. After 130m, by the last house in the village, at another fork, again go left — now on a field track. Just follow this track downhill, past some fenced-off fields, but ignore all turn-offs. In the distance you can see the aquapark on the Ortakent/ Bodrum road. Some 25 minutes down the track you cross a streambed. Three minutes later the track forks: keep left (to the right is the Bodrum Golf Club). Soon, at the end of a fenced-off olive grove, you come to a T-junction, Turn right. At the fork by the first houses of Ortakent, keep right again, to emerge on Kemer Sokak. After a few minutes along a streambed (past some **ancient pillars** which once supported an aqueduct), this leads to the main road and into the centre of **Ortakent** (**4h**), where you emerge opposite the ***dolmuş* stop** to Bodrum.

See map on pages 88-89.
Time: 6h30min
Grade: moderate-strenuous; the footpaths are often stony; there are two ascents to contend with, the harder one taking you up to about 350m.
Equipment: see pages 21-22.
Travel: 🚐 *dolmuş* from Bodrum (Bodrum/Yalıkavak service, departures fairly frequent, journey time 20min. Ask the *dolmuş* to stop at the *'çöp yolu'* (pronounced churp yoloo; *çöp* means rubbish), an obvious track to a rubbish tip seen about 1km downhill, off left on a bend, as the dolmuş starts to descend to Yalıkavak after the windmills. Return on any 🚐 *dolmuş* from Ortakent to Bodrum.
Short walk: *Çöp yolu* — Sandıma — Yalıkavak (2h; easy). Follow the main walk to Sandıma, then use the map to follow Walk 3 in reverse, down past the *sarnıç,* to Yalıkavak. Return to Bodrum by *dolmuş.*
Alternative walks
1 *Çöp yolu* — Sandıma — Yaka (3h30min; moderate). Follow the main walk to Sandıma. Join the route of Walk 3 (page 69), and climb away from Sandıma towards Geriş. But go only as far as the track reached at the 1h20min-point in Walk 3. Turn left here and continue climbing, to reach a track junction about 15 minutes later. Here you rejoin the route of Walk 5 on its return from Geriş. Turn left, using the notes on page 94 to walk on to Yaka. When you join the surfaced road in Yaka, turn left to the main road, where you can catch a *dolmuş* back to Bodrum.
2 *Çöp yolu* — Sandıma — Geriş — Yaka (5h45min; grade as main walk). Follow the main walk as far as Yaka but, when you join the road leading into Yaka, turn left to the main road, where you can catch a *dolmuş* back to Bodrum.

*Windmills (*yel degirmenleri *in Turkish), have a charm of their own, evoking romantic images of a rustic age when sails turned lazily and life moved at a much slower pace. Life still does move at a slower pace at some places on the Bodrum Peninsula, especially in the hill villages and the high* yaylas *(meadows).*

Start out by leaving the *dolmuş* at the ***çöp yolu* downhill from the windmills**: walk down the road towards Yalıkavak, until the high banking on the left dips after about five minutes (50 metres before a track running up to some houses). Take the path sloping up into the field and follow a vague path diagonally uphill towards the wall over on your right. Continue uphill, close to the wall, to skirt a small rocky outcrop. Now head for the wall

View over Yalıkavak

at the left-hand side of the large rocky outcrop at the top of the rise, and find your crossing point — a gap in the wall. Pass through it and note the rising walled-in trail etched clearly along the hillside on the far side of the valley ahead. This is where you are going. To get there, first head left (southwest) — more or less along the contour of the hill, dipping round rocky outcrops. Head towards a large angular rock on the near horizon (Partipanaz Rock, encountered on Walk 8). You meet a track and a wall rising up from the right and reach an area of bedrock at the end of the wall.

The start of the walled-in trail can now be seen below. Turn right and descend the steep field carefully, making for the confluence of streams below and staying fairly close to the wall on the right. The rubbish tip lies over to the left. At the bottom of the field, cross the stream bed about 10m to the left of the large olive tree. Head up diagonally right to the wall ahead (where it meets another wall). Pass through a gap and, 20 seconds later, cross over the low wall on the right. Join a path and turn right. The path dips to cross a stream bed and enters the walled-in trail.

Views open out as you climb to an area of bedrock. Continue along the path as it swings left through a narrow cutting only a minute later, to emerge overlooking Sandıma nestling in the huge valley below. On the left in this striking picture is a white ***sarnıç*** (water cistern; see page 87) and, over to the right, some fantastic rock formations. From the *sarnıç* a motorable track leads down towards the village, described in Walk 3.

As you enter **Sandıma (1h05min)**, keep down towards the bottom of the gully, watching for a sharp left turn where you cross the stream. As you climb into the main part of the village, meet a junction of paths (two minutes after crossing the stream). A left turn leads into Walk 4, but go *right* here, soon reaching a **large grassy area**. Swing left now towards the **eucalyptus trees** *(but keep straight down, past the* sarnıç, *for the Short walk to Yalıkavak)* and, almost immediately, turn left to enter a walled-in path.

Now use the notes for Walk 3 from just after the 50min-point (page 89), until you reach the **junction of tracks outside Geriş (2h40min)**. Turn left here, away from Geriş. The track affords good views over Yalıkavak and rounds the bowl of the valley, below some **ruined windmills**. Eventually a massive angular rock (Partipanaz Rock from Walk 8) dominates the skyline ahead. You cross a shallow saddle and soon enjoy views of a fertile valley and the track from Yaka to Dereköy (Walk 8). Another saddle is crossed, to the left of Partipanaz Rock, then you reach a track junction, where you turn right (*Alternative walk 1 rejoins here.)* Sandıma's valley now lies to the left. At another track junction, where Walk 4 joins from the left, pick up the notes on page 92 (from the 1h45min-point), to follow that walk up right over the saddle, just past the **well**, to **Yaka (5h)** and **Ortakent (6h30min)**.

See map on page 97.
Time: 4h
Grade: moderate; some stony tracks and paths underfoot; ascent of just under 200m
Equipment: see pages 21-22.
Travel: *dolmuş* to the Dağbelen turn-off (Bodrum/Yalıkavak service, departures fairly frequent, journey time about 18min); return from the Bitez turn-off on any passing *dolmuş* back to Bodrum.

This old route across the Bodrum Peninsula is still the only means of communication with the deserted village shown below — Kibrel, where old rose-coloured houses blend beautifully into the surrounding bare rock. The obscure Lelegian town of Side is also thought to be in this region, and the ruins of the tower that you pass on route might be connected with it. An interesting characteristic of Lelegian architecture is the use of roughly-squared blocks for building so, should you stop at the old tower to rest, then you can cast a critical eye and make your own judgement.

Many of the people in this area aim at nothing more than self-sufficiency in their farming and very often have just one or two cows, perhaps a bull or a few goats. In the morning 'rush hour' there is a constant stream of villagers taking their farm stock out to graze, and you may see this in the early part of the walk. Should you see any cows that look as though they may have strayed, then do take note of it — you may well be approached by a distraught villager asking if you have seen his lost cow (inek).

When you give Dağbelen as your destination on the *dolmuş*, you will be dropped off at the end of the road leading into the village. **Start out** by heading along the road to the village (on the same side as you leave the *dolmuş*). Eventually Dağbelen and its minaret come into view, perched on a hillside overlooking fertile land used for cultivation. You pass between an **Ottoman fountain** and huge plane tree as you enter **Dağbelen (30min)**. Stay on the road until it ends at a

Kibrel

T-junction two minutes later (where there is a red brick and stone fountain dated 2008). Go up the track to the left, which is concreted initially (the fork to the right leads to the mosque). Rising steeply, you have lovely pastoral views as Dağbelen is left behind. Ignore the trail descending to the right 10-12 minutes outside the village, and pass a **fountain** on the left just over three minutes later.

Rise up to a high point and views of the northern shore, before starting into a gentle descent. Keep more or less ahead as the main track forks down to the left, ignoring a minor woodland track off right almost immediately. When the track sweeps right to a stone-coloured farm building set some way back, keep ahead on a sunken path. The pink and white of autumn-flowering *Cyclamen hederifolium* and *Narcissus serotinus* add splashes of colour along the route now.

You reach a **clearing with the ruins of an old tower**. Continue past the clearing along the path and spot the section of ancient wall to the left just before the **path from Gündoğan (Walk 7) joins from the left (1h20min)**. The path keeps round to the right and soon starts to rise through a shaded stony section, heading towards the middle of the peninsula. Keep uphill, where a path joins from the right. Olive groves indicate the proximity of habitation, as you walk alongside a wall on the right three minutes later — and a white *sarnıç* (water cistern; see page 87) comes into view. On meeting a crossing path, keep right, towards the *sarnıç*. Two minutes later, follow the main path to the right again, passing a **graveyard** on the left. Just short of reaching the ***sarnıç*** (a pleasant resting spot), your path goes left. Follow it downhill; it is a stony walled-in trail for a short while. Keep ahead on the path as it meanders between shrubs, ignoring a path off to the right. Two minutes later you enjoy a first sighting of Kibrel. When you reach a stone building and a wall on the right, ruined **Kibrel** comes into full view (**2h**). Walk ahead towards the village and, in a little over a minute, meet a path coming from Kibrel. Turn sharp right here. Follow this good path, which leads away from Kibrel, and comes up alongside a wall on the right with a stony field on the far side. Reach a vantage point three minutes later where, if you look back, you can see the village blending well into its rocky surroundings and notice that the path has described almost a semi-circle around the field.

Start heading down a valley on a steadily-descending track. At the bottom of the valley, turn left and continue along a dry, stony stream bed. The sides of the valley slowly close in around you, until you find yourself walking between the vertical walls of a very narrow and beautiful gorge. Out of the narrowest part of the gorge, you pass an old lime kiln on the right. The track then leads to a small **housing development** at the mouth of the gorge, from where you follow a road past a **cement works** and to the main road. Cross the road and head left to the junction with the **Bitez road** (***Bitez yolu;*** **4h**), for a *dolmuş* back to Bodrum.

Walk 7: From Gündoğan to Dağbelen

Time: 3h
Grade: moderate; some stony paths; ascent of 325m
Equipment: see pages 21-22.
Travel: 🚌 *dolmuş* from Bodrum to Gündoğan, fairly frequent departures, journey time about 20min; return on 🚌 *dolmuş* back to Bodrum (Yalıkavak service)
Alternative walk: Gündoğan to the Bitez road (4h; moderate-strenuous). Follow the main walk to the Dağbelen path. Instead of turning right, go straight on: follow Walk 6 (opposite) from the 1h20min-point to the end.

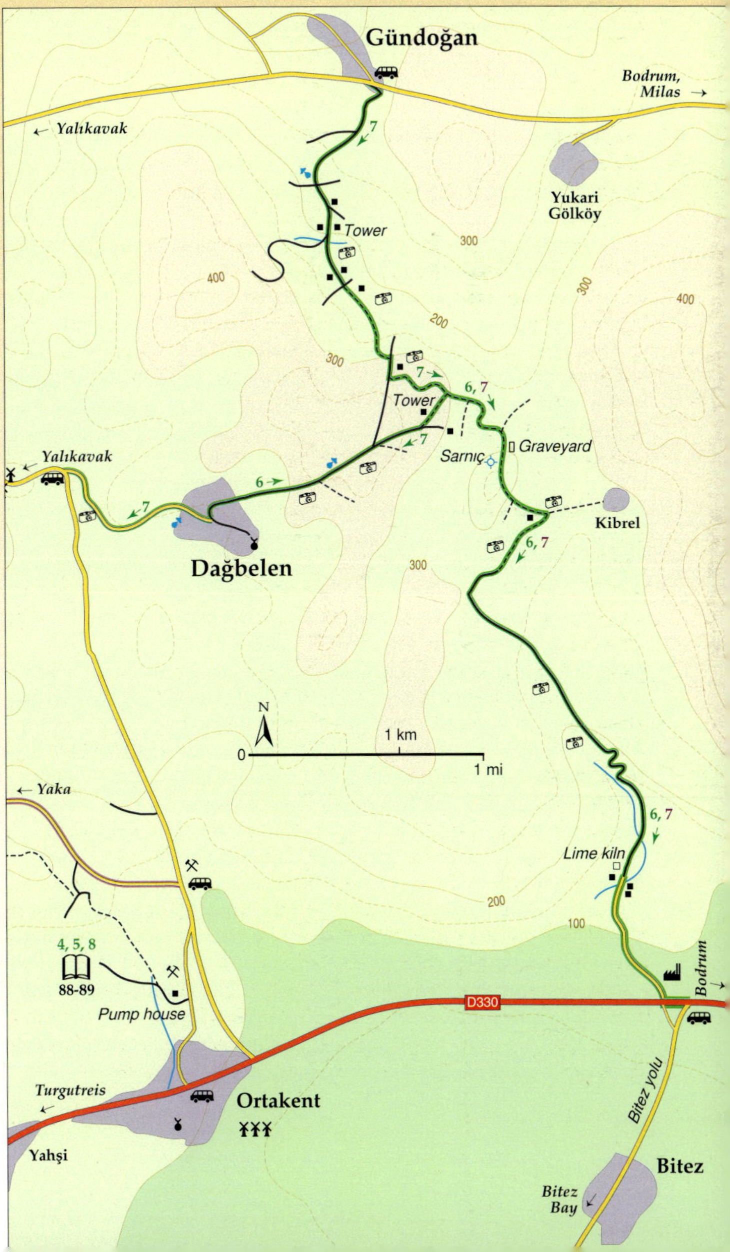

Along any walk on the Bodrum Peninsula there is a reasonable chance of seeing a camel or a train of them. Camels have been used as beasts of burden here for many years. A fully-grown camel is capable of carrying a considerable load, which is useful to both the remaining farmers and the populace in general. Camels move quietly and gracefully, and the sight of one loaded with a refrigerator, tables and chairs seems incongruous in view of their aristocratic demeanour. Camels are treated much as other domesticated farm animals: they are bred, reared and turned out unattended to graze. Tourism has brought change, and the local people are now finding these intriguing animals useful revenue-earners, as at Camel Beach.

Alight from the *dolmuş* just as it turns right off the main road into **Gündoğan**: watch for the village of Yukari Gölköy on the left, 20 minutes from Bodrum, and ask to leave the *dolmuş* just over the next rise). **Start out** by crossing the main road opposite the junction, to find a track which dips down from the road. The track briefly heads left, parallel with the road, then swings right into the countryside. Where a track forks down right, keep ahead uphill, to pass a large **water tank** on the right at the top of the rise. Ignore a left fork just past a renovated farm building (also on the left). Continue uphill, to pass a house on the right and a **stone tower** on the left. A little under two minutes later, the main track swings right and it can be seen carving its way up the hillside; take the lesser track to the left.

The ascent steepens for a while, then a small **hamlet** is reached (**40min**). At the junction of tracks, continue ahead into the woods, along what appears to be a small stream bed at first. Initially leading round to the left, it soon meets an old trail, where you turn right. This lovely shaded section of the route meanders upwards and widens into a woodland track. It rises to a track less than a minute later: turn right here.

Now heading towards Dağbelen, the track passes above a farmed *yayla* (meadow) down to the left. Almost past the *yayla*, turn left down a woodland track. Keep right where the descending track forks almost immediately and soon narrows into a path. The path skirts to the right of the ***yayla* and a farm building** on the edge of pine woods. Soon the path rises again and, although it leads briefly to the right in three minutes, it remains on the edge of the pine woods. When you meet the **junction with the Dağbelen path** (the 1h20min-point in Walk 6), turn right. *(But keep straight on for the Alternative walk.)*

From here continue to Dağbelen by following Walk 6 in reverse: stay on the path; it leads into a track. Keep straight ahead where a track runs back to the right. The track keeps to a high level before descending into Dağbelen, which can be seen for some time on the approach. Once in **Dağbelen**, take the surfaced road off to the right, and follow it to the **main road** (**3h**), where you can catch the Yalikavak/Bodrum *dolmuş*. A couple of restaurants on the right, just before the main road, are a welcome oasis.

See map on pages 88-89.
Time: 3h50min
Grade: moderate; the paths and tracks are usually good underfoot, but there are some stony sections; ascent of about 275m
Equipment: see pages 21-22.
Travel: 🚐 *dolmuş* to Ortakent (using the service from Bodrum to Ortakent, Turgutreis or Gümüşlük), frequent departures, journey time about 10min; return by 🚐 *dolmuş* back to Bodrum (Gümüşlük service).
Shorter walk: Ortakent to Yaka (2h15min; easy). Follow the main walk to Yaka. Turn right on the main village road and follow it out to the main Ortakent/ Yalikavak road, to catch a *dolmuş* back to Bodrum.

As you travel from Bodrum to the start of this walk, you may notice a partly-constructed wooden boat by the roadside (although most are built in shipyards now). Boat-building is an old industry in these parts, given a new lease of life by popularity of the gulet *— taken from the Italian* gouletta *(a kind of schooner incorporating features from the Arab* baggala*). Usually built from local Aegean pine, the hull has evolved considerably, as has the rigging — but the latter is now for show, since the* gulet *is powered by a large diesel engine. You might wonder how the boats are transported down to the sea. If you are unlucky, you might just find out first hand! It is a slow process: greased blocks, which are moved constantly from back to front, are used as a sledge. Given the roads in Bodrum, it virtually stops the local traffic.*

The walk starts off in a region green with cultivation, where trees sometimes arch over the route. You then head into a stark and barren landscape, before returning once again to cultivation. There is a variety of interesting wild flowers and shrubs along the way, including autumn-flowering cyclamen, two different kinds of wild lupins, and mandrakes, Mandragora officinarum, *about which so many interesting tales are told (see Walk 9). Particularly eye-catching, especially in the spring, is the giant fennel,* Ferula communis, *with its spread of light green ferny foliage. It provides a delightful complement to other wild flowers.*

Ortakent, where you leave the dolmuş, *is an old village with interesting tower houses and a row of ruined windmills on the barren*

Landscape between Yaka and Ortakent

hillside. If you have time, it is worth a few minutes looking around. The dolmuş *leaves you in the centre of Ortakent, by a plaza with a taxi rank and PTT.*

Start the walk in **Ortakent**: take the road opposite the plaza (Kemer Sokak), heading inland and then following a stream past some **ruined pillars** that once supported an aqueduct. After 600m, at a T-junction, turn left. Some 250m further on, at a Y-fork by a fenced-in olive grove, bear left. Now simply follow this field track uphill, ignoring all offshoots. You pass the Bodrum Golf Club and eventually cross a streambed.

Reaching the first house in the village of **Yaka** (**1h30min**), keep ahead to join a lane, where you turn left. *(But turn right here for the Shorter walk; this lane becomes the main village road.)* After following the lane to the left uphill for 400m, turn sharp right on another lane. This becomes a track which continues across the top of Yaka, with good views down over the village and beyond it. Some five minutes later, the track goes sharply round to the left, and the village is left behind.

Soon you reach the **highest part of the walk** (**2h**), at the top of the hill between the valleys. From here you can see a hilltop with a mast over to the left. Follow the track into a descent through patches of *Phrygana,* where lavender, *Lavandula stoechas,* can be detected by its aromatic perfume, if not by its dark blue flowers. When the track forks four minutes later, keep down to the right.

Dominating the view now is a large, pitted, angular rock which resembles a wedge of cheese — **Partipanaz Rock**, a useful landmark for other walks in this area. Your way leads down into the valley, to an area of bedrock at the base of this rock. Below it, where there is a dip in the track and a wall to the right, take a path forking left. It curls left towards a white house with a red roof, almost hidden in the trees. Some two minutes later, you pass to the right of the house and head left into a walled-in path, via a rustic gate. Enjoy the flavour of this lovely section of walled-in path, where oleander provides the colour and myrtle the scent, with an accompanying stream to the left — all the time under the watchful gaze of the receding 'cheese rock'.

Cross a dry stream bed and, five minutes later, meet a track by a house on the left. Continue along the track to the right. At a junction of tracks under 10 minutes past the house, keep ahead. Dip down to cross a stream 10-12 minutes later, ignoring tracks off to the left and then right.

The track becomes walled-in, and a track joins from the right before a cobbled section comes underfoot. The track then dips down to cross another stream (some 10 minutes after the last stream crossing). Ten minutes later, fork right on an old trail. Then, almost immediately (by an old, colourful **fountain**), fork left. In two minutes you are in the **centre of Dereköy** (**3h50min**). A minute along the road to the right is a pleasant, shaded *'cay bahcesi'* (tea garden) — a good place to sit and wait for a *dolmuş.*

Old Konacık

See map on page 103.
Time: 4h30min
Grade: moderate; mostly along a track; ascent of about 350m. The diversion to Pedesa requires a little scrambling and agility.
Equipment: see pages 21-22.
Travel: *dolmuş* to Konacık using any westbound service (except Gümbet), frequent departures, journey time 5min. (Konacık is a fragmented series of habitations covering a large area, which can be confusing. If you take a dolmuş serving *only* Konacık, it will drop you off in the *new part* of the village — some 20min into the walk.) Return on foot to Bodrum centre.
Short walk: Konacık (under **2h**; easy). An opportunity to explore the interesting countryside around the old village of Konacık without too much exertion. Follow the main walk to the stony meadow, then return by the same route.

This walk heads into the wild interior, following a valley towards ancient Pedesa, almost hidden in the foliage on its hilltop vantage point. The sense of history is never far away on the Bodrum Peninsula, with flowers as well as ruins around to remind you of past cultures and civilisations. One such plant that you can expect to see on this walk is the mandrake, Mandragora officinarum, *which was referred to back in Biblical times and is associated with many legends. It is recognised by its flat rosette of large, wrinkled, dark green leaves, often achieving a spread up to 50cm or more across, bearing a cluster of short-stalked, usually blue flowers, in the spring, followed by large round berries. Many of the legends arise from the shape of the tap root, which is often forked and strongly likened to the human figure. It was believed to have powers of curing infertility or to act as a love potion. It was also said to shriek when pulled from the ground, and that this cry brought death to those who heard it. The mandrake had a place in medicine, too; both the roots and the leaves have been used in various treatments.*

Unless you are on a *dolmuş* serving *only* Konacık, ask the driver for Konacık *cami* (mosque). The blue-capped minaret of the mosque can be spotted to the right of the main road on the approach from Bodrum. Alight in front of the **Konacık Belediyesi**, and **start the walk** by heading inland along the road alongside this government building. You soon pass the **mosque**, on the right. When the road forks after 10-12 minutes, keep right, to pass through the newer part of the village (the old village is to the left). The road then runs past a **newer mosque** (on the left). Turn left at the next junction, following the brown signpost for 'Pedesa 2K'. If you are walking in spring, look for the mandrake down on the right, near another well, two minutes later.

Beyond the newer part of the village, the road leads through the old, but still inhabited, **hamlet of Konacık (35min)**, then reverts to track. Follow the track as it wends its way further into the countryside and up the hillside: the first indication of the ancient site are early **walls** over to your left as the track levels out. Continue along the track until the ruins on the hilltop come into view, then turn left on a path to **Pedesa (1h55min**; see history opposite). The tower at the far end affords the best views. From this vantage point you can appreciate the prominent situation of these fortifications — occupying a position on a hill in the centre of the Bodrum Peninsula, looking over the north shore just west of Torba and the south shore in the direction of Bitez.

Leave the ruins at the point where you entered them and return to the track, then turn left. Ignore a trail entering from the right as the route skirts to the right of the rocky outcrop and climbs away, giving good views of Pedesa. As the way levels out at the top of the rise, you can see your onward route ahead — a track which dips through an old hamlet (now used for cattle farming), before rising up past a lone building on the left. Descend through the old hamlet (**Gökçeler**). But before rising up past the lone building on the left, turn right and walk along the left-hand side of a stone wall. Head down the field, following the wall. Two minutes later, as the way becomes overgrown, cross the collapsed wall, into an olive grove. Continue down towards the left-hand corner of the field. Some old waymarks may be around to guide you for the next few minutes. Go back over the wall, then cross a dip, to rise up onto a rough path. Go right now, and keep right a minute later, just before reaching a crossing stream bed. With the stream bed on your left, dip down across an adjacent stream bed. Then bend left and pass through a gap in a wall, into a wooded valley. The path edges the stream bed, with short forays onto paths left, then right. The path then rises up to the right and becomes easier to follow. Here the path divides, but keep heading down the right-hand side of the valley, with the **stream bed** on your left (ignore the path entering from the right). You will pass **a number of ruins** — which may have been fortifications along the old route to Pedesa.

Bodrum comes into view as you emerge from the woodland. Four minutes later the path disappears in a **building site**. Drop down to a track/road and descend through woodland. Follow the road to the dual carriageway. Turn left past the Canerler **shopping centre** towards the BP petrol station, cross the road *carefully* and descend into a **concrete culvert**. Keep ahead on the road as you emerge from the culvert, and keep ahead again on meeting the next road. This leads round to the left, passing the **sports stadium** on the left. When you reach the dual carriageway in **Bodrum (4h30min)** turn right. The **bus station** is two minutes to the left.

Walk 10: Bodrum • Pedesa • Bodrum

Time: 4h50min
Grade: moderate; some stony paths/trails; short sections with no path; ascent of about 350m; agility needed to explore Pedesa. ***Route-finding problems likely*** *in bulldozed developments north of Bodrum; you need to have a good sense of direction and to persevere.*
Equipment: see pages 21-22.
Travel: on foot from/to Bodrum

Pedesa is situated in the region once known, and still referred to by the local people, as Gökçeler. It is one of the old Lelegian cities believed to date back to the sixth and fifth centuries BC, when it had greater power than neighbouring Halicarnassus. In the fourth century BC the people were forcibly incorporated by Prince Mausolus into Halicarnassus, and the site was retained as an outpost. It is a fairly large site occupying a commanding position, but there have been few excavations and little reconstruction. There are no roads leading to it; the only way to get there is on rough track. This walk explores some of the interesting and quiet countryside behind Bodrum and reaches Pedesa by what was possibly the old route to Halicarnassus. Sound carries in the peace of the countryside, and the tinkling of bells from the animals can often be heard from distant hillsides. Somewhere along the way in this walk we once heard the pure, sweet, clear voice of a girl break the calm

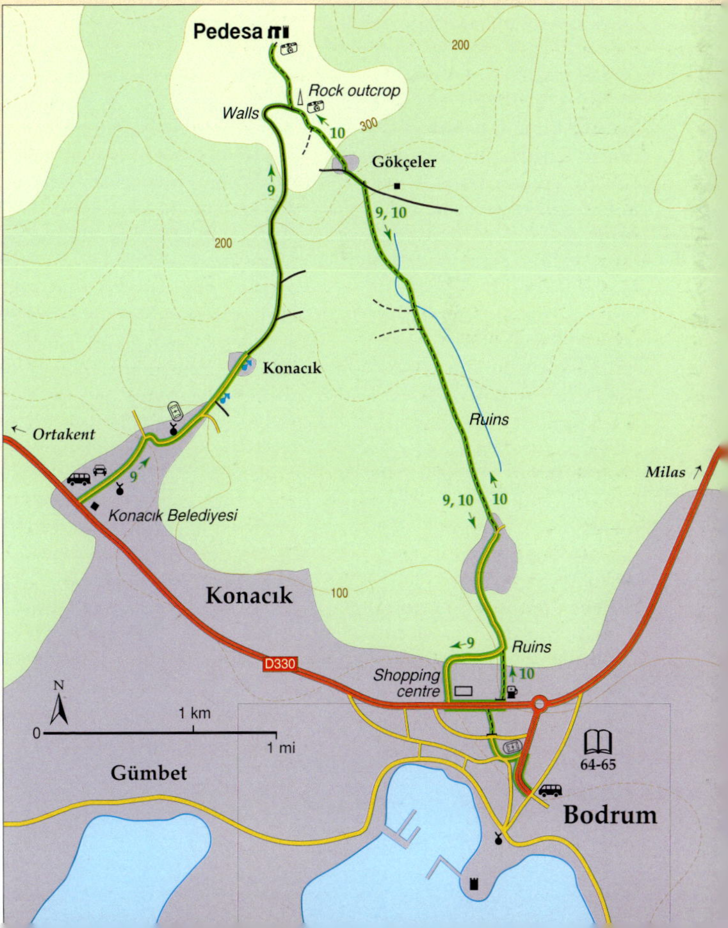

morning air with melodious song — followed in harmonious duet by a shepherd. It was unbearably beautiful and stopped us in our tracks.

Start the walk by leaving **Bodrum bus station** to the left of the WCs, near the ticket offices. Emerging on the dual carriageway, turn right towards the hills, keeping ahead at the traffic lights. Cross the road and in two minutes turn left (*not* the first minor left turn). You pass the **sports stadium** on the right. Follow the road as it leads round to the right, but then keep ahead on a minor road, when the major road sweeps left (three minutes later). Two minutes later, keep ahead into a culvert, rising up left to the busy **dual carriageway**. Cross *carefully*, heading slightly right, towards the culvert between the BP **petrol station** and the Canerler **shopping centre**. Then walk along the culvert/sunken path. A few minutes later you pass some old **ruins**, then the path disappears at the bank of a road. Rise up to this road, turn right, and continue past new developments and up through pine woods. As you head away from the woods, the road veers right. Ahead you can see more **ruins** on the hillside.

Your ongoing path is hard to find because of all the new developments; watch out on the left of the road for a slight dip, where it should be possible to pick up the path heading inland through the woods (you will have a dry ravine below you on the right as you do so). Some 12 minutes along, notice more **ruins** down to the right. At a fork in the path 10 minutes past the view of the ruins, keep right. Two minutes later, the path begins to head along the stream bed, crossing and recrossing, before settling on the left bank and passing through a gap in a wall near the edge of the woods.

Continue alongside the stream, initially heading round to the right. But look for some old waymarks along a rough path up to the left. The route is not very clear at this point, due to invasive foliage, but the rough path heads uphill for a short distance and then over to the left. It dips down and crosses a collapsed wall, near a corner. Turn right and head uphill, with the wall on your right. But a minute later, cross back over the low wall, to continue uphill with the wall on your left. Rise up onto a stony track, with a **solitary building** up to the right and old **hamlet** to the left (**Gökçeler**; now used for cattle), and turn left to walk up through the hamlet.

At the top of the rise the main track forks left, but take the path forking right and keep near the wall on the right. From here the remains of a tower at Pedesa can be seen on the pine-covered hill to the right, as the path descends to become more obviously an old trail.The route becomes a sunken path as it skirts to the left of a **rocky outcrop**, and an overgrown trail enters from the left. As the path levels out beyond the outcrop, Pedesa sits atop the hill to the right, and **Walk 9 joins from a valley on your left (2h15min)**. Follow the notes for Walk 9 from the 1h55min-point (page 102) to visit **Pedesa** and return to **Bodrum** (**4h50min**).

3 GULF OF GÖKOVA

The bays of Çiftlikköy • The bays of Mazıköy • Çökertme • Ören • Akyaka • Sedir Island • Karacasöğüt Bay

Area code: ✆ 0252
Connections: There are up to 5 *dolmuşes* a day from Bodrum bus station (the first leaves at 10.00). Tell the driver which beach you want. The whole run takes about an hour via the inland route, which is more easily motorable.
Tips: Change money before you travel here! Most of the pensions in the various bays are only open from June to September.
Walks: 11-13

The Gulf of Gökova has so far hardly been touched by touristic developments and is still one of the most beautiful stretches of coast in all Turkey. The further you get from Bodrum, the more unspoilt the landscape: hills wooded with pine forests and olive groves alternate with green pastures full of cows in spring or golden stubble fields in high summer. Although signposting is getting better, you're bound to get lost at some point, and a local farmer will hep you on your way. Some idyllic beaches lie at the end of little roads.

The bays of Çiftlikköy

The large farming village of Çiftlikköy is 20km southeast of Bodrum. Surrounded by wooded hills and fields, it's of little interest to tourists. But the stretch of coast a couple of kilometres *before* the village has several attractive bays. Those to the east have some all-inclusive resorts, like Club Med. Those to the west, on the other hand, are partly accessible and free. Coming from Bodrum, the first bit of beach you pass is near the Kempinski Hotel, and it's not always clean. **Yalı Beach**, which follows on, is much more inviting — a sand and pebble beach with several restaurants, surfboard rental and showers.

Getting there: frequent dolmuş *connections to and from Bodrum. If you're driving, follow signposting for 'Çiftlik/Yalı' from the main Bodrum–Milas road.*

The bays of Mazıköy

If you keep driving east along the narrow country roads past Çiftlikköy, after about 35km of nerve-wracking curves and dreadful road) you will come to Mazıköy. Below this sleepy village there are a couple of really fantastic turquoise bays, truly among the most beautiful in the whole country. Even the boat trips and jeep convoys cannot spoil this idyll. So far, these beaches are almost bare of buildings and not overcrowded, even in high season. Once in a while you'll even have a cow watching you swim. It doesn't matter which of the bays you choose — the narrow pebble beach at **Hurma Bay** in the east or the double bay in the west (same access road). The latter is divided in two by a hill— there's the western pebble beach of **Taşlıyalı** and the sand and pebble **İnceyalı Bay** (to the east).

İnceyalı Bay, near Mazıköy

Accommodation/Food and drink

Some new accommodation in the area made a rather unkempt impression in 2010. In high season early booking is a good idea — and usually only available with half or full board.

Hurma Bay

Sahil Pension, just a few metres from the sea. 14 clean rooms of differing sizes with pine furniture. Meals (not always top quality, say readers) are served on the lovely beach-side terrace, then the sweet taken in the garden full of mandarin trees. Per person with F/B £29. ☏ 3392131.

Both the **Mazı Restaurant** (with a large terrace; (☏ 3392121) and the eagles' nest-like **Kayabaşı Restaurant** (☏ 392050) serve first-class fish dishes in lovely settings at decent prices.

İnceyalı Bay

Yalı Turkuaz, somewhat set back in a garden, 5 really narrow bungalows in a row; in good condition. Restaurant with lovely terrace just behind th beach. Per person with H/B £29. ☏ 3392552 or ☏ 0535/7692962 (mobile).

Taşlıyalı-Bay

Eray Pension, just 5 simple rooms with climate control, behind vegetable plots and the sea. Open all year; no sign at the entrance. Doubles with F/B £50. ☏ 0536 2830251 (mobile).

Çiçek Pansiyon also has a nice terrace just behind the beach. 5 plain rooms, but not all with climate control and not all overlooking the sea. Doubles with F/B £54. ☏ 3392039 or ☏ 0544 4433758 (mobile).

Çökertme

The coastal landscape east of Mazıköy is exceedingly attractive. Çökertme is an inland farming village about 50km east of Bodrum, with a little port settlement — not much more than two rows of houses on a small beach more frequented by 'blue cruises' than sun-worshippers; sometimes there are so many yachts that there's nowhere to swim! Still, you may be able to spend the most memorable days of your holiday here — as long as your needs are simple. And when there's too much going on at the beach, just walk along to one of the quieter bays nearby.

Getting there: In high season there are 5 dolmuşes *a day to Milas (Tabakhane Garajı) and 2 a day to Bodrum; outside high season fewer departures. By car, it's most easily reached from Milas: shortly before Ören, turn right by an unmissable power station; from here it's another 12km or so. The route is beautiful, and you'll pass lovely pebble beaches (but, unfortunately, there's a lot of building going on behind them). Driving from Bodrum, keep making for Ören, from where it's signposted.*

Accommodation: There are just a couple of simple guest houses. In July and August, if you haven't booked ahead, you will be very lucky to get a room.

Çökertme Motel/Hotel, belonging to the eponymous beach restaurant (delightful terrace, oriental nook for smoking a hookah, and wooden jetty for sunbathing, but *very* pricey). 24 clean rooms, the older ones in the motel one street back from the beach. The newer rooms (not even finished at the time we did our research) are in a separate blue and white building (Bargasa Konuk Evi) just behind the restaurant and right on the beach: very comfortable, with minibars. Friendly, laid-back atmosphere. Open all year. Doubles in the motel with F/B £46, with breakfast £38; doubles in Konuk Evi (only with breakfast) £83. ☎ 5310156, fax 5310157, www.cokertmehotel.com.

Orhan Pension, bookable at the restaurant with the same name, on the front. The 9 rooms, however, are in a different building one street back from the beach. Family atmosphere. Doubles with F/B £50. ☎ 5310096.

Food and drink: The best restaurant, patronised by the international yachting clientele, is **Captain İbrahim** (☎ 5310012) — always fresh meze and fish (at Bodrum prices).

Ören

Ören, some 12km east of Çökertme, lies on an alluvial plain at the foot of Kocadağ. This 640m-high mountain is very popular with paragliders. So far there are no mega-hotels to spoil the long sand and pebble beach, behind which there are some discreet guest houses and holiday settlements. Unfortunately mayor Kazım Turan wants to make his town into one of the 'most important tourist centres in the world'. But his hopes are thwarted by a coal-fired power station 4km west of Ören. (The building of this power station in the 1990s was the reason why many international hotel chains which had already acquired building sites behind the beach left them undeveloped.)

The actual village centre of 4500 souls (swelling to 30,000 in summer) lies about 1.5km inland from the coast. Here you'll find the post office, a barber's, a couple of shops and, on Wednesdays, a colourful weekly market. Beach and town are linked by a walkway in sumer. Behind the beach there's a promenade lined with young palms, closed to traffic.

Ören was originally built on the site of ancient **Keramos**, first referred to in the 6th century BC and named for the son of Dionysus, God of Wine. Keramos is known as the founder of the potters' art (the word 'ceramic' is derived from Keramos). Only a few unspectacular remains of the ancient city are scattered in and around Ören.

Getting there: In high season there are 2 dolmuşes *a day to Bodrum, frequent runs to Milas (Tabakhane Garajı), 6 a day to Muğla and 4 a day to Akyaka (via Akbük). In summer the* dolmuşes *run as far as the beach.*

Accommodation

Since most of the visitors are Turks staying in their own holiday homes, the choice of accommodation is fairly limited. However, you can find simple aparthotels, motels and guest houses inland. As a rule, you can always find a room, even in high season.

Club Pomalin, just behind the beach and the promenade, is the best place in Ören, opened in 2008. It's not a mega-resort, just a manageable place with 25 tastefully decorated rooms. Friendly personnel. Doubles £58, with H/B £70. ✆ 5322065, ✆ 5322861, www.clubpomalin.com.

Haluk Otel, 100m back from the beach, near the new town hall *(Belediye)*. Old but newly restored hotel with 19 tidy rooms of varying sizes, all with balcony and sea view (but sometimes the views are limited). Lovely roof terrace for breakfast. Doubles with H/B £50. ✆ 5322896, www.halukotel.com.

Food and drink: Fish restaurants and inexpensive bars cheek-by-jowl on the promenade. You get good value for money in Ören.

Practicalities A-Z

Boat trips: You can find various offers at the beach; typically the price is £12.50 per person with lunch.

Akbük

Akbük ('White Beach'), some 22km east of Ören, is well named. Behind the narrow, snow-white pebble beach (which isn't always very clean) there's just a pension with restaurant, a simple campsite, a couple of trees and damp area (beware of mosquitoes!). But this is a great spot to 'drop out'. To escape for a day, you could drive to Akyaka along a little tarred road past lovely wooded coastal scenery, although swimming opportunities are rare along this 22km-long stretch.

Getting there: In high season up to 4 dolmuşes *a day from Ören and Akyaka. Drivers should first follow the Muğla road from Ören village (it starts on the south side of the river, just before the bridge, signposted 'Muğla/Alatepe'). After just under 18km, where the road forks (left goes to Muğla), go right for Akyaka. Turn right after 2.5km (signposted 'Atlaş Restaurant Pansiyon').*

Accommodation: Atlaş Restaurant & Pansiyon, just back from the beach and seaside track, popular with sailors. *Meze*, fish and the obligatory kebabs. They also rent 10 simple rooms with bath and tiled floors, some with their own nice terrace. Open all year. Doubles £33. ✆ 5291146.

Camping: Doğa Restaurant, at the end of the bay, has simple but very romantic camping possibilities. Showers, toilets on side. Open all year. Two people with a camper van £8.50. ✆ 5291010

Akyaka

This small holiday town, at the foot of the Kıran Mountains at the eastern end of the Gulf of Gökova, owes its pleasant character to one man: Nail Çakırhan (1910-2008), a prize-winning architect from nearby Ula (pop. 5200), who revived the traditional Aegean building methods with a lot of wood and oriels. Compared with nearby Marmaris, Akyaka is still a peaceful oasis, made even more pleasant by the constant light breeze. Since mostly Turks holiday here (international tourism has been slow in coming), the peak season is only during Turkish holiday times. Just after this, the restaurants on the narrow, palm-fringed sandy beach start to close, and prices are much cheaper. Akyaka is also popular with ornithologists: in the marshy area south of the river Kadın Azmağı one can see mallards, bee-eaters and little ringed plovers, to name a few. If you head west from Akyaka towards Ören, once past the last houses you come to **Çınar Platjı**, an idyllic little pebble beach with a bar set among oleanders. To get there on foot it's about 1km from the west end of Akyaka, passing the İskele Motel; by car along the new coast road it's about 2.5km.

Getting there: In the summer 2 dolmuşes *a day to and from Marmaris and 4 a day to Ören via Akbük; otherwise* dolmuş *connections every half hour to Muğla bus station, where you can transfer to a bus running along the coast.* Dolmuşes *leave from Belediye Parkı, a bit above the centre (but they make a circuit of the centre, stopping for instance at the large car park near the port).*

Accommodation: There's a good choice of mid-range apartments and hotels, but pensions are thin on the ground. In high season enormous prices may be charged, whereas before and after you should get a 50% discount.

Yücelen Hotel, a pleasant holiday village just off the beach. 2-storey buildings in traditional Aegean style, pool, beach restaurant, all very well kept. Doubles £90 (all in £130). On Kötekli Mevkii, ☎ 2435108, fax 2435435, www.yucelen.com.tr.

Otel Asuhan Çobantur, in a little bay. Pool, mini-beach, terrace restaurant. Lovely mosaic floors in the hallways, 25 rooms (standard hotel type with carpets, minibar and phone) — be sure to ask for sea view. Sauna. At the western end of town (signposted from the route to Çinar Plajı). Doubles with sea view £79, larger suites £83. ☎ 2434550, www.clubasuhancobantur.com.

Hotel Erdem, one street back from the beach. Small, well-kept two-storey building with pool; 21 rooms and 4 apartments for up to 4 people — all with terrace or balcony. Doubles £63. Zambak Sok. 8, ☎ 2435849, fax 2434326, www.erdemotel. com.tr.

Engin Hotel, in the southeast part of town near the open-air cinema (Açıkhava Sineması). Small hotel with quite narrow but very nice rooms with wooden ceilings and massive wooden furniture, most with balcony. From the top rooms there are views to the sea. Restaurant, pool. Doubles £38. From the port follow the river inland. Sefa Sok. 13, ☎ 2435727, www.enginotel.com.

Yener Park, near the Erdem, just

200m from the beach. One of many holiday places for rent. Four well-equipped apartments with climate control and balcony. The landlady only speaks Turkish. For up to 4 people from £38. Zambak Sok. 7, ☎ 2435853.

Camping: **Gökova Orman Camping**, owned by the Yücelen Hotel. Beautifully landscaped site in a shady pine wood with its own beach. Basic sanitation. Bungalows, too — not of the classic log cabin type, but real little houses with baths and terraces. Idyllically sited restaurant. Open all year. From Akyaka drive towards Ören/'Apple Beach'. Two people with camper van £8.50, with tent £6.75, bungalows for 2 from £42. ☎ 2434055, ☎ 2435435, www.yucelen.com.tr.

Food and drink: Simple restaurants both at the beach and in the village. Very good, reasonably priced restaurants at **Kadın Azmağı**, the stream at the south-eastern end of Akyaka. Both **Kordon Restoran** (☎ 2435251) and **Nadir Usta** (further upstream, best reached by boat arranged at the port; ☎ 2435629) offer a huge selection of *meze* and tasty fish.

Practicalities A-Z

Boat trips: At the port you'll find offers for day trips for about £10.50 with lunch. There are also 35-minute river trips; £12.50 is charged for the whole boat.

Car hire: Little on offer, since most visitors have their own cars.

Sedir Adası

This touristic island, in the south of the Gulf of Gökova, is also known as **Cleopatra's Island**. An endearing legend has it that Mark Antony had the bay filled with white sand from Egypt for his beloved Cleopatra… The remains of the ancient city of **Cedreae** are here, including the ruins of a theatre, a temple dedicated to Apollo, an agora, a necropolis, etc. According to Xenophon, the inhabitants of Cedreae were semi-barbarians and were all enslaved in 405 BC by Sparta.

Getting there/prices: Easiest with an organised tour from Marmaris, but cheapest by dolmuş *(6 times daily in high season). The fare per person for the crossing is £4.75; there is then an additional 'island entrance' fee of £5. The turn-off to the ferry mooring is signposted 'Sedir Adası' at the village of Çamlı on the road to Muğla. Note: It is illegal to take any sand from the beach.*

Camping: **Boncuk Camping**, about 7km past the ferry departure point, the last 2km on unmade road; signposted. 24km from Marmaris. Gorgeous setting — on a narrow, sandy beach dotted with palms. Average sanitary facilities; also very well-kept rooms for rent with private balconies. Mobile home or camper van £11. ☎ 4958116.

Food and drink: On the road to the ferry you pass the atmospheric **Çınar Restaurant** (lovely garden). Fresh fish at fair prices. Very popular. They also rent nice rooms. ☎ 4958080.

Karacasöğüt Bay

This bay, south of Sedir Island. It's a meeting place for yachtsmen. If you only want to swim, it's not worth the long trip; there are more beautiful bays closer to Marmaris.

Getting there: From Marmaris take the road towards Muğla and after approximately 14km turn left. From there it's still about 12km to the bay. No dolmuş *connections.*

See map on page 113.
Time: under 4h
Grade: moderate-strenuous, with a tough ascent in the middle section of the walk, and some very stony terrain underfoot. Be prepared for encroaching foliage!
Equipment: see pages 21-22.
Travel: 🚐 *dolmuş* from Marmaris to Çetibeli (either the Muğla or Fethiye service, frequent departures from the *otogar*, journey time 22min); return by 🚐 any coach or *dolmuş* returning to Marmaris.
Short walks
1 Çetibeli circuit (1h35min; easy). Follow the main walk to the point where the track swings right (about 15min past the water deposit). Instead of forking left here, stay on the main track as it swings right. Keep right at the fork of tracks three minutes later, and keep down right again at the next junction. The next small track off left is where you rejoin the main walk: pick up those notes at the 3h-point, to get back to the main road.
2 Çetibeli to Çamlı (2h30min; easy-moderate). Follow the main walk until you emerge on the track above Çamlı. Then turn left, instead of right, and follow the track downhill, to join the road to Çamlı. Turn left here and walk back to the Marmaris road, to await the coach or *dolmuş.*

Natural woodlands, farmed areas, glimpses of old ruins, and wayside flora and fauna all contribute to the kaleidoscope of ever-changing landscapes between Çetibeli and the Gulf of Gökova. Wherever you find water, particularly slow-moving or brackish water, keep an eye open for terrapins, which are commonly seen basking on stones or swimming about lazily. It's likely that you'll pass beehives too. Usually arranged in neat rows, the square boxes are seen in great numbers — possibly in the fields or orange groves, or even lining the tracks, especially in the pine woods.

Alight opposite the Caglayan Pinarbasi restaurant as you enter **Çetibeli**, and **start the walk** by crossing the road. Take the track which leads uphill by the left-hand side of the restaurant.
Almost from the start, the way climbs through a peaceful, pastoral setting. Keep up right when the track forks in one minute, and pause a minute later by a small **cemetery** on the right. Closer inspection of the neglected building with a verandah reveals it to be the old village mosque. The rich purple blossom of the Judas tree shines out from the hillsides in spring, while neighbouring shrubs like myrtle and storax quietly await their turn to bloom. You pass a **water storage deposit** on the left and continue uphill for another 15 minutes or so, until the track swings right. Fork *left* here, towards a gap opening into farmland. (*But keep right, staying on the track, for Short walk 1.)* Having forked left, take the footpath which leads up into the woods on your left, skirting the cultivated land.
The woodlands which flank the path to the left are brightened in early spring by a display of blue and white *Anemone blanda* and a lesser number of lovely yellow *Fritillaria bithynica*. Once beyond the *yayla* (meadow), the path heads more into the woodland and starts to descend a little, before a fork is reached some

seven-eight minutes along. Ignore the fork rising to the left, take the fork *descending* to the left — a **sunken path** through a tunnel of vegetation. A pine-covered valley falls away to the right, with the sea in view further to the right. *Take care* some 10 minutes from the fork: it looks as if the path continues ahead, but follow it round to the right, still skirting the valley on the right. When the charcoal burners are active in the nearby village of Çamlı, it is possible to catch the aroma even at this distance, as you start a steep descent (take care on the slippery pine needles). At a fork, continue ahead towards a ruined building, ignoring the path off to the right. Pass the building a minute later and emerge on a track above the plain. Turn right in the direction of the sea *(but turn left for Short walk 2).*

Continue along the track contouring around the base of the hillside above **Çamlı** (**1h40min**). The track starts to rise; when it swings to the right, be sure to take the footpath leading up into the pine woods. The path joins a wide track under five minutes later. Turn right to continue uphill on a **bulldozed firebreak**. The firebreak rises up the centre of the ridge, descends a little, then continues to climb the hill ahead. Views open up: across the water, to the left, are the cliffs on the far side of the Gulf of Gökova. The firebreak narrows as it sweeps right, eastwards, and then rises to the **highest point of the walk** (**2h45min**).

Continue along the track; some ten minutes later, looking ahead to the shrub-covered hillside, it is possible to make out some ruins — including part of a wall and a doorway. Several forts, both ancient and medieval, as well as some amphora factories, are recorded for this area; this may be one of the forts. (The amphora was a double-handled vessel used by the Greeks and Romans as liquid containers.)

Just over 10 minutes down from the high point, turn right at a junction. A minute later, take the minor woodland track off left. You meet a crossing track in two minutes. Turn left here, below the **hill with the ruins** (**3h**). *(Short walk 1 rejoins here.)* The track descends towards a *yayla,* but take a path forking left *before* reaching this meadow. This skirts the edge of the woodland to the left of the *yayla.* As you descend into the pines, a path joins from the right. You pass a water trough on the left and reach a confluence of paths with a small stream bed over to the left. Keep ahead here, ignoring a path joining from the right and two paths on the left which merge to cross the stream (the route of Walk 12). You cross the same stream bed immediately afterwards. Follow the path to the right, along a small gully —the stream now on your right.

The path turns sharp left with the Marmaris road in view ahead. You have a very steep final descent down a firebreak, to a track junction. Take the track out to the **Marmaris road** (under **4h**), close to the **mosque**. A right turn here leads to some restaurants. Coaches and *dolmuşes* pass at some speed, so give an early and clear signal if you wish to stop one!

Time: 4h20min
Grade: moderate-strenuous; fairly good paths underfoot, but a steep descent of almost 300m down a stony trail, with a corresponding ascent to return. *Routefinding skills required from the 15min-point to the 45min-point, where the paths are confusing.*
Equipment: see pages 21-22.
Travel: dolmuş to Çetibeli (Muğla service, frequent departures, journey time 23min; return on any *dolmuş* or coach bound for Marmaris.

The little-visited shores of the Gulf of Gökova provide a spectacular setting for this walk, which penetrates a fairly remote region. Images of an azure blue sea lapping a green shoreline will provide you with a taster of solitude. Unfortunately, the farmsteads here have been abandoned, and it is no longer possible to continue along this superb coast on foot — the paths are hopelessly overgrown.

Ask to leave the *dolmuş* at the mosque *(cami)*, which is located just beyond some restaurants on the left as you enter **Çetibeli**. **Start the walk** as you leave the *dolmuş* by crossing the road and taking the track at the right of the mosque; it heads directly for the hills. After six-seven minutes, at a junction of tracks, keep ahead on the path up the steep, wide **firebreak**. A minute later, stay on the path as it forks off left. You

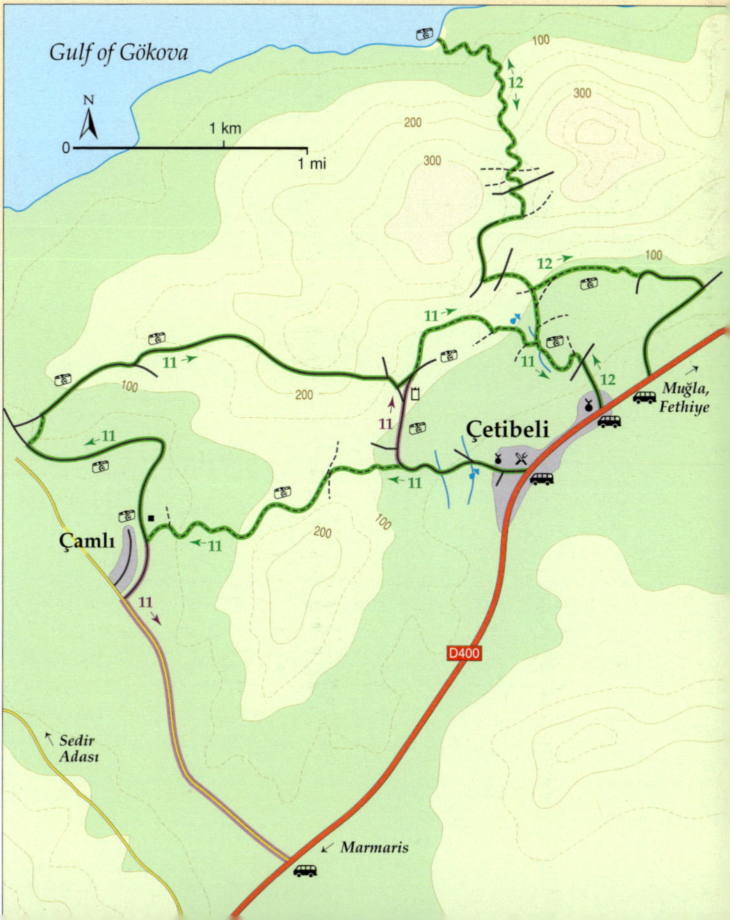

enjoy good views back over the fertile valley, to the pine-covered hills beyond, before turning sharply right into a narrow tree-lined **gully (15min)**. Six-seven minutes along, cross the **stream bed** on the left and immediately take the path off right, to cross back over the stream bed a little higher up. Continue along the edge of the woods, keeping left at a fork a couple of minutes later. At the next fork, shortly afterwards, there is a stand of tall American aloes on the far side of the right-hand fork (easily recognised by their huge rosettes of thick, succulent, spear-shaped leaves). Keep left uphill again here, into the woods.

Brush aside encroaching *Pistachio lentiscus* shrubs and rise up to meet a strong crossing path in just a few minutes. *(NB: your return route will head downhill to the right at this point.)* Head straight across towards a *yayla* (meadow), to meet another path. Turn left to skirt the edge of the *yayla*, which is soon left behind as the path leads away from it and continues climbing. When you meet a track (five-six minutes from the *yayla*; **45min**), stay on the path which continues across the track in a steady ascent. (Watch out here for the purple limodore, *Limodorum abortivum*, the curious saprophytic orchid which finds a home in this woodland habitat.)

Turn right as you emerge onto a

Wherever the land is suitable, regardless of its isolation or difficulty of access, olives feature strongly as a crop. This walk is a classic example: having descended on a difficult, stony path for a considerable time, through heavily forested land, you arrive at the edge of the Gulf of Gökova to find … an olive grove.

woodland track five minutes later. *(Since you will be returning this way, take note at this point of the start of your (waymarked) path for the return — just before the track descends into a dip.)* Continue up through the woods to a large grassy *yayla*. Follow the track as it leads into this meadow, but keep right (now on a path) across the bottom end of the *yayla*. This path takes you back into woodland. The slender flower spikes of the man orchid, *Aceras anthropophorum,* are never easy to spot, but when it grows in the middle of the path, as here, then it is hard to miss! You descend to another meadow two minutes later and head slightly right, across the narrow part, to continue on a stony path.

This path leads to another *yayla* but, before it is reached — *or even seen* — you reach a fork and take the left-hand path. You emerge from the woods alongside a strong track and rise up onto it (by a waymarked white rock). This marks the **highest point of the walk (1h10min)**, and from here the way descends fairly steeply to the seashore. Turn right along the track for half a minute, then look for your waymarked path off left. Keep right at the first fork you come to (three minutes down); then keep ahead over a crossing path. You can already see the Gulf of Gökova through the trees, as the path crosses the head of the valley and leads down its right-hand side. The waymarked path descends the right-hand side of the valley and only edges more to the left as it nears the shore. *Care is required* in places, where the path drops more steeply and takes on the appearance of an old trail at times, vague in places. Although footwork demands concentration in this steady descent, keep an eye out for bee orchids such as *Ophrys holoserica.*

An **olive grove** announces your arrival at the bottom of the valley. The seashore is visible on the far side of the olive grove and is soon reached by bearing right across the grove, past a ruined farmstead. A small shingle beach at the **Gulf of Gükova**, shade from olive trees, a vista of dark green wooded slopes sliding into turquoise blue, the smell of pine, and the sound of the sea combine to provide an irresistibly relaxing setting ... but if you swim, beware of sea urchins.

Return the same way until you come to the right turn at the bottom of the *yayla*. Here you meet the strong crossing path encountered earlier. Instead of turning right, however, continue along the path skirting the meadow; almost immediately you join the crossing path, slightly lower down. Follow it to the left downhill; a path joining sharply from the right in three minutes leads back to the fork with the American aloes — an alternative route back).

Skirt the edge of pine woods, with cultivated fields and scattered houses on the right, as the path zigzags down. Meet a track and turn left. Then, at a T of tracks, turn right and continue through a small farming community. You reach the main road just outside **Çetibeli (4h20min)**. Flag down any passing coach or *dolmuş*. (Or turn right, to some roadside restaurants.)

Time: just over 3h
Grade: easy, with good terrain underfoot; ascent of only 125m
Equipment: see pages 21-22.
Travel: 🚌 *dolmuş* from Marmaris to Akçapınar (Muğla service, frequent departures from the *otogar*, journey time about 30min); alight at the end of the road into Akçapınar (over the hill after passing through Gökçe). Return by 🚌 any *dolmuş* or coach bound for Marmaris.

Short walks

1 Akçapınar to Gökçe (2h35min; easy). Follow the main walk to the 30min-point, but take the track off to the right and start climbing. In about 25-30 minutes, just after a track has joined from the right (and where you can see a track junction ahead), take the path on the right — a short cut to a higher track. Turn right on this higher track to continue up through pine woods. When you meet cross-tracks, keep straight ahead, picking up the main walk again from the 1h50min-point.

2 Circular walk from Akçapınar (under 3h; easy). This is particularly suitable for those with their own transport. Follow the main walk to the cross-tracks on the saddle (the 1h50min-point). Turn right to continue downhill (the reverse of Short walk 1). As you approach a track junction five-six minutes later, take the path down to the left — a short cut to the lower track. Turn left and continue downhill, to meet the road used on the outward leg, where you turn left to head back to Akçapınar. (Under 10 minutes along the road, you could cross the bridge on the right and continue back along a track on the far side of the river.)

A great area of plain stretches eastward from the head of the Gulf of Gökova. Mountains rise all around it, but it is the foothills to the south which are the setting for this walk. The views over the green and cultivated plains make a pleasing contrast to the scenery on walks closer to Marmaris, and the bird life is different too. Particularly noticeable is the abundance of storks: they find plenty of food on the swampy fields here. This migratory bird becomes evident in spring, particularly in April/May, when on the nest. Storks are regarded by the local people as harbingers of good fortune, so their presence is encouraged, and their huge nests are never disturbed, even when built on top of chimney stacks. No matter where the nests are built, their size always makes them look incongruous, but especially so when on top of a telegraph pole… Starting at Akçapınar and running in a direct line across the plain, crossing the main Muğla/Fethiye road and continuing beyond it, is a magnificent 3km-long avenue of eucalyptus trees. If you want to have a closer look, make a short diversion from Akçapınar.

Leave the *dolmuş* at the end of the road into Akçapınar. **Start the walk** by heading into **Akçapınar**. Walk through the village and, where the road bends left across a bridge to the **avenue of eucalyptus trees**, turn *right*. Almost immediately there is a rural feel to the walk, with red-roofed houses dotting the hillside, citrus groves and views of the green plain. As the road leads in a gentle ascent above the plain, it provides the opportunity for watching for birds — the storks being easily spotted. Some 12 minutes or so along, the **bridge** over the river is an *alternative return for Short walk 2.*

Ignore a firebreak and then a track rising to the right (**30min**). *(But take the track if you are doing Short walk 1).*

Continue into the village of **Sirinköy** and keep right at the next two junctions. Then, 120m past the second junction, take the narrow track to the right. Just near a **cluster of eucalyptus trees**, on a bend, take the path up into the pines. This rises steeply and emerges on a firebreak. Continue uphill all the way to a crest, then descend to a track. Turn right on this high-level woodland track, enjoying panoramic views over the plain.

On reaching a **crossing of tracks on a saddle** (**1h50min**), turn left into woodland. *(But head right downhill for Short walk 2.)* Grey-green leaves that rustle in the wind and sparkle silver in the sun announce yet more olive trees — this time buried deep in the pine woods. At the junction of tracks reached some 10 minutes from the saddle, turn right. From here you catch glimpses of the red-roofed houses of Gökçe through the light pine woods. Nearer at hand are masses of the small, white *Gagea graeca* which grows so freely in the dry stony areas and is seen at its best in April. Down left, through the woodland, you can see a river in the valley bottom and, gradually, the views open to reveal more of Gökçe and the main road.

Eventually you reach an open area. Stay on the track as it swings right and then runs parallel with the main road below. Starting to descend, you enjoy good views over well-ordered citrus groves and towards the Gulf of Gökova. Once on the main road, turn left into **Gökçe** (just over **3h**). Any *dolmuş* or coach heading back to Marmaris can be stopped here — or walk into the centre, where there is a shop and restaurants.

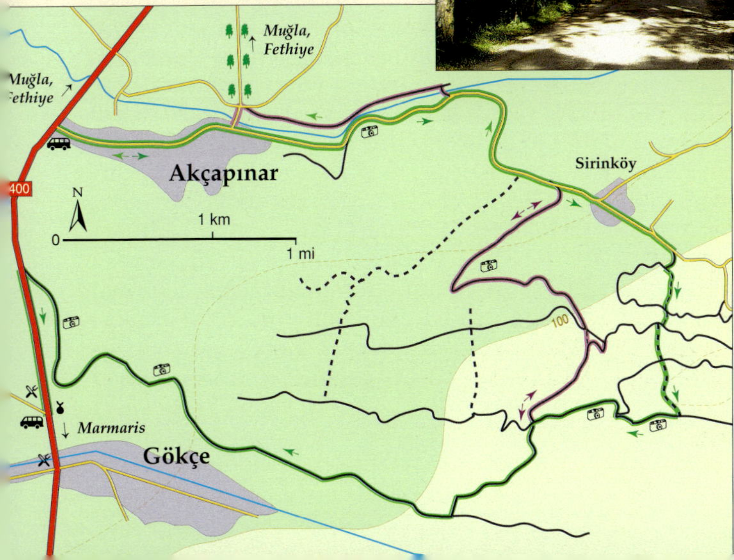

4 MARMARIS

Orientation • History • Accommodation/camping • Food and drink • Nightlife • Beaches and diving • Sights • Practicalities A-Z

Area code: ✆ 0252
Information: The Tourist Office is on the promenade near the castle. Professional staff. Open summer daily 09.00-17.00, in winter Mon.-Fri. 08.00-17.00. İskele Meydanı, ✆/✆ 4121035.
Connections: The **bus station** is somewhat outside the centre, on Mustafa Münir Elgin Bul. Branches of the different bus companies are located in the Tansaş supermarket building on Mustafa Muğlalı Cad, from where all of them operate a shuttle service to the bus station. Buses several times a day to Denizli/Pamukkale (4h; £10), Datça (1h30; £4.20), Ephesus (with transfer at Aydın, 3h; £8.50), Fethiye (3h; £8.50) and Antalya (6h30; £17).
Havaş buses run 5-7 times a day to **Dalaman Airport**; exact times from travel agents or www.havas.com.tr. £11 per person.
Dolmuş: Constant departures to İçmeler and Uzunyalı Beach from the front of Tansaş supermarket on Ulusal Egemenlik Cad. (get on *dolmuşes* heading seaward); they also stop along Atatürk Cad. *Dolmuşes* to Cennet Adası and the bus station stop opposite Tansaş. *Dolmuşes* to Turunç, the villages on the Bozburun Peninsula and Sedir Adası leave from the *dolmuş* station somewhat further north on Ulusal Egemenlik Cad.
Water *dolmuşes* to the beaches around Marmaris leave from several places on the shore promenade; they go every 30 minutes to İçmeler and every hour to Turunç (£3.30 one way).
Taxis: Taxis are everywhere. The fare to Dalaman Airport is about £50, to Datça about £42, to İçmeler £12.50 and to Turunç £23.

In Marmaris you can *really* 'take a holiday' and dispense with all formalities — jacket, tie, shirt and trousers. In Marmaris you can eat out in bathing shorts (which at least has the advantage that you cannot be dragged by your T-shirt into a shop). This informality appeals a great deal to some people; others prefer a more refined atmosphere.

Many other customs, none of them Turkish, prevail in this small town of 30,000 inhabitants. With its sunshine guarantee (300 days of sun annually) comes the 'anything goes' of mass tourism. On the well-kept esplanade which runs round the old quarter by the castle, painters, jugglers and musicians are lined up cheek by jowl. Luxury yachts and tour boats lie moored on the sea side; opposite, waiters tout for business, inviting you to a candlelit dinner on their pretty restaurant terraces. Tourists stroll between the yachts and the restaurants, parading their sunburned bellies, which have shaded their still-white feet for most of the day. Marmaris the town is more chic than its tattooed, thirsty visitors. Every evening the masses flood into the centre from the hotel suburbs (especially when no Premier League games are on TV at the suburban bars). They roam through the modern bazaar, which is anything but oriental: everything on sale carries the trademark of well-known designers.

All the above aside, Marmaris is both an excellent walking base and a brilliant yachting centre — there are well over 1500 berths in the bay. The largest marina, and the most chic, is the Netsel, east of the castle. This is where Turkey's smart set meet. They virtually never go into the centre: The Turkish jet set wants nothing to do with the international proles.

Orientation

The old centre with its bazaar, restaurants and bars, lies around the castle. K. Seyfettin Elgin Bulvarıs runs west from here, towards İçmeler, before becoming Kenan Evren Bulvarı. To the right and left of K. Seyfettin Elgin Bulvarı is the hotel area called Siteler, from where you can catch a *dolmuş* to the centre day and night. If you get off by the Atatürk statue at the beginning of Kordon Caddesi, you can stroll around the castle to the marina.

History

Marmaris, founded as Physcus around 1000 BC by Dorian immigrants, was once a commercial port and Asia Minor's gateway to Rhodes and Egypt. In the 6th century BC the settlement came under Lydian rule. And by the 5th century BC Herodotus had already named it Marmarissos; it is assumed that this name was derived from the marble found in the area. From the 4th to the 2nd century BC Rhodes dominated the port. Marmaris was then constantly exposed to the changing balance of power, until finally in 1408 the Ottomans occupied the whole area. Since then Marmaris has been Turkish. The Bay of Marmaris has always played an important strategic role: where once Süleyman the Magnificent started his expedition to Rhodes and Lord Nelson prepared his fleet for the attack on the French at Abukir, there is now a NATO base (Aksaz Bay east of Marmaris is a restricted military area).

The largest changes in Marmaris's history were brought about however neither by the Romans nor by NATO military strategists, but by tourists. At the beginning of the 1980s only a few globetrotters stayed in the bay overnight; today some 100,000 holidaymakers sink into their beds every night during the summer. The once-sleepy fishing town has become one of the largest international fairgrounds in Turkey. All the gaps between the buildings on the coast have disappeared, as have those in the second, third and even ninth or tenth streets in from the shore — there is not a single strip of green left. New buildings and shells of buildings continue to spread ever further into the hinterland and testify to an optimistic view of the future, and it helps that the

woods around Marmaris are now a national park.

Accommodation/camping

(see plan above)

The bulk of accommodation developed over the past decades was created for cheap mass tourism. There are almost no more friendly guest houses or small hotels with any style left. Individual travellers take a big detour around Marmaris. Most hotels are located west of the old

town behind Atatürk Cad. and further west, around K. Seyfettin Elgin Cad. in the hotel quarter of Siteler, where the highest density of accommodation can be found. In the shoulder seasons prices fall between 30-50%. Recommended alternative places to stay are Akyaka, Turunç and the Bozburun Peninsula. There are some 800 different places to stay on offer.

Hotels/pension: Maritim Hotel Grand Azur (27), on the road to

Marmaris — the yachting fraternity's Mecca

İçmeler, on the left. Extravagant five-star hotel. From the outside it looks almost futuristic. Beautiful entrance with marble pillars and minimalist décor. 288 comfortable rooms and suites, each with balcony. Large pool, indoor pool, private beach, tennis. Doubles £200. Kenan Evren Bul. 17, ✆ 4174050, ℻ 4174060, www.grandazur.com.tr.

Royal Maris Hotel (5), on the seafront road near the centre. 71 rooms: those at the front facing palms and the sea, but noisy. Those at the back are peaceful, but the outlook is the sad hotel next door. Modern fittings. Roof terrace with pool and bar. Doubles £63, singles £50. Atatürk Cad. 34, ✆ 4128383, ℻ 4124112, www. royalmarishotel.com.

Pupa Yacht Hotel (15), about 6km outside the centre in a lovely quiet location. Well run, and right on the sea. 19 little rooms with turquoise furniture, all with super views. Somewhat dated, but OK. Garden with hammocks, idyllic bar, small private beach. Easy to find if you're driving, so recommended in preference to hotels of the same price range in town. To get there, leave town on Ulusal Egemenlik Cad., heading for 'Otogar/Günlüce'; keep following the coast road, it will be on your right. Doubles £58. Adaağazı Mevkii Yalancı Boğaz, ✆ 4133566, ℻ 4138487, www.pupa. com.tr.

Candan Otel (10), 38 classical-modern, pleasant rooms (better quality than one would expect in this price range). Well-kept and comfortable. Friendly entrance area, although one can't always say the same for the receptionists. Good view at the front; in the back it's quiet, but dismal. Good value for money. Atatürk Cad. 44. Doubles £42, singles £29. ✆ 4129302, ℻ 4125359, www. candanhotels.com.

Manolya Otel & Apart (26), the first (and only!) hotel in this neighbourhood when it was opened in 1983 — now it's in the middle of the Siteler hotel district, but in as quiet location (2km to the centre, 150m to the beach). German/Turkish management. The friendly owner, İlyas Bublis, is very eco-conscious — all 18 rooms are decorated with organic paint. 12 apartments. Good, healthy cooking if you wish. Pool area. Open mid-Jun. to Oct. Access: follow Atatürk Cad. and its continuation towards İcmeler, and when level with the Maritim Hotel Grand Azur turn right on 138 Sok. Doubles £42. Manolya Sok. 9, ✆ 4174022, ℻ 4174014, www.manolya-hotel.com.

Gülşah Pansiyon (10), one of the few family-run guest houses remaining in a central location. Somewhat set back from Atatürk Cad., so not nearly as noisy as the others. 20 well-worn but tidy rooms for 2-4 people; laminate floor covering and balconies, relaxed owners. Free tea and coffee. Doubles £33. Atatürk Cad. 52, ✆ 4126642, ℻ 4126641, www.gulsahpansiyon.com.

Öktem Motel (4), 156 Sok. 1. Under 10 minutes from the beach and centre. Clean house with 14 small, rustically decorated rooms with tiled floors and climate control. Somewhat old-fashioned bathrooms, but OK. Pool. Doubles £29. ✆ 4125383.

Apartments: There are a lot of aparthotels (with apartments starting at £25), especially a few streets back from the coast, but they have little capacity for individual travellers as they are usually booked out by tour operators. In general, however, one rule holds true: you can't tell the book by its cover — what they promise on the outside is not usually delivered inside. But one good place is **Manolya Otel & Apart** (see above).

Camping: Fa Beach Club (7), 7km east of town (5km from the bus station). The former Pekuz Camping, today it's mostly a terrace restaurant with garden behind a private beach. There's parking for camper vans, but nowhere for tents. Moderate sanitary facilities. Also 7 bungalows with climate control, TV, small verandah with sea view. 2 people with camper van £15, doubles £50 without breakfast. Leave town on Ulusal Egemenlik Cad., then head for 'Otogar/ Günlüce' and continue till it's signposted. ✆ 4128216, ℻ 4125563, www.fabeachclub.com.

There are, however, far lovelier places on the way to Datça (see page 151) and near Sedir Island (see page 109).

Food and drink

(see plan on pages 120-121)

The selection is enormous: everything is available, Turkish, English, French, Italian, and Asian food, even international fast-food — something for every budget. The most expensive restaurants are those on the esplanade around the castle, where a Coke costs three times as much as anywhere else. But beer is almost always cheap.

On and behind the promenade: There are many restaurants on the promenade between the Tourist Office and marina. Almost all serve fish (not always fresh outside high season) and international food. One long-established place is **Fellini (24)**. Pizza, steaks, Turkish dishes and fish. You'll recognise it from its

Marmaris Bay

yellow chairs. Mains £8.50-21. ☎ 4130826.

The simplest place on the promenade is **Fiskos Bar (22)**, under friendly family ownership for 25 years. Turkish cooking, like tasty *güveç;* fish and grills. Mains from £3.50. ☎ 4131258.

At the eastern end of Bar Street (head towards the Netsel Marina on the promenade, then turn left before the bridge) is the restaurant **Azmak Başı (11)**. Small, a couple of tables in front, lots of Turkish customers. Reasonably priced fish dishes (*levrek* with salad £5.50). ☎ 4131206.

Mazgal (21) is simple, rather quaint. Portion of fish with salad from £4.20. Ali Hafız Çıkmazı 165 (50m back off the promenade, on the way to the marina, on the left, just behind a carpet shop). ☎ 0530 3464059 (mobile).

Drunken Crab (14), unpretentious, lovingly decorated family-run place with just 5 tables (reserve!). Small choice of *meze*, fish and seafood, as well as paella and the house speciality, 'Drunken Crab Soup'. Mains £5.50-12.50. Closed Mon. Bar Street 53a, ☎ 4123970.

At the Netsel Marina: The more refined restaurants here cater for the yachting crowd. One of the best is **Pineapple (19)**, looking out to the yachts. Lovely roof terrace. Excellent *meze* £1.50-7 and international cuisine £6.50-13. In summer they serve some of the best *döner* in the southern Aegean. ☎ 4130431.

In the business centre: There are many simple places, but watch out: the *lokantas* in and around the bazaar look really reasonable from the outside, but many are rip-offs: if there are no prices posted, you are advised to ask the price of every single thing you buy — even a Coke — before you order!

Alin's Restaurant (13) in the bazaar, is beautifully kept and has a huge choice. Also sandwiches, pizzas, crêpes. Daily menu changes; very economical — except for beer (deliberately priced high to keep out the down-market Brits). Many locals; very full at lunch time. Çarşı Postanesi Sok. (turn into the road by the post office and keep straight on, then it's on the right). ☎ 4132525.

Özyiğit Lokantası (9), by the post office. Tasty casseroles and good kebabs. Friendly, inexpensive, open 24 hours. 44 Sok. 40.

You can eat well and cheaply too in the *lokantas* opposite the Tansaş Supermarket on Ulusal Egemenlik Cad. For instance, **Ali Baba (2)** is very nicely furnished and decorated for a *lokanta* and has *döner*, great *İskender kebap* and casseroles. Friendly service. Inexpensive. The only down-side is that it's on the noisy street.

Outside town: **Uçurtma (17)**, 7km east of the centre, is a pleasant place with a terrace and private beach, hammocks, laid-back atmosphere. *Meze*, fish and pizza at good prices. ☎ 4123986. Somewhat more up-market is **Orange (18)**, two doors further on. Good *meze* (£2-3.50) and international dishes (mains £7-12). ☎ 4121583. Access for both places: leave town on Ulusal Egemenlik Cad., then head for 'Otogar/Günlüce' and follow signs for Fa Beach Club; they are about 200m past the club, on the right. *Dolmuş* connections every 30min. from opposite the Tansaş Supermarket (*dolmuş* towards 'Yalancıboğaz').

Sweets: Karen Patisserie (10), on Atatürk Cad. near the Candan Hotel is a modern cake shop with delicious cakes, pastries and other sweets. They also serve breakfasts.

Nightlife

(see plan on pages 120-121)

There are two centres. One is **Uzunyalı Beach** (parallel with Seyfettin Elgin Cad.) — full of identical bars (with the same music and sometimes even the same seating plans). This is where many Brits settle in for the night. The most popular place there is the **Talk of the Town (25)** where the transvestites party. Nearby are places with names like **Red Devil of Manchester Bar**, **Everton Bar**...

The second night spot is **Bar Street**, which runs parallel with the shore promenade towards the Netsel Marina (signposted) and has countless bars and discos. Most charge no entrance fee, unless there is a big 'event'. Three popular places are the quite tastefully decorated **Green House (16)**, with aquariums (and occasional laser shows), **Back Street (6)**, an outdoor bar (only open in summer) where you can dance under palm trees, and the nearby **Club Areena (6)**, supposedly the third largest club in Turkey and also used for big events like 'Miss Russian Queen'. The **Beach Club (8)** is here too, where you can have fun dressing up as Tina Turner or Freddie Mercury and where a lot of concerts are held.

Those who prefer Turkish music to electrobeats, will find some **Türkü Bars** in Bar Street — oriental taverns where traditional Turkish folk music is played. Those in search of quieter surroundings head to the **Ali Baba (20)** hookah café, with its oriental atmosphere and backgammon players.

Beaches and diving

Marmaris Beach, jammed between the sea and the hotel blocks, is so full of beach chairs in summer that there isn't even room to build a sandcastle. So it's a much better idea to take a *dolmuş* or a boat trip to one of the beaches in the area.

Çiftlik is one of the most beautiful beaches around Marmaris. It's best reached by boat, and you pass Kumlubükü Bay (see page 139) on the way. Driving there it's a long way (see 'Bozburun Peninsula' on page 136).

İçmeler Bay (see page 136) is a beautiful beach, but it's plastered with sunbeds.

Sedir Adası (see page 109) in the Gulf of Gökova is most easily reached by organised tour, but there are also *dolmuş* connections.

Diving: Various companies offer dives to wrecks, caves and reefs. You pick these boats up at the port, and prices are much the same whoever you choose — about £42 for two dives with lunch. One of the best places offering dives with English-speaking instructors is **Paradise Diving Centre** (☎ mobile 0542 4133916, www.paradisediving.net). Always ask in advance how many participants there are — with some companies, you'll see about 50 people diving at the same time!

Aquapark: Atlantis Waterpark at Uzunyalı Beach near Point Centre (shopping centre). Large slides. Entry fee £12.50, children £7.50.

Sights

Marmaris has very little to offer in terms of cultural or historical sites. On a hill in the north of the city are a few meagre remains of walls from ancient **Physcus** (see Short walk 14). A visit to **Marmaris Kalesi** is worthwhile — a medieval castle which was extended by Süleyman the Magnificent in 1522. There is a beautiful view over the old town and the port. The castle houses a museum with oil lamps, pots, vases, bowls, amphorae and the like (open daily ex. Mon, 08.00-12.00 and 13.00-17.00, entry fee £1.20). At the foot of the castle, by the Tourist Office, Süleyman built a **caravanserai** in 1545; today the arches shelter a few cafés. A bit further on is an old **market hall** *(Bedesten)*, now housing souvenir shops and a café.

Practicalities A-Z

Boat trips: At first sight, the hundreds of offers at the port look identical, but be sure to ask in advance whether you will have 30 minutes on the beach or three hours, and whether you have to sit on wooden planks or there are comfortable seats. Some boats have live music — you'll love it or hate it. Normally the boats leave at about 10.00 and return between 17.00-19.00. Moonlight cruises begin at 22.30 and end at about 0.30. Reckon on paying from £11 per person for a boat trip with lunch.

Car hire: There are countless agencies; with the national firms you pay about £37 per day; with the internationals about £56 (including insurance). **Avis** is at Atatürk Cad. 8/E, ☎ 4122771, www.avis.com.tr; **Europcar** at Yunus Nadi Cad. 125, ☎ 4174588, www.europcar.com.tr.

Doctors and dentists, English speaking: The private **Ahu Hetman** clinic (167 Sok., ☎ 4177777) has English-speaking staff. Otherwise, ask at the Tourist Office.

Events: There is a week-long international **Yacht Festival** at the beginning of May, with exhibitions and lectures; a spring festival, **Marmaris Bahar Festivalı**, takes place at the same time, with a lot of music and sports. At the end of June there's the **Channel Regatta** from Marmaris to Rhodes. August sees a lot of **concerts** and **theatrical events**. At the end of Oct./early Nov. there's the international regatta, **Marmaris Race Week**.

Ferries: Marmaris has **ferry connections to Rhodes**. A **catamaran** sails from the mid Apr. to end Oct. twice a day (at 09.00 and 16.30; journey time 1); no sailings in winter. There is also a **car ferry**: sails Tue./Fri./

Sun. from May to Oct. Both catamaran and car ferry leave from the terminal east of the Netsel Marina and cost £38 per person one way or same day return. The price for the car itself is £100. For information contact **Yeşil Marmaris**, Barbaros Cad. 13 (shore promenade), ✆ 4122290, www.yesilmarmaris.com.

There is also a **ferry to Bodrum** (see page 72). Information at Agora Turizm, 102 Sok. (on the river), ✆ 4123488, www.bodrum expresslines.com.

Launderettes: There are several, like **Çağdaş Laundry** on 33 Sok., near the marina; £7.50 per load.

Newspapers: English papers etc. are on sale along Atatürk Cad. and Seyfettin Elgin Cad.

Organised tours: There is a huge choice of both coach and boat tours. The going rate for a trip to Dalyan/Caunos is about £17, to Ephesus or Pamukkale £29, a two-day trip to Ephesus and Pamukkale £58, and a 'Turkey' trip or 'Village' trip (meaning to a rural village, which just happens to be a carpet-selling centre) £12.50.

Post: The post office is set back off Kordon Cad. in the bazaar.

Police: There are several stations, for instance one set back off Atatürk Cad. ✆ 155.

Shopping and souvenirs: The lanes in the old town, roofed over with glass and steel, make a huge, if somewhat sterile **bazaar**, brightened by Turkish fast-food kiosks and some cafés.

A rather naff shopping centre with name brand clothing stores and a supermarket is **Point Centre (23)** behind Uzunyalı Beach. Of course the really chic fashion shops are at the **Netsel Marina**.

One of the best souvenirs from the area is the famous **pine tree honey** *(çam balı);* a good place to get it is at **Bayırtat Bal Honey Market (1)** at Ulusal Egemenlik Cad. 7.

Excellent organic olive oil can be bought at **Sabuncu Dede (00)**, 33 Sok. 25A (about 50 varieties).

There is also a weekly, covered **Thursday market** east of Hasan Işık Cad.

Travel agent: **Avalon Turizm**, 99 Sok. 21 (somewhat set back off Atatürk Cad.) cover most airlines. ✆ 4122629, avalonturizm @hotmail.com.

Turkish bath (Hamam): There is a nameless historical bath in the old town behind the mosque near the old caravanserai. Entry with massage £17.

Two-wheel hire: **Best Motorcycle Rental** on 158 Sok., ✆ 4129436, www.bestmotortr.com. has mountain bikes at £8.50 per day, scooters (100 cc) at £22, and motorcycles from a Honda XLR 125 at £35 to a Harley Davidson Sportster 1200 at £120. Usually prices are cheaper if you hire for a longer duration.

Yacht charter: In yachting circles it is almost a matter of course to hire a yacht with captain and crew for a week — the best way to see the Turkish coast. You can hire at one of the travel agencies or directly from the owners at the marinas. One well-known charter company is **Eser Yachting** at 35 Sokak 21. Reckon on £250 per person per week if you take one of the last-minute offers: this includes full board, but not drink. ✆ 4123527, www.eser-yachting.com.

Sailboats without skippers can be hired from **Sun Charter**, with an office in the Netsel Marina.

Walking: Walks 11-20 are all well within reach. For just a long strol, visit **Cennet Adası**, the 'Paradise Island' in the south of Marmaris Bay. Take a *dolmuş* labelled 'Yalancıboğaz' from opposite Tansaş supermarket and get off at the last stop, then walk.

Water sports: There's water-skiing, canoeing, banana-boating, etc. at all the larger beaches.

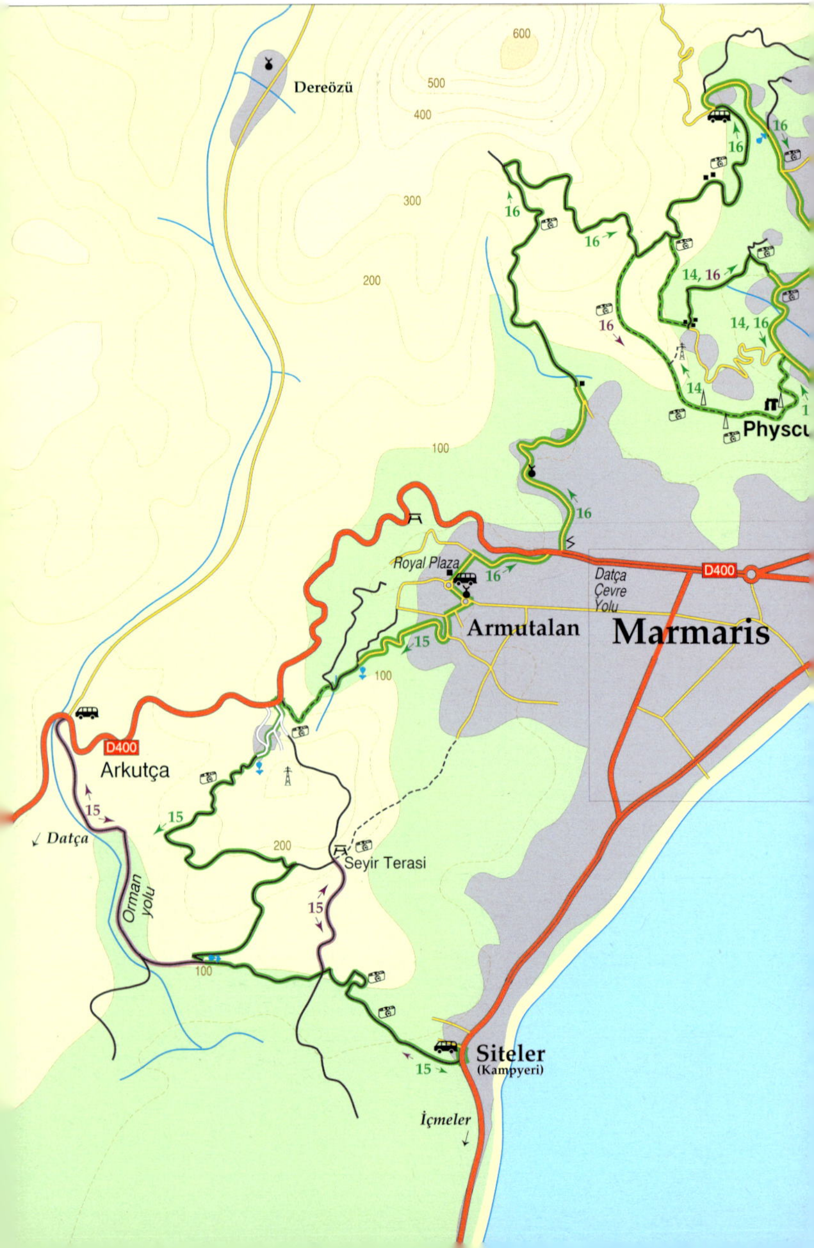

See also the town plan on pages 120-121.
Time: 2h40min
Grade: easy-moderate; reasonably good terrain underfoot; ascent of 200m
Equipment: see pages 21-22.
Travel: 🚐 Catch the Beldibi *dolmuş* from Marmaris *dolmuş* station and note the start of the Beldibi road at traffic lights between the BP and Opet petrol stations (it is under 10 minutes on foot from this point to the start of the walk). Alight very shortly, about 300m past car workshops lining the road, near a cluster of short pylons on the right (just before the stadium). Catch a return *dolmuş* or taxi at the same place.
Short walk: Physcus (1h; easy). Use this walk just to see something of Physcus and enjoy the fine views over Marmaris. Follow the main walk to the saddle (30min); return the same way.

Marmaris now occupies the site of ancient Physcus, a dependency of Rhodes, but little remains of that era — only some walls dating back to the Hellenistic period. These are set on a hillside overlooking Marmaris. They are overgrown with shrubs, and it's difficult to get close to them, but the compensation for the effort required is the splendid view over Marmaris. From here the route of the walk takes an interesting course, as it follows the line of a ridge of mountains separating Beldibi and Armutalan. The path switches from side to side along the ridge, with constantly changing views, before dropping down to Beldibi.

Start out where you leave the *dolmuş:* facing in the direction of Beldibi, turn left off the **Beldibi road** onto a narrow street (İsmail Mustafa Keleş, later 2 Sok), close to the **cluster of short pylons** on the right. Cross Emecikli Cad. and veer right, still on the same street. Fork left on 105 Sok. (later Kenan Evren Cad.), which then swings right along the side of the valley. A few minutes later, just before the road dips and a road forks up left to a housing estate, take a path forking up left along the rock-face, into woodland. The path follows a water pipe which you hurdle several times before it disappears into the shrubbery. As you wind up the hillside there is a small valley to the left, mostly obscured by foliage. Keep right at a couple of forks a few minutes into the climb. Leave any brushwood gate encountered as you find it.

Keep ahead as the path levels out, to reach a **saddle (30min)** with a terrific view of Marmaris, the sea and the islands. Looking left, you can see huge blocks of stone — remnants of the old Greek wall; sadly, these remains of **Physcus** are totally overgrown and unapproachable.

Leave the saddle by taking the uphill path to the right; it is not very clear at first, but it skirts to the left of the large rocky outcrop ahead. A couple of minutes later, the saddle comes into view just below. Keep heading up through a rocky area, with Marmaris Bay over to the left. The narrow path, edged with holly oak, leads towards another rocky outcrop on the left. The path passes to the right of the outcrop, from where there are good views to Physcus and the saddle. From here the path levels out a little, skirts a third rocky outcrop (on the right), and swings inland to a grassy meadow.

You now find yourself on a **ridge**, with Armutalan to the left and Beldibi on the right. From here, the onward route basically follows the line of the ridge. Head across the *yayla,* to follow the path along the left-hand (Armutalan) side of the ridge, from where you can see the start of Walk 16. The path descends a little and continues towards a pylon ahead. Cross another saddle and pass close to the **pylon**, still traversing the left-hand side of the ridge. When the path forks just past the pylon, keep to the lower path, by the side of the ridge. The meadows are left behind now, as you enter light woodlands of pine, wild olive and holly oak. Keep uphill and reach another grassy saddle. Cross it diagonally and continue along the Beldibi side of the ridge. A minute later you emerge on a small *yayla* with a fine panorama over Beldibi, Physcus and Marmaris marina.

From here the path continues directly up the centre of the ridge, trailing fine views of Marmaris. As you reach the top of the ridge, bear slightly right and join a grassy track: it takes you down to a **main track (1h20min)**, where you turn right. *(Walk 16 joins here.)* From here on, the way back is all downhill. Just before a rocky outcrop on the right, take the faint **woodland track (1h25min)** which sweeps back down to the right. This shrinks to a path as it skirts to the right of a valley.

Head down into a cluster of farm buildings, turn left to join a track, and leave the farm through a gate. Initially, the track heads away from Marmaris, but it soon swings right and then down to the road. Turn right here. After 10 minutes you pass the path up to Physcus. Meeting the **Beldibi road (2h40min)**, wait for a *dolmuş* or passing taxi, or walk back.

See map on pages 128-129.
Time: 3h
Grade: moderate; mainly on track; ascent of about 200m. The walk is in the Marmaris National Park, with information boards and maps (there is also a signposted trail to İçmeler).
Equipment: see pages 21-22.
Travel: 🚐 *dolmuş* from Marmaris to Armutalan, frequent departures, journey time about 10min; return from Siteler or İçmeler by any 🚐 *dolmuş* bound for Marmaris.
Short walks
1 Armutalan — Arkutca (2h15min; grade as main walk). Follow the main walk as far as the crossing track (1h45min), but turn right here to the Datça road at Arkutca (also called Arkutcha) and stop a passing *dolmuş* or coach returning to Marmaris. There is nothing at this point in the way of shade or refreshments.
2 Arkutca to Siteler (1h45min; easy). Catch a 🚐 *dolmuş* bound for Hisarönü, Orhaniye or Turgut or catch the Datça bus (all leave from the *otogar*). Ask to alight at Arkutca (also called Arkutcha), in the bottom of the valley, after the descent over the hill from Marmaris. (This is where the road goes off right to Dereözü; see map pages 128-129). At the point where the road curves over the bottom of the valley, take the track forking down to the left. Follow it alongside the stream to the right. In under 30 minutes you pick up the main walk at the 1h45min-point (by a fountain on the corner, where the main walk track enters from the left). Follow the main walk to the end.
Alternative walk: Seyir Terasi (3h15min; moderate, with an overall ascent of 120m). Catch the 🚐 Siteler *dolmuş* and alight at the terminus. Continue along the main road towards İçmeler but, in a minute or less, look for a large wooden board on the right: *Yuruyus Yolu Sonu* ('end of the walking trail'). Head along the forestry track *(orman yolu)* to the right of the sign, *not* the tarmac road to the left. Follow the Kampyeri/Seyir Terasi trail to a viewpoint and picnic spot, then return the same way.

Walks 15, 16: the liquidambar tree is endemic to Rhodes and southwest Anatolia. Its leaves are like those of the plane tree, and it occupies similar habitats.

Climbing the yayla *above the small stone building overlooking Armutalan*

This is a pleasing short walk which follows a forestry track (orman yolu) *through quiet countryside and offers fantastic views of Marmaris along the way. One special feature of the walk is the liquidambar tree,* Liquidambar orientalis, *which is endemic to Rhodes and southwest Anatolia. It is particularly common in the region around Marmaris and can be seen along many of the other walks in this area, as well as in Günnücek Milli Parklar just to the south of Marmaris. It is a member of the witch hazel family and is closely related to the American gum tree,* L styraciflua. *The name derives from 'liquid amber' and is a reference to the fragrant gum it produces, similar to the American gum tree, which is used in perfumery, as an expectorant, inhalant and in the treatment of skin diseases. Its leaves are rather like those of the plane tree, although generally smaller. It does tend to occupy similar habitats to the plane, by streams and rivers, in ravines and on flood plains, but they are not commonly seen growing together.*

Start the walk at the *dolmuş* station in **Armutalan** by heading south along the road, passing the *belediye* (council offices) and **mosque** on your left. You reach a large **roundabout** in a minute or so. Head right here, towards the road on the far side of the roundabout (Sht. Ahmet Bender Cad.). A few minutes later, rise up and follow this road (same name) off to the left, continuing to ascend. Just below the brow of the hill, turn sharp right into a narrow surfaced road (Sinan Cad.). Armutalan and the Datça road are now over to the right, as this road wends its way up the left-hand side of the valley. You reach a **fountain** on the left in 10 minutes or less; then the road reverts to track. A dry stream bed meets the track on a U bend five minutes later. Half a minute past here, head left up the hillside on a waymarked path/trail.
This becomes very stony as it winds through the shrubbery, with the valley of the stream bed crossed earlier over on the left.

Ever closer, on your right, is the Datça road, but the traffic is mostly heard, rather than seen, and does little to disturb the tranquillity of your surroundings. Encroaching foliage may cause a moment's uncertainty some 10 minutes up, but press on uphill: the path/trail swings right and then left. Within five minutes, as the path/trail again swings to the right, go left and rise up onto a small *yayla* (meadow).

A stone building with sheet-metal roof perches at the bottom of the *yayla,* to your left, looking down over Armutalan. Turn right and head up the *yayla* towards a hut; another hut is now visible over to the left. Keeping to the left of the hut ahead, cross a gully and ascend onto a woodland track. Turn right on the track and follow it to the **Datça road** (**55min**). (The path/trail joins here from the right.) Turn left, being wary of the traffic, as the road crests the brow of the hill. In half a minute, take the next track to the left. This track leads straight ahead to a small radio mast. Don't follow it up to the mast however; instead, soon take the motorable track forking down right towards a **small village**. Keep right as the track forks again on entering the village. The people here are friendly, and the village is an amazing microcosm of life before tourism … especially considering that it is so close to Marmaris. But it is not a museum, so please respect their privacy.

After you pass through the lower end of the village, the track sweeps right, alongside the valley on the right. A fountain is passed on the left. An open area, from where there are good views over the terrain ahead, is reached some five minutes later. Keep on the track as it bends round to the left. When the track forks (under 10 minutes beyond the open area), go down to the right, along the left-hand side of a wooded valley. The track turns sharp left about 10 minutes later and descends to a **crossing track** (**1h45min**), where you turn left. *(Short walk 1 goes right here; Short walk 2 joins here from the right.)* Liquidambar trees find a home in the stream bed along this track.

Keep ahead along this pleasant woodland track *(orman yolu)* and ignore tracks off to the right, until you come to a fork of tracks in well under 20 minutes. (The left fork rises up to the Seyir Terasi viewpoint and picnic area which are visited in the Alternative walk; beyond the viewpoint a path leads back to Armutalan.)

The main walk forks *right* here, following the sign **'Kampyeri' (campsite)**. Rise up around the hillside, initially not far above the left-hand track. On reaching a high point, begin the descent towards Siteler. Good views to the Bay of Marmaris and Cennet Adası begin to appear through the trees, becoming more open as you descend, but disappear as the track snakes down through the wooded valley towards the sea. Emerging on the main Marmaris/İçmeler road at the bottom, turn left. In a minute you reach the *dolmuş* station at **Siteler** (**3h**), located on the same side of the road.

See map on pages 128-129.
Time: 4h
Grade: moderate; almost entirely on forestry tracks which are good underfoot; ascent of just over 200m
Equipment: see pages 21-22.
Travel: 🚐 *dolmuş* from Marmaris to Armutalan, frequent departures; journey time around 10min; the walk ends in Marmaris, at the junction with the Datça road.
Alternative walks: This walk joins Walk 14 and, when you meet that route, two possibilities present themselves. Since they are of equal length, make your choice depending on your preference for walking on forestry tracks or on paths. The path walk demands some navigating skills.
1 Armutalan to Marmaris *mainly on forestry tracks* (3h40min; grade as main walk). Follow the main walk to the 2h05min-point, then pick up the notes for Walk 14 (from the 1h25min-point, see page 130) to walk down to Marmaris.
2 Armutalan to Marmaris *partly on paths* (3h45min; grade as main walk). Follow the main walk to the 2h-point, where Walk 14 comes in from the right. From here use the map to return to Marmaris following Walk 14 in reverse, referring to the notes for that walk if necessary.

Rosy-hued, pine-clad hills form a green mantle around Marmaris. This walk explores with ease this seemingly impenetrable barrier. The number of rivers and streams in the whole of this region may come as a surprise to you — as well as the waterfalls along the walk, which passes through two distinct geological areas. The landscape in the early part of the ramble shows barely a trace of the imprint of man; there are no signs of cultivation and no great profusion of wild flowers. Wild flowers give a clue — indeed many clues as you learn to read them — to the infertile nature of the soil generated by the underlying serpentine rock. Serpentines cover large tracts of this peninsula, from the area to the north of Marmaris and westward, sweeping down the Datça peninsula. Although the area is extensive, it is not always exclusively serpentine, and pockets of fertility (associated mainly with the limestone series of rocks) do occur. Villages and farming communities are few and far between in the serpentine region; usually regions of more fertile land of a different geology are cultivated. The high concentrations of metals like iron, magnesium, chromium and nickel from the serpentine render the soils infertile, and it is the high iron concentration that gives the rosy hue to the hills around Marmaris. Certain wild flowers are not only able to survive these soils, but actually flourish because of the lack of competition. The lovely cyclamen with the propeller-like flower, Cyclamen trochopteranthum, *is one easily-recognised example of a flower which is only found on the serpentine soils in this region and, similarly, the liquidambar tree survives competition on this substrate. Should you find bee orchids or the evergreen* Cupressus *trees, then you have definitely wandered back into a limestone region … and you could be near the end of the walk.*

Start the walk at the *dolmuş* station in **Armutalan**. Facing the Royal Plaza Hotel opposite, turn right and follow the road round to the right, to join the **Datça road** in a little over 10 minutes. Keep ahead, back in the direction of Marmaris, and take the first road on the left a few minutes later. Follow this road past an **electricity sub-station** on the right and go past a **new mosque** as the road contours round the hillside. When the road sweeps sharply back toward the sea, turn left past new developments, beyond which the road reverts to track. Just past a house on the right (currently orange), you cross a stream bed. Stay on the main track, heading up an isolated valley. Masses of oleander paint the banks of the stream a cheerful pink down on your left and, all around, the tall yellow spikes of the mullein vie for attention.

The track starts to rise higher above the stream on the left, and in winter and spring there is the sound of water tripping over small waterfalls. There are larger **waterfalls** ahead along this delightful woodland track. Liquidambar trees add a splash of bright green by the water and confirm that this early part of the walk is taking you through a region of serpentine rock.

Eventually your route swings right into an ascending loop (ignore the track off left). You head back in the direction of the coast, with your outward track down to the right.

A sharp left turn in the track leads you away from the waterfall valley, as you continue parallel with the coast, through beautiful woodland and past meadows. Reach the **high point of the walk** (**1h45min**) and start into a gradual descent. Walk 14 joins this walk briefly, at the point where a grassy track comes in from a **knoll on the right** (**2h**; just before the track swings left). *(Alternative walk 2 descends to Marmaris here.)* Keep to the main track, to pass a **rocky outcrop** five minutes later (**2h05min**). *(Alternative walk 1 descends to Marmaris here.)* Fine views open out over Beldibi's valley below. The track heads north now, leading you away from Marmaris and keeping the Beldibi valley down on the right for quite some time. A small group of buildings is passed as the track weaves along the side of this lovely valley.

When you reach **a new development on the right** (**2h35min**), you emerge at a *dolmuş* stop, where you could catch a bus back to Marmaris. Otherwise, follow the road round the small village and down past the local college.

Now heading towards Marmaris along the right-hand side of the **Beldibi valley**, you pass a **fountain** on the right. At a fork under 20 minutes past the fountain, keep right uphill. You pass the point where the track from Walk 14 joins on the right and, 10 minutes later, the **path up to Physcus** (Walk 14). Reach the junction with the **Beldibi road** (**3h35min**). You can wait here for a *dolmuş* or passing taxi. Or turn right, back to Marmaris (note that some shops among the car work-shops sell drinks). In less than 10 minutes you reach the petrol stations on the main road. Go right here, into **Marmaris** (**4h**).

5 AROUND MARMARIS AND THE BOZBURUN PENINSULA

İçmeler • Turunç • Amos and Kumlubükü Bay • Bozburun Peninsula

Area code: ☏ 0252
Connections: Vary from very good (to İçmeler and Turunç) to fairly good (to Bozburun); otherwise nil. See details with individual entries.
Walks: 17-19 (Walks 11-16 are nearby).

The landscape around Marmaris is just delightful — particularly the inviting Bozburun Peninsula (named after its largest village), with its isolated bays and villages, forests, and valleys where trout jump about in the streams. There are also some idyllic spots in the Gulf of Gökova, north of Marmaris (see page 105). As a rule of thumb, the further out you go from Marmaris, the more pleasant and tranquil the surroundings.

İçmeler

The Muğla Tourist Board tells visitors that 'In bygone days there was allegedly healing water in İçmeler, but don't try looking for it now, stick with mineral water'. İçmeler was also once an unimportant village at the western edge of Marmaris Bay. But don't look for that today; with its 10,000 inhabitants, it's a busy holiday centre. Its beach used to be an unspoilt paradise, today it's a forest of sunshades with hardly anywhere to put down a towel. İçmeler is very popular with British and Dutch package tourists, many of whom stay in the identikit (but very well-equipped) hotels and never make it further than the beach, where there is a large selection of water sports, or the beachside cafés. For those who want to see more, various tour operators and car and two-wheel hire firms from Marmaris have branches here.

Connections: A *dolmuş* runs to Marmaris every 10 minutes from 07.00-01.30; it starts and ends in the south side of the bay. But the trip by **water *dolmuş*** is much prettier (also from the south end of the bay, every 30 minutes, £3.50 one way). There are also taxi boats to Turunç (hourly in season, otherwise very limited) and at 10.00 to Amos, Kumlubükü and Çiftlik (return at 16.30).

Accommodation: While there are a great many hotels, most cannot be recommended for individual travellers since they are pre-booked by tour operators.

Food and drink: There's a lot on offer in the centre. Our tip is the **Mona Titti** restaurant, signposted on the road to Turunç. This tranquil, jasmin-scented place has a pleasant terrace and tables around a little pool. They serve tempting dishes like 'spaghetitti', 'chicken titts' and 'Moby's Dick' — let them surprise you! Everything is simply beguiling. It's best to book (☏ 4554046). Open from 19.00; they can collect you from your hotel. Main courses £10-19. And while you're having an apéritif, don't forget to read the 'History of Mona Titti'!

View to İçmeler from Marmaris

Nightlife: The 'in' place at present is the **Pleasure** mega-disco.
Market: On Wednesdays there is a big **market** on Çevre Yolu (the road to Turunç and Datça).

Turunç

Turunç is the Turkish name for a type of bitter orange.and compared with Marmaris or İçmeler, this well-kept former fishing village of 2500 inhabitants is still quite sweet. But for how long? Over recent years it's been caught up in mass tourism more than any other place in the area. Located south of İçmeler on a long bay with some fine-sand sections, the village is no longer only a day trip destination, but increasingly a popular place to stay, especially among British and East European package holidaymakers. Very comfortable resorts have been built to the left, the right and above the bay. The number of smaller, simpler and friendly places to stay falls every year. Cumhuriyet Caddesi, the main street behind the beach, becomes a pedestrian zone in the evening. Here's where you'll find jewellers and carpet dealers, karaoke bars and restaurants with identical menus.

Connections: A *dolmuş* runs to Marmaris every hour. In the summer there are **water** ***dolmuşes*** hourly to Marmaris and İçmeler, and once a day to Amos, Kumlubükü and Çiftlik (out at 10.30, back at 16.30).

Accommodation

The **International Academy Marmaris**, above Turunç, is a place for creative visitors near the Loryma Resort hotel complex (they fetch you with a tractor-shuttle). It's an art and culture centre where you can also stay overnight. The complex was set up by Turkish artists and has workshops and an even an amphitheatre. You can breakfast by the pool listening to classical music. There are 22 very pleasant rooms with bath, most with balcony. Since IAM is a non-profit organisation, it's all very economical. It's passed on Walk 19. Double rooms with H/B £50, singles £34. ☎ 4767818, www.akademionline.net.

Barbaros Beach Hotel, old but well-kept 4-storey hotel in a quiet spot an the north end of the bay. Only separated from the bay by its own small pool. 31 large bright rooms with tiled floors, just under half of which have a sea view. Doubles £30. ☎ 4767040, ℻ 4767008, www.barbarosbeachhotel.com.

Motel Han, right on the sea. 15 plain, but tidy and clean rooms with climate control — those in the front with fantastic sea views. Cosy restaurant. Friendly service. Doubles £38. ☎ 4767006, hanrestaurant@hotmail.com.

Şule Pansiyon, on the shoreside road (but a bit set back — look out for the post office). It'is a wonder that this guest house hasn't been made into an expensive hotel. The 9 rooms (with bath) are spartan, so the place would be nothing special were it not for the beautiful terrace overlooking the sea. One can only hope that this 'fossilised guest house' will stay in business for some time yet! Double rooms £25; no breakfasts available, but there are shared kitchen facilities. ☎ 4767314 or ☎ 0555 6521120 (mobile). If no one is there, ask at the Burak Aparthotel 100m inland.

Food and drink

Everywhere you see 'Full English Breakfast', 'Pizza', 'Burger', 'Chicken Wings'. Most good restaurants have disappeared in the face of down-market tourism. So for eating out, it's worth going to Amos, Kumlubükü Bay (see opposite), or the Bozburun Peninsula.

But our tip for Turunç is the **Yakamoz Restaurant**, near the Barbaros Beach Hotel at the far north end of the bay, is an idyllic garden restaurant, set under old trees above the beach. Choice of dishes is limited, but they always have fish and *köfte*. Friendly service and economical.

Nightlife: Nightlife is focused on several music bars — especially **Fidan** on the main road behind

Sometimes you have to work quite hard for the best views, as here on Walk 19 between İçmeler and Turunç.

the beach. It has a restaurant facing the sea and terrace facing the road (sometimes with football on TV). Open till 4am in season.

Practicalities A-Z

Car and two-wheel hire: This rental business is run by tour operators and estate agents. Scooters from £22 per day and cars from £40.

Organised tours: Various companies offer the same coach and bus tours as in Marmaris.

Water sports: Everything is on offer, from sea kayaking to parasailing.

Amos and Kumlubükü Bay

From Turunç a side road heads south, high above the coast. After a few kilometres a narrow little road branches off to the left, and goes steeply downhill to small, beautiful **Amos Bay**. First you pass the little holiday homes belonging to the staff from the universities of Marmara and Anadolu (with the 'Profesörler Sitesi' sign), then you come to the sand and shingle beach, just 100m long, where you can hire sunshades and sunbeds, and enjoy a meal at the good restaurant.

If you ignore this turn-off to Amos, you soon pass **Asarcık Hill**, which separates Amos Bay from Kumlubükü Bay. On top of the hill lie the stony remnants of **ancient Amos**. Surrounded by the impressive remains of the **town wall**, are a **temple** in quite poor condition and a fairly well-preserved **theatre**. Apollo, who was called Samnaios in this area, was the city's god.

In wide, peaceful **Kumlubükü Bay** an enormous, unwalled villa immediately comes into view — it belongs to the chairman of the Garanti Bankası. Otherwise the bay hasn't much to offer, as its shingle beach isn't among the most beautiful in the area. There are some restaurants and accommodation. Approximately two kilometres south of the bay, you can visit a cave — ask someone to point the way out to you.

Connections: **Taxi boats** make the trip from Turunç and İçmeler to Amos (see under Connections, pages 136 and 137).

Accommodation/Food and drink: **Dionysos Sea Club Restaurant and Villa Florya**. The first is a chic terrace restaurant with beach club in Kumlubükü Bay, ideal for a romantic meal. Small but well-chosen menu (fish carpaccio, grilled prawns or squid in garlic butter, etc.). Top quality cooking in the season. Main courses £9-18.50. ☎ 4767352. Just behind it is Villa Florya, a boutique hotel with 12 rooms. All rooms have sea view and lovely terraces, but the decorations are far from stylish. People staying here can use the beach club free. Doubles £105. ☎ 4767553, fax 4767554, www.villaflorya.com.

Amos Beach Restaurant, a lovely place behind the eponymous beach; popular with day-trippers, but nice and quiet in the evenings, when there is a boat service from Turunç (departs from the quay at 19.30, returns at 22.30 — look for the boat called 'İpek', or call ☎ 4767294). Large variety of dishes, including *pide*. Fair prices.

Bozburun Peninsula

Connections: By *dolmuş* the bays and villages on the Bozburun Peninsula are served by minibus up to 6 times a day in summer, but there's no service on weekends or in winter.

Bozburun

The sleepy little town of Bozburun (*No banks and no ATMs!*) is about 54km from Marmaris and has long been a centre for boatbuilding. In recent years the place has had a bit of a face-lift, in order to catch the attention of the lucrative tourist trade. In the hopes of attracting the yachting fraternity, they have built a new marina and eschewed hotel blocks. So the place has retained some charm and authenticity; it's a peaceful spot with a relaxed little esplanade.

Accommodation: There is a good choice of simple, friendly guest houses and hotels along the shore promenade. But most visitors to Bozburun spend the night on their yachts.

Sabrinas Haus, a dreeam address for those who can afford it. 15 large, very chic and lovingly decorated rooms and suites with wonderful sea views (even from the bathtub!). Heavenly beds. Lovely garden with palms, wooden jetty. Restaurant with both international and Turkish cuisine. Minimum stay 3 nights. It can't be reached by car; they will send a boat to collect you. Doubles from £205. Koru Mevkii (south of Bozburun), ☎ 4562045, 📠 4562145, www.sabrinashaus.com.

Aphrodite Hotel, a very nice place, but more pension than hotel. Praised by readers. 15 simple, pleasant rooms, all with balcony and sea view. Good restaurant, large book corner, small private beach, hammocks. Open Apr.-Oct. Only accessible on foot or by boat (they will collect you; see under Orfoz Restaurant below). With H/B £36 per person. South of Bozburun, near Sabrinas Haus, ☎/📠 4562268, www.hotelaphrodite.net.

Club Buena Vista, popular restaurant with sailors; nice bar on the water. Simple camping place (£4.20 per van) and 3 rooms to rent (£42 per person with H/B). On the west side of Bozburun Bay (walk along the beach), ☎ 4562599, www.club-buenavista.com.

Yılmaz Pansion, a friendly very clean family-run place. Newly equipped rooms with good baths. Shared kitchen and terrace with sea view. Doubles £29 per person, breakfast extra. On the shore road on the eastern side of Bozburun's bay (if it's full up, there are other pensions along here), ☎ 0538 3730993 (mobile), www.yilmazpansion.com.

Food and drink: The quality of the **restaurants** is good everywhere, but prices are on a par with Marmaris.

A really special place is the **Orfoz Restaurant**, where you sit in an enchanted garden in front of a beautifully restored old stone house. It has a lot of flair — almost Greek. Excellent fish and seafood. Of course it's fairly pricey. You can get there on foot or by boat (they will collect you from the Hotel Mete). ☎ 4562209.

Ad Astra Café & Bar, a cosy 'living room' café on the shore road. Mini-verandah in front and sometimes a couple of tables right over the water. Small, beautifully presented dishes. Praised by readers.

Söğütköy

Apart from Bozburun, the villages on the Peninsula are predominantly farming or fishing communities — or both. For example, one half of Söğütköy is located high up on a hillside; the rest of the houses are spread around two bays, Kızılyer in the north and Saranda in the south.

Accommodation, food and drink:

Octopus Aşkın Pension, at the Kızılyer boat dock in Söğütköy. Quiet and peaceful. 12 well-kept rooms, some with a little garden in front. The place is only 20m from the sea but, the little strip of sandy beach is only big enough for a couple of sun loungers. Doubles £58. The adjacent restaurant, right at the water's edge, has excellent fish. At Kızılyer, ☎ 4965093, 📠 4965451, www.askinmotel.com.

Denizkızı Pansiyon, clean rooms with laminated floors and pine furniture. Nicely sited restaurant, bathing platform and sun terrace. Double room £50. At Saranda Bay. ☎ 4965032, 📠 4965804, www.sogutdenizkiki. com.

Yakamoz Pansiyon, 13 plain but tidy rooms divided among 3 buildings, all with balcony (but not all have sea view). Bathing platform, very good restaurant. Doubles £42-63. At Saranda Bay. ☎ 4965185, 📠 4965544, www. pension-yakamoz. com.

From Söğütköy to Selimiye Bay

In the south of the peninsula, where the pine forests are replaced by barren landscape, lies the forgotten village of **Taşlıca** with its space-age mosque. Just the drive from Söğüt to Taşlıca is an experience, with views to the offshore islets and the Greek island of Sými. Shortly before Taşlica a sign points to **Serçe Limanı**, 9km away, a small fishing port with a restaurant (popular with sailors, who sail from there to the ancient ruins of **Loryma**). Still surviving are thewalls of a fortress built to protect **Bozukkale Bay**.

Heading north, there is **Bayırköy**, once a sleepy place, now a popular stop for excursion groups — there were 15 teahouses set around an ancient plane tree at time of writing! Supposedly, the tree is 2000 years old. To amuse themselves in the old says (since nothing much ever happened) here — the old men of the village fixed a sign to the tree to the effect that anyone who walked around it would have a lucky life. At first they used to have a good laugh watching tourists circle the tree, but now they no longer pay much attention.

Past Bayırköy you come to delightful **Çiftlik Bay**, which has one of the best beaches around Marmaris. Sadly it is no longer the idyll it once was; today there are just too many visitors — an armada of boats sails in from Marmaris, disgorging several thousands of tourists every day.

Turgutköy is a popular stop-off for jeep safaris and the coach trips usually called the 'Visit Turkey Tour'. This tour usually includes a stop at the nearby **waterfalls** (signposted 'Şelale'). Don't expect too much here either: in summer the roar of the falls is little more than the flush of a domestic toilet. The water collects in several small pools, where you can swim (entry fee £0.60). There are several trout restaurants along the stream.

Selimiye Bay

The landscape around **Selimiye Bay** is beautiful, with the ruins of an old castle high above. This bay is lovely to look at, but beaches are in short supply. Instead there are seaside restaurants. In recent years some hotels have been built here — small, charming houses rather than blocks.

Accommodation, food and drink: **Sardunya** is a first-class fish restaurant with a romantic terrace right on the sea. Fantastic Aegean cooking with the best olive oil. Good service, but fairly pricey; recommended by readers. The restaurant rents out rooms and bungalows (doubles £63). ✆ 4464003, www.sardunya.info. **Les Terrasses de Selimiye**, a lovely place high above Selimiye. Opened 2008, run by the young French woman, Solenne Moal, who has followed her dream. Terraced, with 10 pretty rooms without unnecessary things like TV! Each room has a huge balcony or terrace. Wonderful view over the bay of Selimiye from the pool area. They will cook a Turkish-French meal on request. Excellent value for money. Doubles £56. Signed in the village (the last bit is gravel). ✆ 4464367, ✆ 4464362, www.selimiyepension.com

Beside these, there is also a **row of simple, cheap guest houses** in the village. One is **Jenny's House**, with 12 carefully furnished rooms and a shady terrace and pool in front. Very

Seafront promenade at Marmaris, where Walk 17 begins

popular with the British who do *not* want to stay in Marmaris. Doubles £42. On the main road, ✆ 4464289, www.jennyshouse.co.uk

Orhaniye Bay

There's a marina at the entrance to this fjord-like bay, but yachts trying to get further in have to take great care, as there is a sand bank just below the surface of the water. There are just a few simple places to stay and good restaurants.

Hisarönü Bay

This bay has a long, narrow and somewhat untidy beach backed by a few scattered guest houses and hotels.

Accommodation/camping: **Club Rena**, right on the beach. It's a mini-resort — just 5 roomy, simple bungalows (with tiled floors and large windows and glass sliding doors). In front a pool with cosy cushions, restaurant (excellent food in the season, at good prices), palm trees and the sea. Laid-back atmosphere. Doubles £63. ✆ 0537 2640415 (mobile), www.clubrena.com.

6.10.16

Walk 17: *Marmaris to İçmeler promenade*

See plan of Marmaris on pages 120-121 to begin the walk and the map on page 146 to end it.

Time: 3h (or as long as it takes)

Grade: easy. The main Marmaris/İçmeler road is never too far away, and a *dolmuş* or taxi is easily accessed at many points for a quick return.

Equipment: just comfortable footwear and sun protection. Food and drink are available all along the route.

Travel: water taxis and *dolmuşes* ply between Marmaris and İçmeler (and Turunç, but less frequently outside high season).

The promenade between Marmaris and İçmeler provides a traffic-free walking route with a diversity of scenery and interest along the way. At the Marmaris end, all is hustle and bustle with cafés/restaurants and souvenir shops cheek by jowl, but they dwindle out as you progress away from the centre. For much of the way, the promenade edges the shore, so there are plenty of opportunities to sit on the beach and absorb the activity in Marmaris Bay, stop for a swim or engage in an assortment of water activities. Pine woods invade the shoreline on the approach to İçmeler, giving a rural feel to the surroundings, while the setting of sandy İçmeler beach is incentive enough to linger awhile. This is a walk which can be savoured by all, with the chance to opt out at any point along the way. It can be joined at any point between Marmaris and İçmeler but, for the benefit of those travelling into Marmaris from other resorts, this brief description starts in Marmaris.

Start the walk from any point on the **promenade** at **Marmaris** by going right when facing the sea, walking away from the marina. Initially, the promenade is accompanied by the main road but soon forks off left, away from the traffic (just before reaching the Hotel Selen). The first few kilometres, which skirt the deep straggle of tourist accommodation behind the shore, are lively and congested with plenty of interesting distractions.

Towards the end of the Marmaris seafront, as the density of building declines, and pine trees edge the promontory separating İçmeler from Marmaris, a gentler ambience prevails. Those who wish to beat a retreat to the main road need to consider doing so before this point is reached, as the main road becomes less accessible for a while. This last section is the most delightful of all. The promenade meanders amongst shady pine trees where scattered café/bars offer a chance to sit and enjoy the view.

İçmeler comes into view once the headland is rounded, sitting at the back of a deep bay. It is hard to imagine being able to find a foothold along the steep green slopes of the hills across the bay here — but Walk 19 from Turunç finds a way!

On reaching **İçmeler**, the promenade continues left, to pass behind the beach with its facilities. The main road, from where it is possible to catch a *dolmuş* to Turunç or back to Marmaris, is close by to the right at this point. (You are also close to the starting point for Walk 18 here.) But the *dolmuş* for Marmaris actually *starts* from the far side of the beach, which is the best place to board at busy times, as they leave when they are full.

Walk 18: From İçmeler to Turunç

Time: under 4h
Grade: strenuous, with a fairly steep ascent of some 425m; mainly on paths which are often stony and overgrown in places. *Only recommended for keen hikers with route-finding experience (and perhaps secateurs!); Walk 19 is a far more straightforward option.*
Equipment: see pages 21-22.
Travel: 🚌 *dolmuş* from Marmaris to İçmeler, frequent departures, journey time about 20min. Another option is to catch the *dolmuş* to Turunç (less frequent out of season, so check at the *dolmuş* station), and start the walk at the 'Turkish House' restaurant. For the return from Turunç you can either catch a 🚌 *dolmuş* or ⛴ water taxi; access points for both (with timetables for the water taxis) are located by the mosque on the main street. Both offer a frequent service to İçmeler and Marmaris during the season. 🚖 Taxis are also found in the same location. Out of season, options are: 1) occasional *dolmuş* to İçmeler/Marmaris (check at the Marmaris *dolmuş* station); 2) taxi to *İçmeler*, then *dolmuş* to Marmaris.

This walk between İçmeler and Turunç is probably a very old route dating from long before the road was built. It is still partly used and kept open by the local womenfolk, who climb up almost daily to cut and gather branches from the strawberry trees. The cuttings are used as fodder for cows. The road follows an easier, but longer route to Turunç.
There is a straightforward division in this walk. The first part is constantly uphill, through delightful woodland that hides a host of interesting flowers, and the second part is steadily downhill with a bird's-eye view over Turunç. Some of the flowers to be seen on the walk include three endemic species unknown outside southwest Anatolia: Cyclamen trochopteranthum *grows in profusion in places, but you can only see its propeller-like pink flowers in early spring;* Fritillaria sibthorpiana, *which is a lovely spring-flowering fritillary with a pendulous bell-shaped flower in bright buttercup yellow, is best identified by its broad, grey-green lower leaf;* Fritillaria forbesii *is named after the British botanist Edward Forbes, who discovered this species in 1842 (it is also a spring-flowering yellow fritillary, but one with very narrow leaves). And there is yet a third yellow fritillary around,* Fritillaria bithynica.

Alight from the *dolmuş* by the taxi rank on the right, as soon as it turns left into the wide road which runs behind **İçmeler**. (If you are travelling on Turunç *dolmuş*, it keeps ahead at this junction, so ask to alight at the 'Turkish House' restaurant and cafe/bar, located where the buildings are left behind and the road starts to wind up the wooded hillside over to Turunç. Then pick up the notes below at the 35min-point.) **Start the walk** by going along the road to the right of the **taxi rank**, with the **Atatürk memorial** on your right. In two-three minutes turn left opposite the **school** *(okul)*. Keep left at the fork a few minutes later. Apartments now line the route which heads towards the old village of İçmeler. Follow the road through **old İçmeler** (**15min**), passing the mosque and then the bakery, both on the right. Towering rocks, decked in blue campanula, and a beautiful natural rock garden, on the left, brighten the way.

Keep ahead as the main road to Turunç joins from the right, following signs to the 'Turkish House' restaurant and cafe/bar. Soon a minor surfaced road goes off to the left, and on your right is the '**Turkish House**' (**35min**). *(Those travelling on the Turunç* dolmuş *join the walk here.)*

Continue along the road towards Turunç, passing another minor surfaced road off left to a small factory. A few minutes later the road swings right to begin its ascent over the hill; turn half-left here on a path heading into the woods (about 50 paces past the 'Caution of fire' sign). This path runs up the edge of the escarpment and passes the **factory**. After about 100m you pass **three big stones**; after the last stone, fork slightly right, *downhill*. The initially faint path now moves off left, becoming stronger as you head up the valley.

Woodlands soon close around the path where *Fritillaria sibthorpiana* graces the way with its dainty nodding bells, as it does at many stations along this climb. The path continues in a winding ascent, sometimes revealing views back down towards İçmeler. While the path is generally easy to follow, sometimes you may be uncertain about the direction. Watch for switchbacks — for instance, some 40 minutes uphill it heads sharply left (where the tendency is to continue straight on). After this sharp turn the ascent gets even steeper, and the path zigzags. Encroaching foliage from storax, strawberry trees and prickly holly oak sometimes obscures the bends of the path but, once you brush (or cut!) it aside, the way is obvious.

Eventually you approach **a high point in a scree-like area** (**1h35min** or so), where the path ascends in a zigzag. The scree is soon crossed and the way is easier going as you reach a more level, open area about eight minutes later. Continue as the path bears left and then right, heading to the right of a just-discernable **white rock** (about 2m high). Unusual amongst the flowers here is the white form of the orchid *Dactylorhiza romana*, normally found in shades of pink or yellow. Keep a tree-filled gully over to your right as the path rises more steeply again, until a **junction of paths** is encountered (**2h**).

Turn right here and continue on an almost-level path, towards a valley scattered with large white rocky outcrops. Wild iris catch the eye along this undulating section of woodland path, which ends about 12 minutes later at a cutting. Here you meet a track. Turn left to follow the track through the cutting, to an entirely different viewpoint over meadows. Continue to descend along the track, until you join the **Bozburun road** (**2h25min**), where you go left. Stay ahead through the cutting a minute later, when the road to Bozburun goes off right. Turunç is down below, but pine trees block the view.

From here the road winds down through a series of extended loops, but a path descends more directly, crossing the road several times on the way down. Once through the cutting, as the road

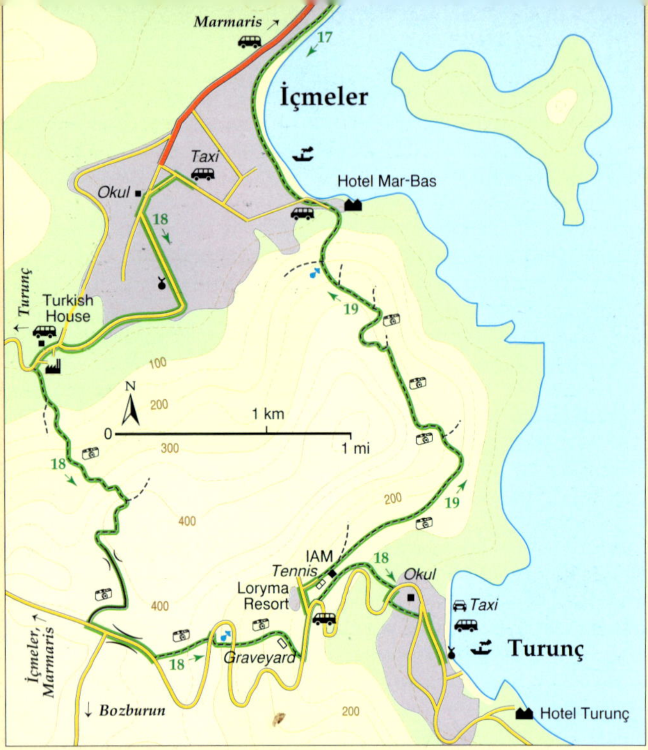

swings right, look on the left for the first part of the path. *Care is needed* negotiating this steep path which descends through the woods. On meeting the road again, turn left and, now with a clear view down over Turunç, look for the path which soon goes down sharp right (beneath power lines). It is a small shale path, which keeps above a concrete-roofed building and through olive groves. Emerging onto the road once more, by a fountain, cross straight over to continue along a stony track which later becomes a walled-in path. Skirt round the **graveyard** on the right and follow a line of pylons towards a building, then keep right to meet the road.

Follow the road to the left downhill, passing the entrance to the **Loryma Resort Apartments** (the start of Walk 19) on the left. When you reach a sharp right-hand bend, take the path off left, to again reach the road. Keeping left, barely touch the road before continuing into a fairly steep descent. This is a very rock-strewn section, and it is easier to walk down the olive grove on the right. Nearing the road again, move diagonally right, away from the rocky area (a high embankment limits access to the road at this point). Head along the road now, above a building with the sign 'Physkos', a bus shelter and a pylon, to locate the path which leads down left into the **school** yard.

Cross the school yard to the right and join the track which leads back onto the road. Turn right and keep ahead to the **mosque** in the centre of **Turunç (4h)**.

11. 10. 16

Red + white waymarks.

Walk 19: From Turunç to İçmeler

See map opposite
Time: 3h15min
Grade: moderate-strenuous, with an ascent of about 230m; well waymarked (see text)
Equipment: see pages 21-22
Travel: hourly *dolmuş* to Turunç during the season (ask to be dropped off at Loryma Resort), or water taxi from the waterfront at Marmaris (near the old town), then either take a taxi or walk to Loryma Resort (see map). Out of season options: limited *dolmuş* service between İçmeler and Turunç (check at the *dolmuş* station); alternatively, *dolmuş* to İçmeler and then taxi to Turunç (12km; alight by the taxi rank as you enter İçmeler; see the start of Walk 18). Return on *dolmuş* from İçmeler, or water taxi in season

Undreamed of views and solitude are the reward for the intrepid who defy the seemingly impregnable hill separating Turunç from İçmeler. Hidden amongst the foliage, which clings tenaciously to the craggy hillside, an old waymarked footpath forges an adventurous route along the contours. It has its gentler touches however, with grassy areas and, in autumn, splashes of colour from the Cyclamen hederifolium. *Surprisingly, there are no vertiginous sections, despite the steep slopes encountered at times along the way.*

Leave the *dolmuş* as it nears the end of its descent into **Turunç**, at the Access road to the **Loryma Resort Apartments**. **Start the walk** by heading along this road. When it forks left uphill just past the pool, keep straight ahead on a gravel road below the **tennis courts**. This ends by a building, the International Academy Marmaris (IAM, see 'Accommodation' on page 137). The woodland path to İçmeler begins here, between a yellow generator and a large tree: a rock to the left of the tree is marked with a green arrow. From here the path is marked throughout with green arrows and/or red dots — sometimes even with cairns — so it is clear throughout. At first it more or less contours eastwards, with fine views over Turunç.

After about 10 minutes the path bends left uphill, to rise to the top of a ridge. Ignore another waymarked path which descends ahead. You are now on the İçmeler side of the ridge.

At a division in the path about six minutes later, keep left uphill, climbing steeply. In 15 minutes you will find yourself looking back down on Turunç. Notice how the route so far has almost completed a U around the contour and along the ridge, with Loryma Resort below. Soon afterwards you reach a **high point** and catch your breath with a wander through pine woods.

There is time now to enjoy some fairly level walking through woodland, gaining a first view of İçmeler through the trees. You emerge from the woods into a more grassy and open area, with İçmeler still in sight. Five-six minutes later you find yourself looking down over the entrance to Marmaris Bay.

A little over 20 minutes from the Marmaris Bay view, the path appears to go straight ahead, but instead turns up to the left. The next 15 minutes or so comprise the **steepest part of the walk**, sometimes involving a little scrambling up the hillside. At the

This walk affords some splendid views towards the bays and Marmaris.

top of this ascent, begin to head downhill on a woodland path made slippery underfoot by leaves. There are some particularly magnificent panoramas towards Marmaris now, as the path climbs again, and İçmeler is suddenly much closer. As the path decends again, you come to a fork: keep left uphill. The ridge ahead now blocks İçmeler from view. Some 15 minutes from the last fork, the path divides again: again keep left uphill, aiming for the dip in the ridge ahead.

Crest the ridge and continue on the path ahead; İçmeler's beach is quite close below you. Soon after passing a **well** on the left, you reach a fork: descend the steep woodland path, to emerge on a saddle under 10 minutes later. The final descent is down a very stony path to the right. Not far down this path, the easier route is the path off to the right alongside a stream bed (keeping ahead here leads to a shale slope with access to the road). The path to the right emerges in a chicken run. Keep ahead, along the right-hand side of the run, to meet the road. A left turn here, opposite Hotel Mar-Bas, quickly leads to **İçmeler** beach and the ***dolmuş* terminus** (**3h15min**).

6 DATÇA AND THE REŞADIYE PENINSULA

Between Marmaris and Datça • Datça • Bays around Datça • Knidos

Area code: ✆ 0252
Information: Datça's Tourist Office is in the 'Kaymakamlık' (district office; near the police); open Mon.-Fri. 08.00-17.00. From mid-Jun. to end Sep. an office also opens in a small wooden house on Cumhuriyet Meydanı (irregular hours). ✆/℻ 7123546, www.datca-turizm.gov.tr.
Connections: Regular **buses** to Marmaris from 06.00-22.00 (1h30; about £4); several times a day to Muğla. For all other destinations, outside high season you must usually change in Marmaris or Muğla. Datça's bus station lies somewhat outside the centre, on the road to Marmaris, but most bus companies have branches in the centre on Atatürk Cad.
Dolmuş: Up to 8 *dolmuşes* run every day to Palamutbükü and Mesudiye (Hayıtbükü and Ova-bükü), in winter 3 a day. Note: On Sundays connections are very bad (non-existent in winter)! The *dolmuş* station is on Atatürk Cad.
Taxis: There is a stand at Datça's *dolmuş* station (among others). A trip to Knidos, with a two-hour stop costs £63, Mesudiye one way £25, Palamutbükü £29.
Walks: Walk 20, circuit of Knidos

The sparsely populated Reşadiye Peninsula is a long and narrow strip of land stretching into the sea west of Marmaris. At the tip of the peninsula are the ruins of the ancient city of Knidos. Driving there you come upon many an unspoilt bay.

Not long ago the only way to Datça, the main town on the peninsula, was via a hilly road with endless hairpins, a test for both driver and car. Now the road has been improved, so all you need is some patience. On the way you have constantly changing views of wild ravines, turquoise-blue bays and steep, bare rock cliffs. Many of the villages en route are still caught in a time-warp, natural and unspoilt — especially when compared with Marmaris! Even Datça, with its 14,800 or so inhabitants, is still a quiet little town. The isolation of the peninsula has long been a deterrent to the development of touristic infrastructure. Whether the improved road will bring change remains to be seen.

Between Marmaris and Datça

If you drive west from Marmaris, for quite a distance you pass little more than a couple of turnings to remote bays and campsites. The best camping is at the **Aktur** holiday centre 50 km along; its beautiful beach is visible from the road. Some 8km further on, the small town of **Emecik**, on a slope to the right, is of no interest to tourists. Nor is the **Bay of Karaincir** 3km further on, since its flat sandy beach is usually full of Turks staying in their nearby summer homes. Then, about 1km past Karaincir Bay, you pass the kilometre-long, undeveloped sandy beach of **Gebekum**: the most beautiful part of this beach is the eastern end. In spring 2010 the first naturist *hotel* in Turkey opened here; in a few weeks it had to close down again ('having contravened building regulations'). Turkey is just not ready for naked tourists. From here it's still about 14km to Datça.

Camping sites between Marmaris and Emecik

Çubacak Mesire Yeri, huge site located in pines by an attractive pebble beach, but the pitch is very close to the Marmaris–Datça road. Caravans £11-15; tents for up to 4 people £9.20-12.50. On the main road, about 21km west of Marmaris. ✆ 4670221, ✆ 4670043, www. cubacakcamping.net.

Inbükü Mesire Yeri, 3km past Çubacak Mesire Yeri, also in pines by a small pebble beach. Set well below the coastal road and really spread out (lots of bamboo stands, so you can often find an isolated spot). Simple; many Turkish guests. But rather dilapidated in 2010. Caravan £7.50; tent £6.50. ✆/✆ 4369119, www.yesil-mavi.com.

Aktur Tatil Sitesi, huge site in pines by a beautiful sandy beach. All facilities of a town, including a bank, ambulance and Turkish bazaar! Excursions, bicycle hire. Also bungalows — from simple huts to 'holiday villa' style. Caravan (£20 for 2 people), doubles with H/B from £54. Signposted. ✆/✆ 7246836, www.akturcamping.com.

Resorts between Marmaris and Emecik

Club Golden Key Bördübet, an idyll in the woods. Beautiful, well-spaced complex with tasteful, comfortable rooms and suites. Hens potter about between the palms; pool and children's play area. Boat to private beach. Many sports facilities. Open May to mid-Oct.; advance booking recommended. On the way to Club Amazon (see below — 12km from the turn-off, all tarred road). Double with H/B £220. ✆ 4369230, www. goldenkeyhotels.com.

Club Amazon: coming from Marmaris, turn right after about 16km towards 'Bördübet Amazon'; it's 16km from the turn-off, the last 4km unsurfaced. Secluded, paradisial place on the Gulf of Gokova. Not on the sea, but an arm of river (you take a canoe to the site's beach). Well equipped and run, friendly and laid back. Good restaurant, large splash pool. Also rent bungalows — from tiny 'stone tents' to larger 'covered wagons'. With F/B from £42 per person. At Bördübet, ✆ 4369111, ✆ 4614231, www. klupamazon.com.

Datça

Datça, the main settlement on the Reşadiye Peninsula, is a small, friendly coastal town, which still has little in common with the mass tourism of the large neighbouring towns of Bodrum to the north or Marmaris to the east.

Located 76km west of Marmaris, it is particularly popular with the yachting fraternity. The small marina is always busy, and a charming ensemble of bars, restaurants and souvenir shops has accumulated around it. The outlying areas look very different

— hotels are springing up in an effort to emulate the holiday metropoli of Marmaris or Bodrum. If Datça is not careful, its frenetic building activity will scare off those who have been attracted to the place for its simplicity and friendliness. So far, however, it's just small beer relative to the large tourist centres. Symptomatic of this is the wholly undeveloped art of touting in front of restaurants — there are virtually no touts to be seen.

Datça, with its lack of culturally interesting historical sites, is trying to be proactive by building a museum which will accommodate finds from Knidos. The plan is to build it on the end of the promontory near the amphitheatre — but the plans have been on the drawing board for years…

So far only a few holidaymakers stray to **Eski Datça** (Old Datça), a restored village with narrow cobbled lanes, from which the coastal town got its name. Old Datça, approximately 2km inland from the coast, is worth a visit; there are even friendly places for an overnight stay and more and more cafés are opening.

Accommodation/camping

(see plan on page 152)

Although there are some simple pensions in the centre, they are hardly inspiring. For places in the new district on the way to Kargı Bay, you really need a car.

Villa Aşina (19), a kitsch palace from the outside, is really lovely inside — there's not a corner lacking something of interest! 17 cosy, tasteful, comfortable rooms, all with own terrace and sea view. Even from the pool area there's a great view. Doubles from £79 including breakfast and afternoon tea. On the way to Kargı Bay, signposted. ✆ 7122444, www.villaasina.com.tr.

Villa Tokur (19), signposted off the road to Kargı Bay. German/ Turkish management. 13 very pleasant rooms with cast-iron framed beds, plus 2 apartments for a maximum of 4 people. All with balconies, air-conditioning and central heating. Welcoming pool area. Open all year. Doubles £54, apartment £79. Koru Mevkii, ✆ 7128728, www.hoteltokur.com.

Bora Hotel (12), middle-grade hotel in the centre; very clean. Friendly lobby with a 'sitting room' touch. 18 rooms with fridge; nice view from the upper floors. Doubles £50. İskele Mah. ✆ 7122040, www.borahotel.com.tr.

Oğuz Pansiyon (13), clean house in the centre. 11 rooms with small new baths, some with balconies and nice views. Doubles £29, İskele Mah. ✆ 7123800, www.oguzpansiyon.com.tr.

Yavuz Apart Otel (4), very friendly, well-run and carefully decorated place between the *dolmuş* station and the sea. 2 double rooms and 8 large, very clean and well equipped apartments, all with climate control, good bathrooms and balconies (half of which have sea views. Family atmosphere. Doubles £25 (no breakfast), apartments for up to 5 people from £50. ✆7123578, www.yavuzapart.com.

Esenada Otel (11), Datça's first hotel — now 60 years old — and not a lot has changed. A lovable quaint hovel with the simplest of rooms, where one shares baths and loos. Terraces and a court-

yard. Run by two friendly sisters, ideal for women on their own who don't need 'home comforts'. If no one is there, ask in the fabric shop next door. £6.50 per person. Near the amphitheatre, ☎ 7123014.

***Camping*: Ilıca Camping (20)** is a lovely campsite at the south end of (pebbly) Taşlık Beach. New sanitary facilities. They rent large bungalows with bath and small ones without. Nice bar. 2 people with camper van £15; bungalows for 2 with bath £50 (without £33). İskele Mah. ☎ 7123400, ilicacamping@hotmail.com.

***Outside*: Dede Garden Hotel**, in idyllic Eski Datça, signposted off the road to Datça. 6 different, colourful suites, each individually and lovingly equipped. Little pool with palm trees, café/bar, everything very well kept. Doubles £83. ☎/fax 7123951, www.dedegardenhotel.com.

Doğa Pansiyon, also in Eski Datça (signposted), a reader's tip just received. 10 very large clean rooms with kitchenette and fridge. Good breakfast. Doubles £39, ☎ 7122178, www.dogapansiyon.com.

Pigs Bay Camp, super-idyllic but totally spartan. 20 plain but nice bungalows with bath, somewhat set back off the beach. It's at the 'end of the world' — Domuzçukuru Bay, only accessible by boat or a three hour walk. Open May-Oct., but that could change (the place changes hands quite often!). Generator-powered electricity (solar energy planned), but there's always cold beer. Boat transfer three times a day from Hayıtbükü Bay. Bungalow with H/B £25 per person, treehouse £21. With your own tent £12.50. Domuzçukuru, ✆ 0535 3270241 or ✆ 0533 5701549 (both mobiles), www.pigsbaycamp.com.

Food and drink/Nightlife

(see plan above)

The bulk of the restaurants in Datça, including many small, reasonably priced *lokantas*, can be recommended. The prices throughout are around 20 to 30% lower than in Marmaris, and the service is 100% better.

Emek Restaurant (14), at the port. Excellent grills and fresh-caught fish, plus such a huge selection of *meze* that it's hard to choose. Lovely terrace. Good prices: *meze* from £1.70, mains £5-10. ✆ 7123375.

Culinarium (14), near Emek. German/Turkish management. The menu has a small but good choice of excellent Turkish/ Mediterranean fusion cuisine. Every dish is freshly prepared and makes a great change from kebabs and grilled fish. Good steaks. Well-spaced tables, delightful roof terrace with a hint of 'ship's deck' atmosphere. Mains £10.50-15. ✆ 7129770.

Yeşim Bar Restaurant (16), idyllic beach restaurant at Kargı Bay. Well-kept terrace, lovely garden. A nice place for an evening mean with the sound of the sea. Delightful breakfasts. Mid-range prices. ✆ 7128399.

Beyaz Amca (16), 'White Uncle' (the proprietor has white hair), at the port. Large choice of extra-ordinary fish dishes with extra-vagant sauces. Very tasty seafood pasta. Mains £5.50-13. ✆ 7122258.

Fevzi'nin Yeri (5), tiny, popular fish restaurant with a pretty terrace outside and fish net decorations inside. Small selection of *meze*, good fish. Middle price range. 70. Sok., ✆ 0535 9595419 (mobile).

Mocca (10), cosy bistro with terrace at the port, popular with both locals and tourists. German/Turkish management: Gabriele does the baking, Erdinç makes the pizzas and pastas.

Zekeriya Sofrası (9), a *lokanta* on İskele Cad. A couple of tables outside on the street and a couple more inside. You can check the casseroles and see what's cooking before you order. Tasty *köfte* too. Cheap and very popular. There's a similar choice next door at the **Korsan Restaurant (9)**.

Café Inn (8), little café with European 'city-style' décor and a nice terrace on the sea. Lavazza coffee — a welcome change from so much *neskafe!* İskele Cad., opposite Zekeriya Sofrası.

Nightlife is concentrated in a small area around the marina, where there are some nice bars. The top meeting places are the **Marin Bar (15)** and **Bambu Bar (15),** where you sit under trees and slurp stylishly presented cocktails. If you want to dance, go to the **Dance Club Gallus (17)** near the marina, on the road to Kargı Bay.

Beaches and diving

Datça has three public beaches: child-friendly **Kumluk Beach** north of the port, **Taşlık Beach** south of the port and **Hastane Altı** below the hospital.

The most beautiful beach within walking distance of Datça is **Kargı Bay** to the south. Up to 10 *dolmuşes* a day go there as well. Further south is beautiful **Armutlu Bay**; Walk 20 (page 161) describes these bays in more detail. But the most beautiful beaches around Datça are only accessible on boat trips or after a long walk. **Domuzçukuru Bay** (or 'Pigs Bay') is perhaps the loveliest, with a long sand and pebble beach. It's possible to stay overnight there; see page 153.

Diving: Datça Diving runs daily trips with two dives, equipment and lunch for £42. Information from the dive boat in the port or ☎ 0539 6598907 (mobile), www.datcadiving.com.

Practicalities A-Z

Boat trips: Of the various tours, one of the most popular is to Knidos (see 'Getting there' on page 158). In high season there are also sailings to various beaches on the Reşadiye Peninsula (prices £13-17 per person, including lunch). In the shoulder season there is little on offer, andprices depend on how many people book. One of the most extensive programs is offered by **Seher Tour** (at the port), ☎ 7122473, www.sehertour.com

Car ferries to Bodrum: From mid-Apr. to mid-Jun. and mid-Sep. to end Oct. there's a small car ferry on Mon./Wed./Fri. at 09.30 from Körmen Limanı (9km north Datça) to Bodrum. Returns from Bodrum at 09.30 on Tue./Thu./Sat. In summer this ferry runs twice a day (09.30, 17.30). The trip takes about 2 hours. Buses run from Datça to Körmen Limanı to coincide with departure times. Tickets cost £8.50 per person one way, inclusive of the bus to Körmen Limanı (reservations recommended). Car with driver costs £29 one way, each additional passenger £4.20. You can buy tickets in the **Datça Ferry Boat Office**, in an alley off İskele Cad., near the mosque. ☎ 7122143, www.datcaferryboat.com

Sailings to Symi and Rhodes: Some years there are regular timetabled sailings, other years it's impossible to get details. Usually the following holds true: In Jul./Aug. frequent connections to Symi (either daily or every other day); sometimes the ferry goes on to Rhodes. In Jun. and Sep. either irregular service or none at all. Tickets to Symi cost £21 one way, £42 return. Information from Seher Tour (see 'Boat trips' above).

Doctors: The local hospital is at the corner of Hastane Cad. and Çetiner Cad. Friendly Dr. Taner Karaman has a practice there. ☎ 7123082 or ☎ 0532 6950942 (mobile).

Car hire: Local firms like **Seher Tour** (see under 'Boat trips' above) charge from £33-38 per day. Sixt has an office far out of town, at the Knidos turn-off. Cheapest model £58 per day. Dörtyol Mevkii 190, ☎ 4440076, www.sixt.com.tr.

Events: The **Almond Festival**

usually takes place in the second half of August (**Datça Knidos Badem Festivalı**). — with rock and folklore concerts, dance performances, sporting competitions and even bullfights.
Launderette: **Laundry** (by the WCs at the marina, only busy in the evenings. Per machine £5.
Newspapers and magazines in English are available in **Çağlar Market (3)** on Atatürk Cad. near the *dolmuş* station.
Police: located in the centre on Atatürk Cad.; ☎ 155.
Post: also in the centre on Atatürk Cad.
Shopping: Compared with other holiday resorts, the choice is modest. Datça thyme honey and and some other kinds of honey are available at **Uğurlu Balları (7)** on İskele Cad. near the Ziraat Bankası. **Natural Active (8),** at İskele Cad. 43/B, is a lovely shop with natural products from Datça (soaps, olive oil, honey or sage tea). On Friday evenings there is a **fruit and vegetable market**; on Saturdays a large general **market** (both near the post office). A small selection of English books is stocked at **Civan (3)** at Dr. Turgut Dündar Cad. 12. There's a large **Migros Supermarket (1)** near the bus station.
Turkish bath (Hamam): **Belediye Hamamı**, simple, new bath set a bit back off Ambarcı Cad. Open daily 08.00-22.00. Entry and 'the works' £25.
Two-wheel hire: You can usually get a scooter from the car hire firms. **Eriman**, on Atatürk Cad., also has scooters from £17 a day. ☎ 7123206.
Yacht charter: One of Datça's largest charter agencies is **Knidos Turizm** at the port. ☎ 7129464, www.peri-tr.com. **Seher** (see above) also offers *gulet* trips, including last-minute bargains (if places are free) from £42 per person per day.

Ovabükü Bay

Bays around Datça

Hayıtbükü and Ovabükü: These two bays lie 13km west of Datça, below the scattered settlement of Mesudiye. **Ovabükü Bay**, the further west of the two, has a wonderful beach, behind which are a few simple guest houses. **Hayıtbükü**, a quiet bay east of Mesudiye, is a little reminiscent of the idyllic bays in the Greek islands and is becoming ever more popular with yachtsmen. There's a small beach, most inviting for a swim (can be quite full in summer). Many people only plan to spend the day here, then stay for a whole week. The two bays are connected by a narrow road.
Getting there: There is a dolmuş *connection in summer to/from Datça* *(see page 149).*

Accommodation/food and drink in Hayıtbükü Bay

Gabaklar Pansiyon, in Kızılbük, a small, palm-studded bay near Hayıtbükü Bay. 24 rooms, 12 of

Sunday afternoon bullfight on the Reşadiye Peninsula

them in spacious bungalows with modern plumbing, climate control, fridge and nice verandahs. Super-idyllic, with a lot of greenery and flowers, lovely restaurant. Walks organised. Doubles in bungalow £83, simpler versions in the main building £63. ☎/℻ 0252 7280171, www.gabaklar.com. (The web site is only in Turkish, but very well done with many photos.)

Altun Motel, at Hayıtbükü, one street back from the bay. 10 comfortable, small rooms with good baths, fridges, standard furniture and verandas. Unfortunately, no sea views. Helpful management. Doubles with H/B £63. ☎ 7280073, www.altun pansiyon.com.

Pansiyon & Restaurant Ortam, at Hayıtbükü Bay. Just behind the beach in two 100+-year-old Greek houses. In the main building (with restaurant) there are 4 small, plain rooms (2 with private bath, 2 with shared bath). In a neighbouring building 3 roomy, tastefully equipped rooms for 4 people, with fridges and comfortable baths. All guests can enjoy two lovely terraces and excellent meals (the speciality is octopus done many different ways). The hosts, Süleyman and Mahmut, take special care of their guests. One of our favourite places, open all year. Double without bath £22, with bath £30, rooms for 4 people £78. Hayıtbükü. ☎ 7280228, ℻ 7280091, www.ortamdatca.com.

Accommodation/camping/food and drink in Ovabükü Bay

Ada Pansiyon, 11 very clean, well-furnished rooms, 9 of them with balcony (some with nice sea views). Very tasty dinners in the restaurant on request. Welcoming family atmosphere. Terrace just behind the beach. Doubles £54. Just off the little coast road at the western end of the bay, on the beach. ☎ 7260102. www.adapansiyon.com.

If Ada is full, readers recommend trying the nearby **Bağevi Apart Otel** (www.bageviapart.com).

Hoppala Pansiyon, at Ovabükü Bay. Long-standing family-run place with lovely rooms, top-class baths and climate control. Nice garden. In the restaurant just behind the beach you can get Turkish home-cooking with vegetables from their own garden and home-made bread; the pension itself is 100m inland. Open all year. Doubles £50. Ovabükü. ☎ 7180148, ℻ 7280259, www.hoppala.com.tr.

Gülbahar Pansiyon & Camping, well-kept bungalows in a grove behind the beach; camping possible (but not if you have a really large vehicle). Bungalow for 2 people £50 per night; camping (depending on the size of tent or vehicle) £6.50-8.50. ☎ 7280029 or ☎ 0532 7328060 (mobile).

Palamutbükü: This bay lies 24km west of Datça on the south shore of the Reşadiye Peninsula. At the western end is a small fishing port with a handful of bars. There are usually a few yachts anchored here. The road has some restaurants and pensions. The beach changes to fine sand the further east you go. The settlement looks a bit makeshift, but not unpleasantly so. Since most trade comes from Turkish tourists, it's purgatory here from the end of June till the beginning of September, otherwise the place is dead (and prices fall). From Palamutbükü a little road goes east to Ovabükü Bay, past small sand and shingle beaches which are often deserted.

Getting there: There is a dolmuş *connection 8 times a day in summer to/from Datça; see page 149.*

Accommodation: There are over 20 places to stay, mostly simple narrow wooden bungalows. All those listed below are right behind the beach.

Otel Mavi Beyaz, the loveliest and most comfortable place; opened as a boutique hotel in 2010. Everything is blue/white, with a Greek flair (simple, but beautifully decorated, baths with lovely tiles, many rooms with balconies and fine sea views). Greenery in front, with cushions for lazing about. Restaurant, bar. Doubles from £83. At the far east end of the bay. ☎ 7255555, www.otelmavibeyaz.com

Bük Pansiyon, 34 tidy rooms, 4 of them in a new wooden building near the main building: roomy, good baths, generous balconies, fridges. Restaurant with terrace just behind the beach, where you could spend the whole week. Doubles £42-50. Near the Hotel Mavi Beyaz. ☎ 0546 2452786 (mobile).

Aylin Ahşap Evler, 18 rooms with baths divided between wooden bungalows and huts, all in a row behind the restaurant. Well-kept; opened in 2009. Doubles with H/B £70. Near Bük Pansiyon. ☎ 7255248, www.aylinahsapevler.com.

Food and drink: Dostlar Restaurant on the waterfront; good and economical. The beach is the 'terrace' here, where you enjoy *meze* or grilled octopus under shady trees. ☎ 7255092.

Jardin de Semra, with a lovely terrace. They also sell works of art. Dishes are shown on a blackboard. Mains £5-10.

Café Bük, at the western end of the bay by the port. Good snacks and terrific *mantı*. Friendly; family-run.

Knidos

Knidos, the ruined and only partly excavated site at the tip of the peninsula, attracts many visitors. While the ruins themselves are unspectacular, the combination of stony remains and wild landscape is really spellbinding. The ruined city is a beautiful destination for a trip and, after your visit, there is a small beach with crystal-clear water for a swim. The two ports at Knidos have been orphaned for two millennia. There's nothing stirring in the War Harbour these days (thankfully), but the commercial port is coming back to life, attracting boat trips and yachts.

An earlier place called Knidos, forerunner of today's Datça, was

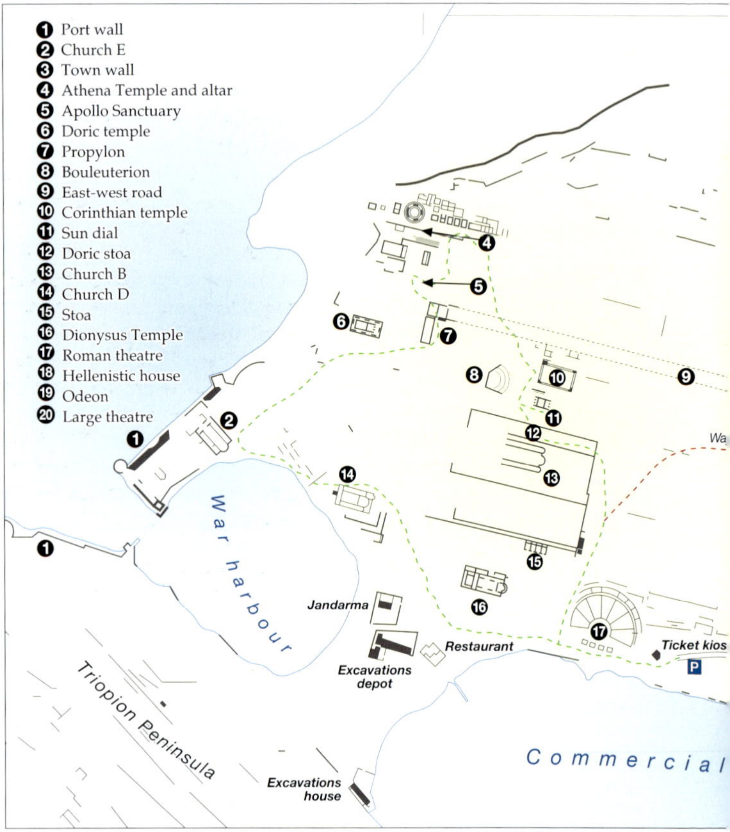

mentioned for the first time in the 7th century BC. Due to the increasing population, a new city of the same name was built in the 4th century BC on the western tip of the peninsula. This was laid out according to a Hippodamic grid (after the Greek architect Hippodamus), with right-angled roads. Inland, a 4km-long wall surrounded the city. For even greater protection from land-based aggressors, plans were made to close off the whole peninsula (it measures only 800m across at its narrowest point some 30km west of Marmaris). In its heyday the port city supported more than 70,000 inhabitants. Within its walls stood the Sanctuary of Apollo, the centre of the Dorian Hexapolis, where festivals were held every four years. Knidos was also known for its Asklepieion, one of the top four medical schools of the ancient world (the others were Pergamon, Kos and Epidauros). Knidos was a stronghold of science at the same time: the engineer Sostrates sketched out the Alexandria Lighthouse here, one of the Seven Wonders of the Ancient World. Art also blossomed in this wealthy city, although most of the works have

been lost over the course of centuries (some treasures are in foreign museums — the famous statue of Demeter, for example, is in the Louvre). The stability of the Hellenistic era allowed Knidos to flourish. St. Paul the Apostle stopped here on his journey to Rome, creating an early Christian community. Knidos was first investigated by English archaeologists at the beginning of the 19th century; the last excavations (2006) were carried out by the University of Konya Selçuk.

Getting there/opening times/prices: 35km west of Datça by road. Boat trips sail from Datça daily in summer at 10.00, stopping several times at bathing beaches; about £17 per person including lunch (in the shoulder season you can negotiate the price). Boats also sail here from Marmaris. By taxi it costs about £52 return from Datça (including two hours for a visit).

Two dolmuşes *a day from mid-Jun. to Sep.; depart Datça 10.30, 12.00; return 14.00, 17.00). Otherwise take a* dolmuş *to Yazıköy (3 a day at 12.00, 15.00, 17.00), from where you have to walk or hitch the rest of the way (almost 8km). In summer Knidos is open daily 08.00-19.30; in winter from 08.00-17.00; entry fee £3.50. There is a restaurant at the commercial port.*

Short walk round Knidos

(allow 1h30min)

From the car park, follow the path down to the bay and the one-time **commercial port**. When there was a northery wind, ships sailed in here from the Aegean; a southerly wind brought in those from the eastern Mediterranean. From here you have a marvellous view over the Triopion Peninsula (not to be confused with the Apollo Sanctuary called the Triopion, which was discovered during excavations near Emecik).

The path goes past a **small theatre**, known as the Roman theatre, which once offered seating for about 5000 people and is still in quite good condition. A short way west are the foundations of a **Dionysus Temple** which was later converted into a church — as were all the other temples in the city. Behind this, a few rebuilt columns catch the eye; they were once part of a **stoa**. Two officials in the *jandarma*

The two harbours at Knidos

station opposite make sure that no stones disappear!
On the way to the **war harbour** (which was once connected to the commercial port by a channel that could be closed with an iron chain if it came under threat), you come to **church D**; the floor of the middle apse was once covered with geometric two-tone mosaics. If you continue to follow the path along the bay, **church E** soon appears; it was also decorated with mosaics.
The path now heads uphill along the coast past the foundations of a **Doric temple**; its substructure was built using rose-coloured limestone. The **propylaeum**, which also forms the entrance hall to the **Apollo Sanctuary** on the hill, is a bit further east. To the north is an altar with a base of grey-blue marble. The steps where the spectators sat to watch the rituals are still visible.
If you go further uphill to the next terrace, you come to the impressive round base of the **Athena Temple**. It was long thought that this temple was dedicated to Aphrodite and housed the famous statue by Praxiteles (350 BC), one of the most famous sculptures of the ancient world. Praxiteles had the courage to model the Goddess of Love unclothed for the first time. Originally this monumental work was to be installed on Kos. But the conservative island did not want the statue, and so Aphrodite came to Knidos, where she was venerated as Goddess of the Sea and protectress of sailors. It is said that because of the naked Aphrodite, the Asklepieion of Knidos attracted more visitors during the following period than Kos. Where the temple actually stood is still in dispute.
From here the path leads gently downhill away from the coast. Just before the main road, a sign points the way to the **Demeter Sanctuary** and the **acropolis**. If you make this tiring climb, you will be rewarded with spectacular panoramic views and will pass the fairly unspectacular **large theatre**.
If you instead follow the path further downhill, you come to a heap of rubble that was once a **Corinthian temple** from the 2nd century, behind which (on the sea side) is a Hellenistic **sundial**. To the west of the temple was the **bouleuterion**. Continue further downhill and you reach the remains of the 114m-long **Doric stoa**, as well as **church B** with its three apses and figurative floor mosaics. Once past the small theatre, you arrive back at the commercial port. Before finishing your circuit of Knidos, don't miss the remains of the nearby **odeon** — below the access road, about 300m west of the town wall. It was built in the 3rd century BC and used for smaller events.

Time: 4h
Grade: easy-moderate; the roads and footpaths are generally good underfoot, except on the section just beyond Kargı Beach (where you must be sure-footed and have a head for heights).
Equipment: see pages 21-22.
Travel: coach from Marmaris to Datça, regular departures, journey time 1h30min. See plan on page 152: the coach stops at the bus station *(otogar)* on the outskirts of Datça, where a *dolmuş* connects with the centre. Return the same way.
Short walk: Kargı — Armutlu — Kargı (1h40min; easy, but you must be sure-footed and have a head for heights on one short stretch at the outset). Access by *dolmuş:* up to 10 times daily from Datça. Follow the main walk from Kargı Beach to Armutlu and return the same way.

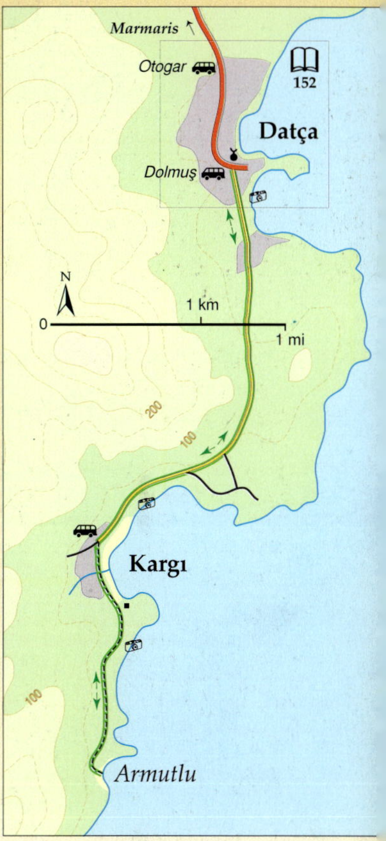

Datça is a delightful coastal village west of Marmaris, about halfway along the Reşadiye Peninsula. It's very picturesque, so you are sure to leave with some treasured photographs. But it is quite small — too small to keep you occupied for a full day. This walk has been designed to fill the time, to make the whole day a more enjoyable experience. It explores the region to the south of Datça, largely following the coastline, and it visits two lovely bays. Kargı is the first and the larger, where some of you might be content to spend the whole day. However, the second bay, Armutlu, has the intimate charm of seclusion and is well worth the extra effort to get there — even if you just do the Short walk.

Start the walk at the *dolmuş* station in **Datça**, near the harbour. Turn up the road on the right, opposite the mosque (Kargı Cad.). It quickly leads away from the village into countryside and gives some of the best photographic viewpoints back towards Datça. In about 20 minutes the road leads away from the shore and cuts across the headland towards Kargı.

It is hard to believe that the surrounding countryside, seemingly arid and shrubby, could hide a wealth of interesting spring flowers but, if you keep your eyes to the right, you could expect to see a number of bee orchids — including the yellow

On the way to Armutlu Bay

bee orchid, *Ophrys lutea ssp galilaea* and the sombre bee orchid, *O fusca*. The small yellow *Gagea* species are everywhere and add plenty of ground colour, but look twice if you see a red anemone, for it may really be the red turban buttercup. They are similar in size and colour, so the only way to be certain is to inspect beneath the flower, to see if there are green sepals immediately below the petals; if so it is the buttercup, *Ranunculus asiaticus*. It has limited distribution, with the yellow and white forms only growing on Crete and the red form on Rhodes — and now near Datça.

The road crests the hill and, as you begin your descent to Kargı, the bay spreads out before you like a map. Follow the road beside the shingle beach and the sparkling sea. Kargı is still little more than a farming community enjoying a very fine location beside this enchanting bay, but it is surely destined for a greater role in tourism. Leave the road/track when it swings away from the shore and continue along the shingle beach, crossing a small stream on a **plank bridge**. Pass **Kargı Restaurant (1h10min)** and continue to the end of the beach. Then follow the path around to the right, by the wall, and head inland. As you pass a small building on the left in about a minute, turn left, and then diagonally right, to climb a small hill, heading for the centre of the saddle.

Crossing the **saddle**, you descend a well-defined path leading through a boulder-strewn area, just above the sea. The path becomes a little obscure as you cross an area of bedrock, but head upwards to find a clear path. Again, a minute or two later, you must climb a little to continue along the path. *Care is needed* where the path narrows on the steep-sided bank, and some walkers may find this section unnerving.

The path meanders around the coastline, giving fine views — especially as you approach a cove. The next cove looks particularly inviting, with the ultramarine sea lapping the shingle beach, and the path leads down to it. This is **Armutlu (2h)**, a delightful place to relax — either in the sun or under the shade of the nearby trees.

From here return the same way to **Datça (4h)**.

7 EXCURSION TO PAMUKKALE AND HIERAPOLIS

History • Accommodation/camping, food and drink, nightlife • Sights * Hierapolis

Area code: ☎ 0258
Information: The Tourist Office is at the southern entrance to the travertines. Information in English. Open daily 08.30-12.00 and 13.30-17.30 (in winter 08.00-12.00 and 13.00-17.00). ☎ 2722077, www.pamukkale. gov.tr.
Connections: There are few ***dolmuş*/bus** connections to/from Pamukkale Köy. Long-distance buses usually stop at Denizli bus station, from where you can catch a *dolmuş* to Pamukkale Köy every 20 min. between 07.00 and 19.00 (then hourly till 22.00). Various large bus companies — like Metro, Kamil Koç and Pamukkale (with booking offices in Pamukkale Köy) also offer transfers to Pamukkale. From Denizli there are good bus connections to all the main tourist resorts in the area (for instance Selçuk, 2 hours or Marmaris, 4 hours).
Opening times/Entry fees: The **travertines** are open round the clock, the **Hierapolis Museum** is open daily in summer (except Mon.) from 09.00-19.00, in winter from 08.00-17.00. An entry fee of £8.50 covers both the travertines and Hierapolis, but the museum costs £1.25 extra.
Organised tours: In Pamukkale Köy you can book a day trip to Aphrodisias or other attractions in the area for about £11 (excluding entry fee).
Access to the travertines and Hierapolis: The area has three entrances. One is at the foot of the travertines by Pamukkale Köy (small parking area). From here you climb on foot up to the plateau and the Hierapolis site (mostly on a road through the terraces). Or you can drive up. At the top there are two entrances: the southern entrance, about 250m from the terraces, and the northern entrance, near the road to Karahayıt — about 1200m from the travertines. On the way from the northern entrance to the travertines you pass the impressive necropolis. From the northern entrance there is a free shuttle service to the travertines; from the southern entrance it costs £2.50 (including parking). *Dolmuşes* run from Pamukkale Köy to the northern entrance every 15 min. from 08.00-19.00.

Be aware before you go: if you expect to be able to bathe in the beautiful turquoise waters of the travertine terraces you are going to be disappointed. Bathing has long been forbidden, and today you have to enjoy this tourist magnet by walking single file behind coachloads of other visitors. A visit to the ancient site of Hierapolis above the terraces is some compensation…

The emergence of these unusual white lime travertines is based on a simple chemical reaction. A hot spring (53°C) contains large quantities of dissolved calcium bicarbonate. When it cools on the surface, it is converted into water, carbon dioxide and calcium carbonate (lime). The carbon dioxide escapes, while the travertine lime is deposited and clogs the drainage canals for the water. The water then overflows and spreads fan-like over the slopes, thus forming the white travertine terraces — enormous, graduated basins like oversized bath tubs, one above the other. From below, with a little imagination, the 120m-high incline resembles a large frozen waterfall.

Directly below the travertine terraces is Pamukkale Köy, a settlement consisting of guest houses, hotels, restaurants and bars, frequented by individual travellers. Karahayıt, a few kilometres north of the terraces, is where the bus groups stay in large hotels and the more conservative spa guests in simple pensions. The next nearest city is Denizli with some 480,000 inhabitants — a lively, provincial centre 18km south of Pamukkale, usually covered in smog. It's of no real interest for tourists, since all its historical buildings have been destroyed by earthquakes.

History

For thousands of years, the inhabitants from the surrounding area knew about and appreciated the healing properties of the Pamukkale spring.

The Hittites and Phrygians established altars here, while the Pergamon King Eumenes II founded the city of Hierapolis here, as a countermeasure to the nearby Macedonian city of Laodikeia (the meagre ruins of which are signposted off the Pamukkale/Denizli road). The rivalry between the two cities, whose wealth was based on the wool trade, was so great that they hindered each other's development. Only after integration into the Roman province of Asia did Hierapolis attain greater importance. In the year 60 AD the city was destroyed by an earthquake, but was rebuilt shortly afterwards. From its early years it had a strong Christian community, and during the Byzantine era it even became a bishopric. Following an invasion by the Seljuks, the city was deserted. Carl Human, the discoverer of Pergamon, undertook the first excavations in 1887. Since 1957, systematic work has been carried out by Italian archaeologists in particular.

The travertines at Pamukkale

Accommodation/camping, food and drink

The infrastructure at **Pamukkale Köy** is primarily geared to individual travellers. At one time there were over 100 places to stay, but the decline of the travertine terraces (see panel overleaf) also meant the end for many guest houses. Even though the condition of the travertines is improving again, many places are fighting for survival. The money for renovations is lacking, no matter how urgent the need. The accommodation described below offers you a good choice, although some places can be hard to find, since touting is not as pronounced as elsewhere in Turkey. Nearly every guest house has a channel bringing water from the springs into its own pool. The more luxurious places to stay are on the north side of the Hierapolis ruins, at the edge of **Karahayıt**; sometimes they offr large discounts.

Accommodation in Karahayıt: Spa Hotel Colossae, a five-star hotel; classic hotel rooms with balconies. 'Wellness centre', thermal treatments, several restaurants, large choice of sports. Singles £115, doubles £135. ✆ 2714156, ℻ 2714250, www.colossaehotel.com.

Accommodation in Pamukkale Köy: Venüs Hotel, 14 well-kept, high-class rooms, nicely furnished, with flat screen TV and climate control (some with

Once upon a time, there was a white ...

Pamukkale is usually translated as 'cotton castle', but this is not strictly correct. Pamuk, the Turkish word for cotton, is used in this context as a synonym for 'white' (just as 'snow' in 'snow-white' might be). So Pamukkale (kale = castle) would be better translated as 'cotton-white castle'.

But today you would look in vain for the wonderful Pamukkale white on the terraces — even though it is referred to in tourist brochures as often as Bordeaux red! For decades this natural phenomenon was subject to thoughtless commercial exploitation. Hundreds of thousands of visitors were coached in along a purpose-built road which went right through the centre (today this has been replaced by two new approach roads) and these visitors were then allowed — without taking off their shoes — to trample across this splendid 'white'.

Even more devastating was the construction of luxury hotels on the plateau directly above the terraces, which fed their pools with the hot spring water. Too much precious liquid was taken in this way, so that no more lime was deposited on the terraces. Eventually word got out that Pamukkale was no longer 'worth a visit', since the radiant white had been replaced by a dirty grey. Even then, it took washing-baskets full of letters protesting the situation and pressure from international environmental protection organisations before the authorities began to act. In the year 2000 the last hotel above the terraces was razed to the ground — and now the few modern foundations are mixed with those from antiquity. The entire area has become a UNESCO World Heritage Site. The condition of the travertine terraces has improved substantially since then.

balconies and tiled floors). Restaurant, pool, nice oriental. nooks in the lobby. Pool. Recommended by readers year after year. Doubles £25. ☎ 2722152, www.venushotel.net.

Pansiyon Beyaz Kale, the 'White Castle', with 11 spotless rooms, great bathrooms, climate control and colourful walls arranged round a cosy pool area. Readers have praised the good cooking and the warm-hearted owners for years. Singles £15, doubles £25. ☎ 2722064, 📠 2722568, www.beyazkale pension.com.

Hotel Pamukkale, tidy, clean rooms with climate control and carpeted floors. Pool. Nice roof terrace, own restaurant (good quality and choice). Family atmosphere. Camping in the grounds. Doubles £25; camping for 2 people £12.50. ☎ 2722090, www.hotelpamukkale.net.

Dört Mevsim Hotel, a small hotel with a nice pool area in the garden. Simple, clean rooms — friendly atmosphere. Camping in the grounds. Doubles £17. Hasan Tahsin Cad. 25, ☎ 2722009, www.hoteldortmevsim. com.

Camping: Many pensions welcome campers, including:

Seyir Camping, on the through road from Pamukkale Köy (at the exit towards Karahayıt). Huge restaurant attached, catering for

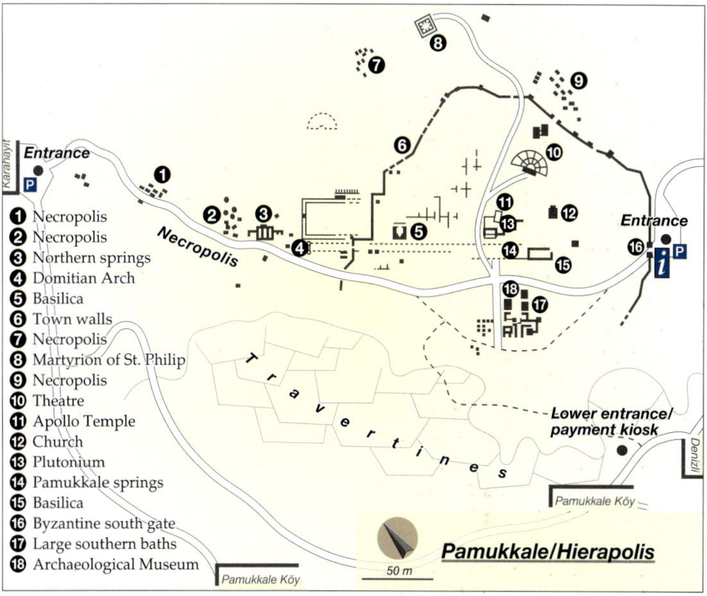

coach tours. Nice green area in front of a pool (but no shade). So not idyllic, but well kept and okay. Open all year. 2 people with caravan £12.50. M. Akif Ersoy Bul., ✆ 2722471, ✆ 2722155. **Tepe Camping**, some 7km from Pamukkale Köy, on a hill with far-reaching views. You can pitch a tent on the grass in front of the pool; caravans park on a terraced slope above. Okay sanitary facilities (2 showers and loos). But the place could be better kept. They also rent musty-smelling rooms. 2 people with camper van £8.50. On the way to the southern entrance to the travertines, signposted. ✆ 2653973, www.tepecamping.com.

Food and drink: The fact that most visitors only come to Pamukkale once in a lifetime and then mostly by coach and for only two-three hours, doesn't help the catering trade. Annoying touts, sluggish service, small portions, high prices, and food prepared quickly and on the cheap complete the picture. You're best off eating in the pensions and hotels.

Sights

The travertine terraces are *the* sight. They totally cover a slope 100m high and over 2km wide. The spring is as vigorous as ever, and someone is employed to divert the water along the broad channels, so that the central terraces slowly regain their 'cotton-white' appearance. In summer each terrace is flushed once a week, in winter every 20 days. The water is then collected at the bottom of the slope, and supplied first to the guest houses and afterwards to the fields on the plain. Some basins are lit at night. Whether during the day or at night, *before walking over the*

terraces you must remove your shoes! But you are allowed to paddle in the attractive pools alongside the main path.

Pamukkale baths: Since bathing in the travertine terraces is now a thing of the past, a bath in the Pamukkale hot spring is today's alternative. The main spring lies in the open inner courtyard of the former Pamukkale Motel. It feeds a beautiful pool studded with palms and ancient columns — hence the name 'Antique Pool'. Bathing in this warm 35°C water is a really pleasant experience — as long as you're not alongside a coachload of tourists (which, unfortunately, is usually the case). The water allegedly helps with stomach ulcers, bronchitis, heart and circulation complaints, intestinal disorders, and much more besides…

Opening times/prices: open daily from 08.00-19.00 (in winter until 17.00); entry £10.50, children £4.20.

Above: bathing in a spring-fed pool; below: a corner of the huge necropolis at Hierapolis

Hierapolis

Almost everything of interest lies scattered over the plateau above

the travertines. The ruins of the **large baths** lie just off the road to the hot spring and are impossible to miss. Their massive arches were once faced with marble. Today the building accommodates the small, but beautiful and quite interesting **archaeological museum**, which contains finds from Hierapolis and Laodikeia, particularly richly ornamented sarcophagi, statues and reliefs.

Apollo Temple and Plutonium: In A 2.5m-high platform with a small staircase, as well as some sections of capitals scattered among the ruins, allow you to mentally rebuild the Apollo Temple (around which excavations were taking place in 2010). In front of it lie the imposing ruins of what used to be an enormous fountain area built from large rectangular blocks. A few steps further on you come to the Plutonium, a grotto dedicated to Pluto, God of the Underworld. This is where the spring originally gushed forth. Poisonous gases contaminated the large entrance hall, and unauthorised intruders (like birds and even oxen) died. Only the priests could enter unharmed: they crept along the ground holding their breath. The grotto is largely buried, only a chamber with an arch above the door remains. The entrance (recognisable from its arched doorway) is blocked, since sulfurous gases are still leaking out.

Theatre: The almost completely excavated theatre (2nd century BC) is still in relatively good condition. With sides measuring over 100m in length, 20 rows of seats in the first tier, 25 rows in the second, and eight staircases, it seated up to 10,000. Marble friezes and statues by the carefully restored fly tower give an impression of the former splendour.

Martyrion of St. Philip: St. Philip's mausoleum (signposted as 'San Filip Kilisesi') lies 600m north of the theatre. The grave has never been found, so it is not clear whether the saint was really buried here. This most unusual building was constructed at the beginning of the 5th century and destroyed less than one hundred years later by an earthquake. Sections of the walls are still head-height, while the square layout is also visible. Adjacent to the outside walls are eight rectangular chambers, which are only accessible from the outside, and thought to be lodgings for pilgrims. There's no sign of an altar, but the semicircular seating for the bishop and community elders is still recognisable.

Necropolis: If you walk along the main street of Hierapolis from the Pamukkale baths, you first pass the foundation walls of a **basilica**, then a **Byzantine city gate** and a **colonnade** dating from the reign of Domitian which terminates at an arch dedicated to him. Once you reach the **northern baths**, which were converted into an enormous **basilica** during the 5th century, you are at the **necropolis**, the largest ancient graveyard in Anatolia, extending for some 2km, with more than 1200 tombs from different epochs — temple tombs, circular barrows which were once crowned with phallic-shaped stones, sarcophagi, etc. … some lying half-sunken in the travertine lime.

8 EXCURSION TO APHRODISIAS

History • Accommodation, food and drink • Circuit of the site

Area code: ☎ 0256

Connections: Organised tours to Aphrodisias are often coupled with a visit to Pamukkale. In addition, travel agencies in Pamukkale offer day trips to Aphrodisias.

If you are going by **private transport**, coming from Aydın turn right towards Karacasu about 16km past Nazilli. From Karacasu the way is signposted (it's another 38km). There's a large car park on the main road just before the site. Transfer from there to the site is included in the parking fee (£3).

There are good **bus** connections from Selçuk (1h30min) and Pamukkale (1h30min) to Nazilli, from where you can take a *dolmuş* to Karacasu. In summer there are hourly *dolmuşes* every day from Karacasu to Aphrodisias in summer (fewer in winter).

Opening times: The site and museum are open daily from 08.30-19.00 in summer, 08.00-17.30 in winter. Entry fee £3.50.

'Imagine arriving in a city so rich in archaeological treasures that sculptures roll in front of your feet, and marble heads fall from the walls or lie one on top of the other in the irrigation channels!' Thus enthused the Turkish archaeologist Kenan T. Erim in the *National Geographic* magazine, having made research into Aphrodisias his life's work (he died in 1990). Another time he is quoted at having answered the question 'Why did you never marry?' with 'Marry? Me? I am married. Where would I find a better wife than Aphrodite?'

Aphrodisias was one of the main centres of the Aphrodite cult. The Goddess of Love, Beauty and Seduction left her mark on the city. The cult and its followers often arranged raucous festivities for visitors who came to Aphrodisias from all over the ancient world. The goddess was eventually dispelled by the Christian God, and purged from the city.

The ruins at Aphrodisias are somewhat less spectacular than those at Ephesus, but you can enjoy them without the crowds. Moreover, its location in the middle of a plateau is far more pleasant to the eye. The most beautiful time to visit is in spring, when the flowers bloom between the ancient monuments, and the surrounding mountain peaks are still covered in snow.

History

The nearby Maeander River with its fertile valley was already attracting human beings in distant past. The first traces of a stable settlement at Aphrodisias date from the 7th century BC. At that time it was a small Assyrian town called Ninoe.

In the 2nd century BC Ninoe was renamed Aphrodisias by decree of the Roman Empire. The Roman dictator Sulla, on the advice of the Oracle in Delphi, paid homage to the Greek Goddess of Love, whom the Romans revered as Venus. From

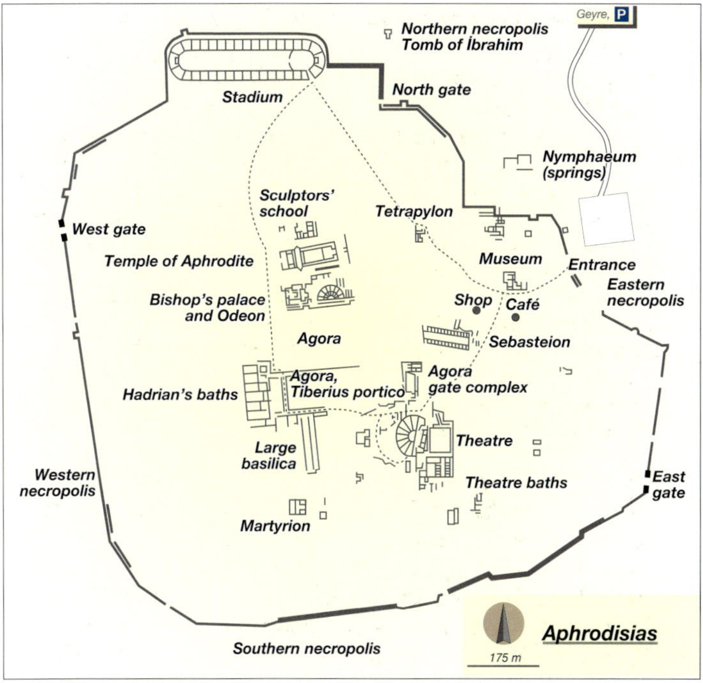

this time Aphrodisias flourished, experiencing its heyday between the 1st century BC and the 3rd century AD. The city was granted many privileges, was independent, and was considered so holy that it didn't even need a city wall until the 4th century AD. But it was not only the cult of Aphrodite that made the city famous during late antiquity: literary and scientific work also made important contributions, while the fame of the local school of sculpture spread throughout the Empire. The raw material, marble of the finest quality from a nearby quarry, was masterfully worked and exported. Sculptures from Aphrodisias adorned Olympia in Greece and Leptis Magna on the North African coast, as well as many places in Rome. The Aphrodisian sculptors successfully relied upon the city's good reputation, replacing their first names with the ethnic adjective 'Aphrodisieus'.

The splitting of the Roman Empire brought about the fall of Aphrodisias. Under Byzantine rule, the city became a bishopric. In the 7th century the Christians tried to whitewash over the pagan past and baptised the city Stauropolis ('City of the Cross'); later it was called Karia, then Geyre. With the Seljuk conquests of the 11th and 13th centuries, the small town, already in a pitiful state due to earthquakes, sank into obscurity.

Accommodation

It's best to plan your trip so that you will *not* have to stay

overnight here. Below is one place for the stranded!
Aphrodisias Hotel, the best choice (which isn't saying much). 25 spartan, down-at-heel rooms with outdated equipment and a creepy atmosphere. Restaurant (in the garden in summer). Double rooms H/B £42. Camping possible. Near Geyre on the main road. ☎ 4488132, 📠 4488422.

Circuit of the site

From the entrance the walkway runs past sarcophagi straight to the museum, which is usually visited last. Around the area in front of the museum (with a statue of lions in the middle) there are further sarcophagi, with parts of the frieze from the Tiberius Portico laid out among them. The usual tour runs anti-clockwise, so from the museum head right. Visitors are asked to stick to the designated paths.
Tetrapylon: This is probably part of a large ceremonial gate from the 2nd century, which would have been accessible from all four sides. The gate consisted of four rows of four columns, which have been rebuilt as far as possible, including the timber-work. The artful spiral fluting of the columns deserves special mention — a masterful piece of work by the local stonemasons. The gate was possibly the entrance to the holy groves around the Aphrodite Temple, whose columns can be seen to the left in the background.
Stadium: This is considered the best-preserved ancient stadium in the whole Mediterranean area and is also the most impressive monument in Aphrodisias. With a capacity of 30,000, it could compete with many Premier League stadiums today. The site is 262m long and 59m wide, with semicircular ends, so that all the spectators had a good view. The entrance tunnel, through which the sportsmen came into the stadium, is also completely

---

The excavations at Aphrodisias

The ruins lie within and around the old village of Geyre, whose inhabitants were resettled in the 1960s, as they stood in the way of the excavations. The first dig — plundering would be a better word — was undertaken in 1904 by the French railway engineer and hobby archaeologist Paul Gaudin. Some of the finds ended up in the museum at Istanbul, others somehow made their way to Boston, Brussels, Berlin and other far-flung corners of the world.
In 1937 excavations were made by Italian archaeologists. Pieces of the most magnificent find — the frieze of the Tiberius Portico decorated with almost life-like faces — are in the museum garden at Aphrodisias and the Archaeological Museum in İzmir.
Starting from 1961, Aphrodisias was researched systematically by a Turkish-American team under Kenan T. Erim. They rebuilt a few columns every year and heaved the fallen capitals back into their original positions. The tomb of the famous archaeologist lies next to the rebuilt tetrapylon. The excavations are continuing today with an international group under the direction of New York University.

intact. The emperor would have taken his place in a box in the centre on the northern side. The holes in the rows of seat held poles supporting canopies to protect the crowd from the sun. Originally a circle of columns towered above the top of the stadium. Mainly athletic games, gladiatorial fights, as well as wrestling and boxing matches took place in the arena.

Temple of Aphrodite: Only 14 columns and the front wall of the cella from the famous Aphrodite Temple (signposted as 'Tapınak') are still standing today. Originally 13 columns ran the length of the cella on either side and eight columns the width. The building was torn down during the Byzantine era, and a Christian church built in its place; only the surrounding colonnade was left untouched. Excavations brought several finds to light, indicating an even earlier sanctuary. North of the temple — appropriately — are the rubble remains of what in antiquity was the sculptors' school.

Bishop's palace and odeon: Southwest of the Aphrodite Temple are the remains of what is called the bishop's palace, a stately house with impressive bluish marble columns. The odeon, still in good condition, was built over the southeast end of the palace in the 2nd century AD. Surviving from the original roofed building are the bottom **nine rows of seats** (the upper rows were made of wood), with lions' feet as a symbol of power, the **orchestra** and the narrow **stage**. The marble facing, mosaic floor and many sculptures from the odeon are in the museum.

Northern agora: The city's double agora stretches out to the south of the odeon and bishop's palace — two arcaded squares which formed the administrative and commercial centre of Aphrodisias. Excavation of the 202 x 72m large northern agora has so far been only rudimentary; the archaeologists' most recent discovery has been a fountain and the foundations of a possible altar. Coin finds indicate that trade continued here until the 7th century.

Hadrian's baths: The baths are typical of Roman public baths, with a large cold-water bath, warm- and hot-water areas, as well as a sauna. The two marble basins of the **caldarium** (hot-water bath) are worth a mention.

Southern agora: This square measures 212 x 69m and because of the surrounding Tiberius Portico is also known as the Tiberius Agora. **Diocletian's well-known price edict** was discovered on its western side: with inflation in the empire rocketing, the emperor had tried unsuccessfully to get it under control by publicly posting lists with fixed prices everywhere in the realm. After an earthquake in the 4th century, the gateway to the agora was converted into a **nymphaeum**, which, much to the citizens' annoyance, would flood the agora again and again.

Theatre: The hill against which the theatre nestles is a *höyük,* an enormous heap of debris formed by age-old rubble from settlements dating back as far as 5800 BC. Of the theatre (1st century BC) only the **rows of seats** are almost completely intact; the fly tower is in worse condition. Originally Hellenic, the theatre was rebuilt several times by the Romans. The **auditorium**, with its marble seats, was to a large extent dug into the slope. The semicircular **orchestra** was deepened under Markus Aurelius and the lower rows of seats were removed, so that fights between gladiators and animals could be staged without endangering the spectators. After such fights, the orchestra could be flooded with ditch-water and cleaned. By the stage there was also an entrance tunnel, in which the hunters and hunted waited to appear. Only the lower part of the auditorium and half a row of columns have been rebuilt.

***Tetrastoon and theatre baths*:** After an earthquake in the 4th century, the agora was constantly flooded, so the Aphrodisians built a new market by the theatre. This was surrounded on all four sides by a portico *(tetrastoon)* and connected on the south side to an older, basilica-like hall. On its western side are the theatre baths, which were used up until the Byzantine era. In the middle, still in good condition, is the circular, nearly 10m-high **caldarium** (steam room).

***Sebasteion*:** Named after Sebastos, the Greek equivalent of the Latin Augustus, this once stood at the eastern end of the northern agora; today it's hidden behind the excavation building on the way to the museum. It was used to pay homage to emperors of the Julian-Claudian dynasty from Augustus to Nero. The complex was dominated by two 80m-long rows of three-storey columns along the two longer sides, with an processional avenue between leading to the temple (of which little remains). On our last visit the porticos were being rebuilt. There were once reliefs between the columns on the middle and upper storeys of the south gate; they've made copies for the reconstruction (you will see the sensational originals later in the museum). On the middle floor there were mostly mythological motifs, on the upper floor the emperors. Few reliefs remained from the north portico — on the middle floor there are some depicting subjugated peoples, on the upper floor gods. In the 4th century, when Christianity won the upper hand, this 'cult' hall was converted into an early 'shopping mall'.

***Museum*:** Everywhere you look, it becomes clear that Aphrodisias's fame was not based solely on its sculptors' school. The museum consists of two wings — the old (front) wing and the new one behind, the **Sebasteion Hall**. In the front wing there are mostly busts and statues of various emperors, princes, philosophers, muses and gods, as well as many important citizens and governors. In a hallway there is a relief from the 1st century BC honouring a citizen called Zoilos, who rose from being a prisoner to become a benefactor of the state (donating the theatre's fly tower among other things). The Sebasteion Hall displays the stupendous original reliefs from the Sebasteion — there are about 80, all restored. The only object not from the Sebasteionis a marble sculpture of a galloping horse, a one-off ancient find.

9 EXCURSION TO EPHESUS

History • Circuit of the site • Sights around Ephesus

Area code: ☎ 0232 (Selçuk)
Connections/accommodation: Ephesus is a popular destination for organised tours from both Bodrum and Marmaris. Independent travellers visiting the area usually stay at Selçuk (3km from Ephesus; accessible by **bus** or **train**), a town outside the scope of this guide.
Opening times/prices: The site is open daily from 08.00-18.30 (16.00 in winter); entry £8.50. A visit to the hillside houses costs another £6.50 (tickets at the entrance to the houses); parking costs £2.20 extra as well.
Tip: Ephesus has two entrances, a lower one (accessible from Selçuk via the Pamucak/Kuşadası road), and an upper one (off the road to Meryemana). The upper entrance is considered the 'main' one, simply because most coach tours start there and then collect their groups from the lower entrance. Taxis from Selçuk also aim for the upper entrance— it's further away, so they can charge more! Our tour begins from the *lower* entrance: it's easier to reach if you don't have a car (although it also has better parking): from Selçuk either take a *dolmuş* or go the 3km on foot (past the Artemis Temple). At the lower entrance you may well be greeted with an offer of free transport back from the top, 'to save you having to walk back' (only 15 minutes). Or you may be offered free transport to the top immediately, so you can 'visit the site in the correct order'. *It's all a con:* a relative of this Good Samaritan owns a carpet shop.

Ephesus was a famous city when Athens was still a provincial town and Rome hadn't even been founded. In its heyday the inhabitants of this metropolis numbered a quarter of a million — an almost inconceivable number, given living conditions at that time. Today Ephesus is one of the world's most fascinating ancient sites.

Ephesus was the richest city in Asia Minor and known as the 'bank of Asia'. Its large port was the gateway to the treasures of Anatolia and Persia. But the city didn't only rely on business: Ephesus was the centre of the Artemis cult and was thus an important place of pilgrimage. The Artemision, the enormous Artemis Temple, was ranked among the Seven Wonders of the Ancient World.
Fame and wealth are, however, transitory. The port silted up, and the city declined. Only excavations between 1866 and 1922 brought Ephesus back to life. Few sites in the world offer such an intact city, and in peak times up to 15,000 visit every day.

History

The existence of a settlement in the area goes back to 2000 BC. During that period, the Lelegians established themselves on the hill of the Selçuk citadel, where there was also a sanctuary to the fertility goddess Kybele.
In the 11th century BC, Ionic settlers laid the foundation stone for the city of Ephesus. Their leader was Androklos, who had

asked the Oracle at Delphi where the new city was to be based. The answer read: 'A fish and a wild boar will indicate the place'. Equipped with these instructions, the settlers set off. One day, as they tried to cook a not-quite-dead fish over the fire, it jumped from the grill and, knocking the coals, set some shrubs on fire, out of which jumped a wild boar. The boar took off and only came to a halt at the delta of the now dried-up **Kaystro River**. Here the settlers established their city — at least, so the legend goes.

Ephesus developed quickly into a substantial city due to its port and its favourable location. The Greek cult of Artemis merged with the archaic worship of Kybele into the Ephesian variant of Artemis worship, which found its visible expression in an enormous Artemis Temple: work on it began in the 6th century BC, and it took more than 200 years to complete.

Around 550 BC the city came under attack from the Lydian King, Croesus. Rather than defend themselves, the inhabitants encircled the temples and city with a rope, in order to put themselves symbolically under the protection of the gods. Croesus was impressed: he preserved the unfinished temple and only plundered the city. But scarcely 200 years later the temple was destroyed anyway: in 356 BC Herostratos set fire to the finished building in order to immortalise his name (which he obviously succeeded in doing). When Alexander the Great offered in 334 BC to take on all rebuilding costs for the huge temple, the proud Ephesians rejected the offer. They financed the splendid reconstruction themselves and enlarged the temple asylums, in which the use of force was forbidden. Thus the costs of the temple were soon amortised — rich outlaws found sanctuary here and thanked the goddess with their generous donations.

Artemis of Ephesus

It is thought that starting from 294 BC Lysimachos, one of Alexander the Great's generals and ruler of Pergamon, moved the city, which up until then only extended around the Artemis Temple, to today's location. A new port was dug and the city was surrounded by a 9km-long fortified wall.

In 133 BC Ephesus fell to the Romans and soon thereafter became the capital of the province of Asia. But for a long time Rome was more the inhabitants' enemy than friend, due to the high tax demands. And in 88 BC Ephesus was involved in Mithridates of Pontus's revolt against Roman rule: during the so-called 'Ephesian Vespers', 80,000 traders, tax collectors, and other

Roman citizens were killed throughout Asia Minor. The city nevertheless flourished under Roman rule, becoming a metropolis with more than 250,000 inhabitants. Most excavated sights and objects of interest date from this time.

The visit of St. Paul the Apostle, who stayed here in 55-58 AD on his second missionary journey, also came during the time of Roman rule. Paul's lectures had such an effect that the long-established icon-vendors could hardly sell another Artemis. Thereupon a silversmith called Demetrios mobilised the mob against the Christians: gathered in the theatre, they gave voice to the much-quoted saying 'Great is Artemis of the Ephesians!' After the first tumults Paul left the city. Another apostle who is said to have worked in Ephesus was St. John the Evangelist.

In 262 AD the city and temple were destroyed by the Goths, and the following reconstruction was slow. The port silted up, and other commercial centres surpassed Ephesus in rank. In the 7th century they gave up the settlement on the plain and withdrew to the nearby citadel hill (Selçuk). Here, under the protection of the small Christian town of **Hagios Theologos**, the Ephesians survived for several centuries, while the once-great city next door slowly sank into oblivion. In the mid-13th century the Seljuks conquered Hagios Theogolos. In the 14th century, under the new name Ayasoluk, the citadel city experienced a short rebirth as a commercial centre and residence of the Aydınoğulları, which ended with Ottoman conquest in 1423.

In 1866 the British architect and engineer J. T. Wood discovered the Artemision and began excavations. From 1896 work has been carried out by the Austrian Archaeological Institute. Ayasoluk was renamed Selçuk in 1914.

Circuit of the site

Note that not all parts of the site are always open to the public!

Hidden somewhat off the beaten track are the ruins of the **Church of the Virgin Mary**, a former three-nave basilica. It is assumed that it was developed in the 4th century from a market hall, in which the Third Ecumenical Council took place in 431. All that remains, apart from some ruined walls, are columns and a baptismal font. If you would like to see it, turn right along a path between the ticket office and toilets.

Otherwise follow the shady avenue which leads from the entrance straight to the Arcadiane and large theatre. On your right there was once a 200 x 240m-large courtyard surrounded by an arcade where athletes trained — **Verulanus Square**; not a trace of it remains today. After a few metres the ruins of the **theatre gymnasium** emerge on the left.

Arcadiane (Arcadian Way): This long boulevard once led from the theatre to the port, but today ends in a thicket. It was refurbished in 400 AD by Emperor Arcadius, who had columns and arcades built along the entire length (over 500 metres); it was surfaced with marble and was the first road in the world to be illuminated at night. It has been resurfaced, and many columns

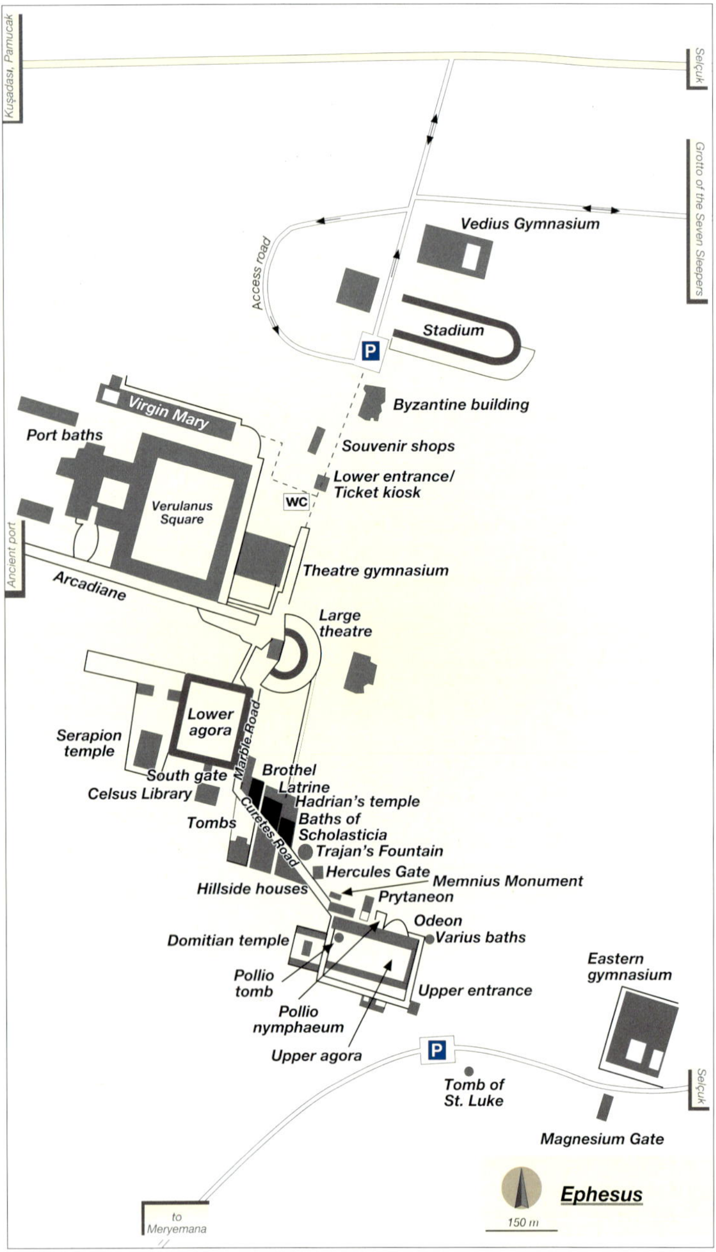
Kuşadası, Pamucak
Selçuk
Grotto of the Seven Sleepers
Vedius Gymnasium
Access road
Stadium
P
Byzantine building
Virgin Mary
Port baths
Souvenir shops
Lower entrance/
Ticket kiosk
WC
Verulanus
Square
Ancient port
Arcadiane
Theatre gymnasium
Large
theatre
Lower
agora
Marble Road
Serapion
temple
South gate
Celsus Library
Brothel
Latrine
Hadrian's temple
Baths of
Scholasticia
Tombs
Curetes Road
Trajan's Fountain
Hercules Gate
Memnius Monument
Hillside houses
Prytaneon
Odeon
Varius baths
Domitian temple
Pollio
tomb
Pollio
nymphaeum
Upper entrance
Upper agora
Eastern
gymnasium
P
Tomb of
St. Luke
Selçuk
Magnesium Gate
to
Meryemana
Ephesus
150 m

have been rebuilt. In order to protect it from the masses of visitors, it is no longer possible to walk on the Arcadiane.

The large theatre: Built impressively into the slope, the theatre held 24,000 spectators. Originally a Hellenistic building from about 270 BC, it owes its current appearance to structural alterations undertaken by the Roman emperors Claudius and Trajan. The theatre has a diameter of 130m, is 38m high, and has 66 rows of seats divided into three tiers. Only the walls of the first floor still stand from the original three-storey stage (18m), in front of which is the forest of columns in the orchestra. The acoustics are particularly impressive — as is the view of the Arcadiane leading to the silted-up port.

Marble Road: This was once an arcaded avenue similar to the Arcadian Way; it runs from the theatre past a pump-house to the Celsus Library (see below). It owes its name to the heavy marble-slab surfacing, under which is a 2m-high drainage system.

Lower agora: This market place, on the right-hand side of Marble Road, is surrounded by colonnades and measures 110 x 110m. The **south gate** of the agora (next to the Celsus Library, see below) is in excellent condition, and is called the **Gate of Mazeus and Mithridates** after its donors, two slaves who were once employed by Emperor Augustus who were released and later made their fortunes in Ephesus. Those who approved of this and those who didn't is clear from the bilingual inscription: The Latin version mentions the Romans, the Greek one leaves them out.

Serapeion: The meagre remains of this temple lie behind the agora and library (when looking from the marble road). Dating from the 2nd century AD, it must have been enormous. Climbing an external staircase, you come into an entrance hall supported by eight 14m-high Corinthian columns. Each individual column was carved from one piece of marble and weighed several tons. The iron gate to the cella was so heavy that it ran on rollers. The basins and large niches in the cella were used for ritual washing.

Celsus Library: This two-storey library was built in 135 AD at the end of Marble Road by the Consul Gaius Aquila as a heroon in memory of his father Celsus, a governor of the province of Asia. A gallery ran around the upper floor, from which one could see into the lower reading hall. Since the Austrian archaeologists found no less than 850 of the original building blocks, they succeeded in completely rebuilding the front over a period of eight years starting in 1970; even the statues are once again standing in their original places. They embody, from left to right: education, honesty, virtue and wisdom. Inside the library there are still some ancient notice boards, but no manuscripts — the Goths burned them to heat the baths.

Curetes Road: This leads from the library to the upper agora (see below). Arcades border it, and mosaics shine in front of the adjacent public buildings. There was also a drainage system under this road. Just at the beginning, on the left, is what archaeologists have long believed to be a **brothel**, since they found a statue of the God Priapos with an outsize penis, as well as the picture of an exhausted-looking mature woman. A public latrine is next door, with a fountain decorated with columns in the centre and toilet seats against the outside walls. Opposite the latrine, on the other side of the road, are three tombs, of which the huge **Octagon** is inscribed. Behind it a futuristic canopy marks the so-called hillside houses.

Hillside houses: These were excavated over several years, during which time frescoes and mosaics were found in amazingly good condition. Restoration is ongoing. The extra fee you pay to visit is well worth it — this is spectacular (and, since coach tours usually omit the houses, you have some peace and quiet). A tour gives you a close-up view of how antiquity's 'top 10,000' arranged their mansions, including under-floor heating, hot baths and flowing water.

Hadrian's Temple and the Baths of Scholasticia (Varius Baths): Continuing along Curetes Road, you come to the impressive, largely reconstructed Temple of Hadrian (130 AD) on the left. The keystone of the architrave shows Tyche, the Goddess of Victory. A frieze depicts the legend of the city's founding. Next to it lie the ruins of the multi-storey baths, built by Varius Valens at the start of the 2nd century and renovated by Christin Scholasticia 200 years later. They offered space for up to 1000 visitors, and even had a library and an entertainment area. The statue of the found is still there, except the head. From the baths one could observe the traffic on the road through a glass window.

Trajan's Fountain and Hercules Gate: A few steps further uphill, also on the left-hand side of Curetes Road, is the skeleton-like rebuilt Trajan Fountain — a magnificent nymphaeum which was dedicated to the Emperor Trajan in 114 AD. Twelve statues were once located in the niches, and a large statue of the emperor stood above it; now only his foot is left as a reminder. A few metres further uphill there used to be a triumphal arch. Since a relief of Hercules adorned the side columns, it was also known as Hercules Gate. Today, however, the upper horizontal stones are missing.

Memmius Monument (Hydreion): A few more steps uphill on the left is the Memmius Monument, which was later transformed into a fountain. It was dedicated to Gaius Memmius, a grandchild of the Roman general and dictator Sulla, who plundered the city in 84 BC as punishment for the Ephesian Vespers.

Domitian Temple: Past the **Pollio Tomb** (Sextilius Pollio was another patron of the city) and the **Domitian Nymphaeum**, which was once, like the Trajan Fountain, richly decorated with statues, you come to the massive foundations of the Domitian Temple. Here archaeologists found the head of a monumental statue of the Emperor Domitian, who was murdered in the year 96. History remembers him as an enemy of Christians. There is a kind of 'inscription museum' in the foundations today, where original Latin texts with English translations are placed opposite each stone slab. Unfortunately, it's not always open.

Upper agora, prytaneion and 'odeon': The 160 x 58m square was the political centre of the city. Somewhat north of it stood the prytaneion, a meeting house. Here the eternal fire of the city burned, guarded by the curetes (priests) and vestal virgins. In this building they found the larger-than-life statue of Artemis, which today is housed in the archaeological museum at Selçuk. From here you can walk through a semicircular hallway to a building which is assumed to be the bouleuterion, the city hall. It is called the 'odeon' because of its shape. The rows of seats are in excellent condition. About 1400 spectators could watch the council meetings from 27 rows of seats. Between the city hall and upper agora are the bases of columns which once lined the 160m-long '**Bulls-head Hall**' (named for their strange capitals).

Sights around Ephesus

Outside the paid-admission area: The sites near Ephesus with no entrance fees are hardly worth a visit. On the right-hand side of the road past the upper exit is the mis-named **Tomb of St. Luke**, a round mausoleum belonging to an unknown deceased from the 1st century, which was converted into a church during Christian times (for a while it was believed that St. Luke was buried here). A little further along is former main gate, **Magnesium Gate**, north-west of which are the scant remains of the **eastern gymnasium**, also called the girls' gymnasium on account of the statues found here.

Near the car park by the lower entrance are the ruins of a **Byzantine building**, probably a palace or baths. Further along the Selçuk road lies a 192m-long **stadium**, built under Emperor Nero; a monumental entrance gate still remains, but all the stone grandstands were plundered to built the hilltop citadel. Some 50m further on, surrounded by a fence, is the rubble of the **Vedius Gymnasium**, donated by Publius Vedius Antonius, a rich citizen of the city. It had, among other things, under-floor heating.

A cave known as the '**Grotto of the Seven Sleepers**' is sign-posted from the approach road to Ephesus. During the Christian persecutions, seven young men are said to have hidden in these caves. Roman soldiers saw them and bricked up the entrance, whereupon the refugees sank into a sleep lasting 200 years. When they were awoken by an earthquake and broke down the wall, Christianity had long become the state religion, and the persecutions had become history. Emperor Theodosius II later established a pilgrimage church here, in which the bodies of the young men allegedly lay buried. The site is fenced, but visible.

Artemision: This once-famous temple is half-way along the Ephesus/Selçuk road. Antipater, when compiling his list of the Seven Wonders of the Ancient World, wondered if the Sun God Helios had ever seen anything similar, except at Olympos. Today Helios still looks down on Olympos, but instead of the Artemision he sees almost nothing —

just the one column shown on page 55 is still standing.
Opening times: freely accessible.

Selçuk Archaeological Museum: This ranks among the most outstanding museums of its kind in Turkey, with some of the most beautiful treasures from Ephesus. In the first hall on the left are **finds from the hillside houses**, a large array of treasures — an Egyptian statuette of a priest from the 7th century BC, a marble fresco of Socrates, a bust of Tiberius, and so on. In the next hall is a **monumental fountain** with a sculpted group of figures in which Odysseus and his men prepare to blind the Cyclops Polyphemus. The next room is dedicated to **Eros**, with a delightful small bronze of him riding a dolphin; he is also shown with Aphrodite and Psyche. In the **garden** there are a few capitals and sarcophagi, as well as souvenirs for sale.
Past the hall containing **objects from tombs**, which illustrates how ancient civilisations buried their dead, one reaches the most beautiful and impressive hall of all — the **Artemis Hall**. Beside an Artemis statue without a head are two Roman marble copies of the cult figure. The largest is 3.2m high (the original must have been made of wood). The most prominent part of these statues is the chest, representing fertility, although experts are divided about whether the protrusions are eggs, breasts or bulls' testicles. A model of the Artemision clearly shows why it was once one of the Seven Wonders of the World. In the next room you're among the **Roman emperors**; a highlight is a bust from the once-colossal statue of Domitian which stood in the temple at Ephesus.
Address/opening times/prices: in the centre of Selçuk diagonally opposite the Tourist Office. Usually open daily 08.30-18.30; in winter closes earlier (and on Mon.); entry £2.50.

Meryemana: This is the house where the Virgin Mary is believed to have spent the last years of her life. Little is known about her life after the birth of Jesus, and her burial place is also unclear. Was it Mount Zion in Jerusalem or Aladağ, 9km south of Selçuk, as indicated by the following story?
A German nun, Katharina Emmerich (1774-1824), had a vision of the house where Mary lived and died. Although she had never been to Turkey, in 1891 Lazarist monks from İzmir discovered a house on Aladağ, 7km south of Selçuk, which matched the description and so became a place of pilgrimage. It consists of a dome-covered sturdy stone building in a parkland setting. In the main room, below the apse, is an altar with a black Madonna: this is said to have been Mary's bedroom. Just below the house is a spring, from where believers can draw holy water. Pilgrims come in droves to Meryemana on Ascension Day.
Getting there/opening times/prices: From the centre of Selçuk take the road towards Aydın and turn right after about 2km (signposted to Meryemana). From here it's another 7km to the house. Parking £2.25. No dolmuş; *taxis about £21 return. Open daily from 08.00-19.00. The entrance fee of £5 is raised by Selçuk to maintain this 'Meryemana Cultural Park'.*

Index

Only geographical names are included here; for all other entries, see Contents, page 3. **Bold type** indicates a photograph; *italic type* indicates a map or plan; both may be in addition to a text reference on the same page.

Selçuk/Ephesus
Aydın/Selçuk
Burdur, Isparta
Altınkum
Iasos
Mylasa
Milas
Kıyıkışlacık
Bodrum (Milas)
Beçin Kalesi
Gulf of Güllük
Güllük
Boğaziçi
Eskihisar
Stratonikeia
Yatağan
Oyuklu Dağı 1892
Muğla
Akçay
Değirmenalanı
İkizköy
Gölçük
Ula
Türkbükü
Yalıkavak
Torba
Güvercinlik
Karaova
Gümüşlük
Karakaya
Ortakent
Bodrum
Kızılağaç
Çiftlikköy
Turgutreis
Akyarlar
Mazıköy
Ören
Keramos
Çökertme
Akyaka
Gökova
Akçapınar
Gökçe
Sedir Adası
Çetibeli
Kabagünlük
Taşbükü Bay
Karacasöğüt Bay
Yalı Bay
İnceyalı Bay
Hurma Bay
Gulf of Gökova
Kos
Hamitköy
Köyceğiz
Köyceğiz Gölü
Sultaniye
Marmaris
Yuvacık
Ekincik
Caunos
Çandır
Dalyan
Ortaca
Dalaman Çayı
Dalaman
Reşadiye Peninsula
Körmen
Emecik
Aktur
Hisarönü
İçmeler
Orhaniye
Turunç
Amos
Kumlubükü Bay
Turgut
Karaincir Bay
Gebekum Beach
Eski Datça
Datça
Knidos
Yazıköy
Mesudiye
Hayıtbükü
Ovabükü
Palamutbükü
Bayır
Çiftlik
Bozburun
Selimiye
Söğüt
Taşlıca
Bozburun Peninsula
Symi
Loryma
Sangerme
Kocagöl
Göcek
Sarsala Koyu
Günlüklü Bay
Katranci Bay
Kargı
Günlükbaşı
Çalış
Fethiye
Gulf of Fethiye
Kayaköyü
Ovacık
Hisarönü
Gemiler Bay
Ölüdeniz
Kıdrak
Baba Dağı 1969
Pınara
Kabak
Eşen
Sidyma
Bodrum to Marmaris
Includes excursions to Pamukkale/Hierapolis, Aphrodisias and Ephesus
Tilos
Rhodes Town
GREECE
Hálki
Rhodes
Lindos
Karamanlı
Karataş Gölü
Tefenni
2421
2272
2294
Dalaman Çayı
Akçay
Çavdır Çayı
Gölhisar
Gölhisar Gölü
Çavdır
Çameli
Karaman Gölü
Koru Dağı 2124
Korkuteli Barajı
Korkuteli
Altınyayla
Yazır Gölü
Söğüt
Yapraklı Barajı
Karabayır
Sarılar
Boncuk Dağı 2418
Ziyaret Tepesi 2598
Patlangıç
Oineanda
Ceylan
Üzümlü
Kadyanda
Kemer
Gebeler
Tlos
Akdağlar
Girdev Gölü
Elmalı
Karataş Semayük
Bey Dağlar
Kızlar Sivrisi Tepe 3070
Akçay
Yesilgöl
Uçarsu
Uyluk Tepesi 3024
Gömbe
Avlan Gölü
Susuzdağ
Kofu Dağı 2469
Arykanda
Arif
Çatallar
Saklıkent Gorge
Sinekçi
Nisa
Bozcaya 2065
Akyazı
Xanthos
Letoon
Kınık
İslamlar
Alaca Dağ 2338
Turunçova
Limyra
Dirgenler
Kasaba
Demre Çayı
Yeşilköy
Gelemiş
Akbel
Patara
Kalkan
Kaputaş
Phellos
Felen Çayı
Çukurbağ
Myra
Demre (Kale)
Beymelek
Andriake
Simena
Gökkaya Bay
Kaş
Aperlae
Üçağız
Kekova Adası
Sıçak Yarımadası
Cape Ulu Burun
Kastellórizo (Greece)
Finike
Gulf of Finike
Gökliman Bay
Kızılsu Barajı
Kocaaliler
Karaca Ören 2 Barajı
Karaca Ören 1 Barajı
Kızılkaya
Köprülü Canyon Milli Parkı
2505
Selge
Beşkonak
Yenimahalle
Gebiz
Karain Cave
Düden Waterfalls (upper)
Kursunlu Şelalesi
Perge
Sillyon
Zeytintaşı Cave
Aspendos
Termessos
Güllükdağı Termessos Milli Parkı
Güver Canyon
Aksu
Serik
ANTALYA
Geyikbayırı
Saklıkent
Düden Waterfalls (lower)
Lara
Belek
Side, Alanya, Alarahan
Gulf of Antalya
Beldibi Cave
Beldibi
Göynük
Olimpos Beydağları Milli Parkı
Ovacık
Kuzdere Köprü
Yayla Kuzdere
Kemer
Kiriş
Çamyuva
Tahtalı Dağı 2366
Beycik
Phaselis
Tekirova
Alakır Çayı
Alakır Barajı
Ulupınar
Yanartaş (Chimaera)
Çıralı
Olympos
Rhodiapolis
Kumluca
Musa Dağı
863
Çavuşköy
Adrasan
Hacıveliler
Mavikent
Karaöz
Kaş to Dalyan
Antalya to Demre
10 km
Bodrum to Marmaris
Highlighted names refer to the principal sights — towns and villages, beaches, ancient sites, natural parks, etc.
Datça
Location of the walks in this book